in the face of economic uncertainty and shifting social values. He spells out the basic purposes and goals of college education; explains how to give clarity and consistency to all college activities—from academic programs to investment policies; and analyzes the qualities and commitments needed for strong leadership, teaching, internal cohesiveness, and external alliances in any college that strives to become a college of consequence. Special attention is given to a curriculum that meets the *total* needs of today's students. Martin's forthright views and practical ideas on the purpose and content of college education should interest and inspire everyone concerned about the dwindling status of humane learning and the institutions of higher education that support it.

THE AUTHOR

WARREN BRYAN MARTIN is scholar in residence at The Carnegie Foundation for the Advancement of Teaching. He has had wide experience as a professor and as an administrator. From 1974 to 1980, he was president and director of the graduate fellowship program at the Danforth Foundation.

A publication of

The American Council on Education

A College
of Character

*Renewing the Purpose and Content
of College Education*

Warren Bryan Martin

A College
of Character

Jossey-Bass Publishers

San Francisco • Washington • London • 1982

A COLLEGE OF CHARACTER
Renewing the Purpose and Content of College Education
by Warren Bryan Martin

Copyright © 1982 by: Jossey-Bass Inc., Publishers
433 California Street
San Francisco, California 94104

&

Jossey-Bass Limited
28 Banner Street
London EC1Y 8QE

Library of Congress Cataloging in Publication Data

Martin, Warren Bryan.
 A college of character.

 Bibliography: p. 199
 1. Education, Humanistic—United States. 2. Church
colleges—United States. 3. Education, Higher—United
States—Aims and objectives. I. Title.
LC1011.M317   378′.012′0973   82-48392
ISBN 0-87589-554-9   AACR2

Manufactured in the United States of America

*Acknowledgment is gratefully extended for permission to reprint previously
published materials:* On p. 13, lines from "Choruses from 'The Rock'" in *Collected
Poems 1909–1962* by T. S. Eliot; copyright, 1936, by Harcourt Brace Jovanovich,
Inc., Copyright © 1963, 1964 by T. S. Eliot. Reprinted by permission of Harcourt
Brace Jovanovich, Inc., and Faber and Faber Ltd. On pp. 55–56, excerpt from
America Revised by Frances FitzGerald. Copyright © 1979 by Frances FitzGerald.
Reprinted by permission of Little, Brown and Company in association with the
Atlantic Monthly Press. On pp. 156 and 197, lines from "The Dry Salvages" in *Four
Quartets*, copyright 1943 by T. S. Eliot, renewed 1971 by Esme Valerie Eliot.
Reprinted by permission of Harcourt Brace Jovanovich, Inc., and Faber and Faber
Ltd.

JACKET DESIGN BY WILLI BAUM

FIRST EDITION

Code 8237

The Jossey-Bass
Series in Higher Education

Foreword

≥0≤≥0≤≥0≤≥0≤≥0≤≥0≤≥0≤≥0≤≥0≤≥0≤≥0≤

I believe, as Warren Martin provocatively suggests, that in the days ahead institutions of higher education must be strengthened and reformed precisely because they have, in their search for truth, a unique obligation to fulfill. The professions of teaching and administration must, once again, be considered true vocations, and those who enter must have both the training and authority required to address the moral crisis in education and the nation.

Warren Martin's claim is that the place to begin this process is the liberal arts college. These institutions are, he argues, small and reasonably manageable. The orientation of faculty and students, despite competing influences, is frequently inclined to be supportive of larger ends. And the liberal arts college can, with imagination, develop connections beyond the campus—with churches, museums, libraries, business and industry, parents, and alumni.

Martin's emphasis on the centrality of the liberal arts college, even more, his confidence in the church-related college, will draw controversy. But nearly everyone will agree that colleges and universities in America must examine their purposes and define their missions more carefully and more accurately. Not everyone will endorse Martin's curriculum plan or his approach to professional development, but nearly everyone will agree that the undergraduate curriculum needs more coherence, even as teaching and learning need more courage and honesty.

The harsh truth is that, today, college administrators are all too frequently preoccupied with budgets, paperwork, and management problems. Many faculty members are trying to survive until the retrenchment war is over. Students, in turn, are working on their own agendas, uninspired by larger visions.

This drift on the campuses reflects, at least in part, our larger confusion as a nation. More than fifteen years ago Walter Lippmann wrote: "[Americans] are left with the feeling that there is a vacuum within them, a vacuum where there were the signs and guideposts of an ancestral order, where there used to be ecclesiastical and civil authority, where there was certainty, custom, usage and social status, and a fixed way of life. . . . Modern men are haunted by a feeling of being lost and adrift, without purpose and meaning in the conduct of their lives" (1966, p. 17).

The tension of living within a void, on the one hand, while feeling the elation of freedom, on the other, is, I suspect, an inevitable condition of our time. When many people celebrate their freedom from tradition, it is necessary to promote institutions in which a disciplined search for authentic forms of community will be nourished and sustained.

Today, hard personal and civic choices must be made, and within such a context, colleges and universities have a special obligation to help students develop "the capacity of judging rightly in matters relating to life and conduct" (the definition of *wisdom* in *Oxford English Dictionary*). The responsibility given scholars and teachers is not only to search for truth, but additionally, to shape knowledge to fit the details of life. They are to apply truth to conduct, or translate knowledge into wisdom.

In this book, Professor Martin views the college of character as an institution concerned with the achievement of what might be characterized as the *educated heart*. This convenient label means the development of an appreciation of beauty, a tolerance of others, a reaching for mastery without arrogance, a courtesy toward opposing views, a dedication to fairness and social justice, an adherence to integrity and precision in thought and speech, an openness to change, and a love for graceful expression and audacious intellect.

Martin helps to focus attention on the central issues by stating his own viewpoint in a straightforward way. A variety of options is discussed, but the reader has no doubt which one the author prefers as he sketches his vision of a college of character.

The Carnegie Foundation for the Advancement of Teaching challenges its staff members, and the Scholar in Residence, to enter into the controversies on basic issues confronting higher education in America. Warren Martin has accepted this challenge and, in his essay, has contributed to the answers that will endure beyond the debates.

August 1982   Ernest L. Boyer
President
The Carnegie Foundation
for the Advancement of Teaching

Preface

The following statements of the times reveal the status of undergraduate education, particularly in liberal arts colleges:

A college president:

> The Board of Trustees hired me to keep this ship afloat. I accepted their challenge. Survival is the goal and good management is the means to that end. I will, therefore, introduce programs that pay and cut out those that don't. Good intentions will no longer in themselves be good enough. Sentimentality pays no bills. We will produce in response to market demand. From now on, "He who pays the piper calls the tune." We will not only survive, we'll prosper.

A faculty member:

> Our enrollments are not sagging as much as was predicted. If this is a market-driven organization, I con-

clude that we should keep doing what we have done—for general education, a distribution requirement; for the upper division, preprofessional majors and some electives in the liberal arts. The old-fashioned curriculum stands the test of time.

An education reporter for a major newspaper:

> The students with whom I come in contact couldn't care less about general education and the liberal arts curriculum. They are job-oriented and pragmatic. Therefore, unless a liberal arts college offers a full-ride, they prefer to go to a community college for a couple of years before transferring to the state university. And along the way, they will take as little general education as possible and do as much career-oriented work as possible. Furthermore, the concern of colleges and universities today for student enrollment means they will offer these students what they want, helping them finesse the liberal arts and feature career training.

A student:

> Faculty members at this college are scared. I can apply pressure and improve my grades. I "contribute" by my presence to the department's FTE and, in exchange, the faculty contribute to my transcript. Students used to be intimidated by faculty. Now the reverse is true.

Such comments suggest basic attitudes and fundamental issues that affect the future of the liberal arts college in America. Are there institutional purposes that transcend "survival"? Are the old ways still the best ways? Have the interests and orientations of most students changed so radically that general and liberal education are anachronistic? Have college faculty and administrators surrendered integrity—institutional, personal—to expediency? Can academe determine the imperatives for integrity when facing relentless changes?

Instruction from Research

These questions were no less urgent in the late sixties when, as research educator, at the Center for Research and Development in

Higher Education, University of California, Berkeley, I directed a study of institutional distinctiveness in American higher education, culminating in a report to the U.S. Office of Education entitled *Institutional Character in Colleges and Universities: Interaction of Ideology, Organization, and Innovation* (see Martin, 1969). Institutional growth and expansion raised questions about what endures despite changes. The new student movement coalesced around problems concerning the social and political relevance of traditional education, and many faculty and administrators questioned whether emerging innovations and experiments conformed to established procedures and stated purposes. While the federal government expanded its support for targeted programs—research, access for minorities, facilities—and while state coordinating agencies proliferated in response to the need for an equitable distribution of funds, educators endorsed and even pressed for these forms of federal and state intervention without considering the effects on institutional independence or the prospect of fiscal dependence. The big words, the gong words, remained *autonomy,* used by college officers, and *accountability,* used by state and federal officials, while actual practice seemed to indicate that institutional purposes were being changed to accommodate categorical programs, that management skills and systems theory were becoming ends in themselves. Were colleges and universities free to innovate, critics asked, only in order to conform more readily? Were the schools allowed to change only to the extent that it made them more alike?

The research project at Berkeley set out to isolate factors contributing to institutional distinctiveness but ended with a collection of data and a range of experiences that, taken together, forced an unexpected conclusion: At the deep level of intent and basic commitments, as compared with appearances and surface arrangements, the main word to characterize these institutions was not *distinctiveness* but *conformity* (Martin, 1969, p. 210). The institutions differed, to be sure, in size and in many other characteristics. The vaunted theme of American higher education's diversity appeared throughout the study. However, another theme, less popular—higher education's uniformity or conformity—was even more prominent. I acknowledged the presence of these two themes, and the dominance of one, in this way:

Every college or university has character in the sense that it has characteristic programs or activities by which the institution can be identified. Indeed, these administrative and organizational differences, plus their quantitative and qualitative effects have been the basis for the claim that America has the world's most diversified system of education. But does diversity in structures and functions mean diversity at the level of basic values? Given the range in types of institutions and the variety of roles for institutions within them, it would seem likely that value differentiation as a consequence of role differentiation would be a conspicuous feature of college and university life and an integral part of the diversity claimed for the system. However, it is precisely this "obvious" outcome that was not supported by the findings of the institutional character research project. Beneath diverse structures and functions we found uniformity in educational assumptions and sociopolitical values across major interest groups and in various types of institutions (Martin, 1969, p. 210).

Many educators, it seemed, wanted to treat colleges as many governmental officials treat budgets: If budgets are numbers to be manipulated, skillful government is a matter of making programs conform to categories of numbers while, it is to be hoped, making the numbers balance; hence, if colleges consist of budgets, numbers (FTE and so on), facilities, and programs, administration is a matter of making activities fit those categories. However, if politicians know that budgets are not merely numbers but also human aspirations, not merely the manipulation of data but a curious mixture of persuasion, pressure, faith, and movement toward consensus, educators should know that colleges are not only enrollment-driven but also motivated by conviction and compromise, by values as much as by programs. The "bottom line" emerges from what is *valued* and is always a goal distinct from its numerical or programmatic manifestations.

Values not only operate beneath surface choices, but also act as criteria or normative standards. Underlying our choice in the personal life is the normative value of self-interest; beneath forms of public behavior is the basic need for social acceptance; behind professional occupations is the deeper commitment to professionalism.

Christopher Jencks and David Riesman reported, in *The Academic Revolution* a study chronicling the rise and triumph of professionalism on campus, evidence in colleges and universities of increasingly convergent goals achieved by ever more similar means (Jencks and Riesman, 1966). The institutional character study at Berkeley in 1969 supported this conclusion. Administrators and faculty members, while differing in sociopolitical orientations, were surprisingly alike in making professionalism the cornerstone of their emotional and institutional values. Whereas the description and style of professionalism were originally intended to help achieve institutional objectives, we researchers found that, increasingly, the purposes of the college or university were tailored to forms of professionalism defined by external faculty guilds and accrediting associations. Also, the academic revolution of 1910 to 1960 had become, by 1970, counterrevolutionary, bent on crushing rival loyalties and blocking further changes. Diversity was still trumpeted but was rigidly contained at the point where it became a threat to the new behemoth. Consequently, credentials became more important than professional competency, even as schooling was equated with education. The legitimate authority of professional skills, we concluded in our report, had succumbed to the authoritarianism of professionalism: "The metaphor for our condition is the maypole dance. Students, faculty and administrators today, in their varying garbs representing their several traditions, are all dancing around a common center. And as they clutch their ribbons and carry out the prescribed dizzying maneuvers, they seem blinded to the fact that they are dancing in an ever-smaller circle and are reducing their individual freedom by binding themselves more and more tightly to the Standard" (Martin, 1969, p. 231).

Today, just over a decade later, the full effects of narrow professionalism in academe can be seen. Pushing everyone into professional categories while discrediting the generalist has contributed to the bifurcation of educators into the camps of the traditionalists and nontraditionalists. In the seventies, the weight of conformity proved unbearable to audacious leaders who had made commitments to innovative or experimental programs—for example, cross-disciplinary, problem and theme curricula—and those educators broke away from conformity to the Standard and tried to make diversity in education much more pronounced. In fact, some persons and their programs have gone so far that the question today is not whether they have the freedom to be different but what are the limits to diversity.

Another effect of professionalism, more evident in the early eighties than in the late sixties, is the fragmentation of teaching and learning that occurred when almost all colleges and universities accepted the specialistic orientation of the so-called research university. This development endangered the notion of community on campus, and it has negatively affected the larger community. Graduates with their professional "isms" have contributed to the fragmentation of professional and social life. The situation is so serious now that education leaders fear that the university and its graduates are too immersed in professional specialties and professionalism to ever again be able to foster in American society a sense of unity and shared purpose.

The Berkeley-based research on institutional character in the sixties, and experiences in the seventies, create a picture for the eighties of the dominance of professionalism in colleges and universities and its diminution of meaningful diversity in the name of procedural specialization. More encouragingly, however, another research finding has held true, a factor tremendously important in dealing with current urgencies: The liberal arts college provides the best setting for cultivating a spirit of community and a sense of shared purpose. The professional Standard was, according to our research data, in place in such colleges. Yet, their faculty and administrators were less comfortable with it and more likely to diverge from it in organizing their own lives than were colleagues elsewhere. Prospects for innovation and experimentation in teaching and learning, examining old purposes and considering new ones, were better at liberal arts colleges than those at other types of institutions.

Furthermore, as mentioned, what we found in the late sixties was confirmed throughout the seventies. During that decade I traveled to scores of colleges and universities as consultant, lecturer, and accreditation team member and, later, as director of the graduate fellowship program, Danforth Foundation. My experiences showed that the educational institution best suited to deal with many of the serious problems besetting colleges and universities, as well as the culture at large, is the undergraduate liberal arts college, including, indeed, emphasizing, the church-related one.

Because this conclusion opposes conventional thinking, I must face throughout this essay the challenging question of the adequacy of the college for the task and the answers a college of character would give to questions that seem to confound higher education and society.

In this essay I quarrel with various aspects of college life in America as well as with political, economic, and religious forces that threaten the college. My thesis is that the liberal arts college is being shunted precisely when its distinctive themes and services, indeed, its character, are needed to moderate the extremes of those educational institutions mesmerized by the model of the elite university that emphasizes narrow research, and those institutions opportunistically following the model of the community college that, when overblown, trivializes education services. Also, developments such as the relocation or dislocation of Americans on two grids of dominance—immensity and intimacy, the usurpation of authority by political and social institutions that persuade people to settle for the life of the masses or of the solitary person—tend to nullify mediating institutions such as the church and the college.

Liberal arts colleges working with churches and synagogues should be revitalized, not deprecated; lifted up, not pushed aside. By their natures, and when functioning at peak efficiency, church-related colleges are best positioned to deal with the ethical crisis in higher education and to provide leadership for the countervailing force that must be recruited if America is to withstand the threat of authoritarian government.

A Personal Statement

Big themes and sweeping claims emerge when a lover's quarrel gets to the heart of the matter, and this essay is a lover's quarrel with higher education. As such, it is not dispassionate, but passionate; not neutral, but opinionated. It is not a typical research-oriented study, calling for more research. The essay is a polemic, a broadside, an exhortation on controversial topics of concern to every lover of American colleges and universities. It is an essay in the classical sense, that is, an interpretative composition with a subject treated in a personal way. Such exposition offers an opportunity to speak from the heart and to set out the chess pieces and try a few moves.

The future of the liberal arts colleges is an explosive topic. Despite their diversity, most opinions on the issue share at least one emphasis—that the college as we have known it is imperiled. Such a prospect causes some observers, including myself, to become so agitated that in comparison with persons who eschew enthusiasm, they seem strident in their arguments. (The ground rule for debate among troubled lovers of the college should be that it can be sharp but must not become acrimonious.)

My essay contains controversial words and phrases: *religion* more often than *values* (in academe, as with the BBC, the word *values* is a polite synonym for *religion*); *moral* and *ethical* rather than *group preferences* and *personal taste; a college of character,* not *the characteristics of a college.* Certain words and phrases will offend some readers as too sectarian or abrasive. These auditors prefer a softer, more ecumenical set of terms, even as they prefer a more agnostic, modest, utilitarian approach to complex issues about which good minds differ. Although the language employed and the education goals defended throughout the essay have honorable traditions, precise definitions, and application to present conditions, nevertheless, the classical style of this essay has the disadvantage of attracting more attention than its spirit of understanding and attitude of good will. I also risk seeming to be pretentious, particularly in daring to talk about the future in ways that imply a perspective from heights inaccessible to mere mortals.

Another important topic, as controversial as the future of liberal arts colleges, is their reform. What changes are needed now to prepare them for their responsibilities in the future? Assumptions and purposes of colleges in general, as compared with colleges of character, are here handled as one would a melon—sniffed for aroma and probed for soft spots. A curriculum for a college of conviction, as compared with a college of convenience, is roughed out and mulled over. This essay discusses the effects that a new orientation in the college and a reformed curriculum would have on professional development programs, on interactions with precollegiate and postcollegiate institutions, and on relationships with churches and synagogues.

In this book, the church-related college is criticized, then embraced. In that encounter, grappling with overpowering issues, I felt as Jacob when he wrestled with the angel of the Lord and begged for a blessing. (But, some will say, I acted more like a lion in a den of Daniels.) The point, despite all the heaving and sweating, is that colleges, particularly church-related ones, have the potential for leadership in education and in the nation precisely because the qualities and skills that characterize these institutions at their best are the ones most needed now.

What is involved here, ultimately, for all of us, is not a breakfast spat but a mandate for decisions on the most fundamental problems and themes. Whatever disputes we have about the format, language, and style of this essay, we cannot escape the larger issues, assuming that you care as I do about the beleaguered liberal arts college. Whether or not you accept my uncompromising commitment to the college, we all make choices concerning the education enterprise, or abdicate responsibility and allow the choices to be made by others. Despite the fulminations in this essay, I have confidence that the right choices will be made at many colleges; that the college of character will emerge, fulfill its awesome mission, and ultimately have, in this epoch as in an earlier one, positive effects on the general culture as well as on its own students. That faith, culminating in this book, stems from the persuasion of several thousand faculty members, students, trustees, and college administrators who, across the nation, demonstrate with their lives this affirmation of faith:

> Let those who must, despair.
> Let those who will, begin again.

Washington, D.C.   Warren Bryan Martin
August 1982

Acknowledgments

This essay, more than most, is dependent on the ideas and experiences of persons other than the author. One of the objectives was to collect, synthesize, and apply useful material that might otherwise remain scattered. Furthermore, because the intended audience is broad (including presidents, deans, trustees, and other community leaders, as well as faculty members, students of higher education, and parents of college students), the essay moves from education theory to practical details as well as from polemical statements to how-tos. For a project as comprehensive as this one, I needed plenty of help.

The scope of this endeavor also required a review process featuring diverse readers—persons likely to be skilled in various elements of the arguments and able to represent contending interest groups. Selected faculty members and administrators at several colleges and universities were asked, therefore, to read the draft manuscript and share their reactions face to face with the author. I am grateful to Kenneth Chatlos, Dean Dunham, and Charles Geilker of

William Jewell College; William Beatie, John Correia, Valeria Gomez, and Paola Sensi-Isolani of St. Mary's College (California); Douglas Moore, Robert Morlan, Kevin O'Neill, and Kent Smith of the University of Redlands for accepting this assignment and faithfully carrying it out.

Church leaders who read the manuscript, in one or another of its incarnations, and provided valuable criticisms, were Emerson Colaw, Bishop, Minneapolis area, United Methodist Church; Robert Bailey and Kenneth Beck, college board members, and Donovan Hull, campus chaplain at Hamline University. Thomas Trotter, general secretary, and Charles Cole of the United Methodist Board of Higher Education, Nashville, were also active participants in the assessment of the book. All of these persons showed Christian charity without the loss of critical judgment.

Leaders in Washington, D.C., to whom I am much indebted, national association officers and scholars, persons generous with their time and willing to respond to early drafts of *A College of Character,* were Dale Parnell of the American Association of Community and Junior Colleges, David Breneman of Brookings Institution, Thomas Stauffer of the American Council on Education, Mark Curtis and Jerry Gaff of the Association of American Colleges, and Gary Quehl and Jack Armstrong of the Council for Independent Colleges. Also helpful was Malcolm Scully of the *Chronicle of Higher Education.*

There were teacher-scholars at colleges and universities who gave me early warning of the pitfalls and minefields into which I was prone to wander. They included Stephen Bailey, Patricia Graham, and David Riesman of Harvard; Harriet Sheridan, Brown University; Martin Marty, University of Chicago; Howard Bowen, Claremont; Martha Church, Hood College; Steven Eskow, Rockland Community College; Martin Meyerson, professor emeritus, University of Pennsylvania; and Roy Niblett, professor emeritus, University of London.

Three colleagues at Carnegie—Arthur Levine, Verne Stadtman, and Michael O'Keefe—read and argued, sighed and shook their heads, but did not withdraw their support. Three other colleagues—William Danforth, chairman of the board, Danforth Foundation; Gene Schwilck, president, Danforth Foundation; and

Ernest Boyer, president, Carnegie Foundation—provided time, space, and sustenance; encouragement, warnings, and magnanimity of spirit.

Signe Lindquist-Martin gave me faith, hope, and love even when only one of these gifts would have been an act of undeserved generosity.

Joanne Erickson edited the manuscript thoughtfully. Kay Watson made sense of the incomprehensible and typed the illegible. Len Boswell and Gracia Alkema authorized and monitored the processes of publication. All of these colleagues persevered when they could have given up. Their skills were exceeded only by their patience and dedication to the task.

To all of these people, for all of their services—criticism and support—I am grateful. They will find that the book still contains much they would have had me forgo. To them, I admit with embarrassment, paraphrasing the Apostle Paul, "That which you would sometimes have me do, that I did not. And that which you would not, that I did." Perhaps their forgiveness will outlast their distress when they learn that ineptitude, not stubbornness, limited some outcomes, and, more, that the quality of their judgments contributed to the best that remains and especially to whatever is likely to endure.

Warren Bryan Martin

Contents

───0⇌0⇌0⇌0⇌0⇌0⇌0⇌0⇌0⇌0───

The Author

Warren Bryan Martin is currently scholar in residence at The Carnegie Foundation for the Advancement of Teaching. He received his bachelor's degree in philosophy from Asbury College in Wilmore, Kentucky (1947), his bachelor of divinity degree in church history from Nazarene Theological Seminary (1950), and his doctoral degree in history from Boston University (1954). He also holds honorary degrees from Westminster College (Salt Lake City) and Western Maryland College.

Martin taught at Pasadena College from 1954 to 1958 and at Cornell College (Mt. Vernon, Iowa) from 1958 to 1962. From 1962 to 1966, he served as provost of Raymond College at the University of the Pacific. He was research educator and director of development at the Center for Research and Development in Higher Education at the University of California, Berkeley, from 1966 to 1972.

In 1972, Martin became provost of the College of Arts and Sciences at Sonoma (California) State University. He served as vice-president and director of the graduate fellowship program at the

Danforth Foundation from 1974 until 1980, at which time he joined The Carnegie Foundation.

Martin has published over fifty articles in professional journals and several books, including *Alternative to Irrelevance* (Abingdon Press, 1968) and *Conformity: Standards and Change in Higher Education* (Jossey-Bass, 1969). He has lectured at more than 100 colleges and universities. His views on innovation and change in higher education, and on American values, have been reported by *Time, Newsweek,* and the major press services.

For William H. Neff,
who faithfully put books
into my hands,
with the hope that worthy ideas
would reach my mind

A College
of Character

⊂⊃○⊂⊃○⊂⊃○⊂⊃○⊂⊃○⊂⊃○⊂⊃○⊂⊃○⊂⊃○⊂⊃

*Renewing the Purpose and Content
of College Education*

1

Crisis of Identity: Old Colleges Serving New Masters

Throughout the eighteenth and nineteenth centuries in America, the liberal arts college dominated higher education's center stage. Every other program or school was compelled to relate to it—the schools of divinity, medicine, and law, the conservatory of music, and all programs in education and home economics.

Not until the second half of the twentieth century did this college lose the limelight. Slowly at first, more rapidly later, the college has moved from the center to the periphery of higher education. Now it provides service courses, if located in a university, for preprofessional and career-oriented programs. If the college is free-standing, it may still retain a commitment to the liberal arts, but more likely, it is compromising with public demands by designing marketable programs. Programs once marginal have moved into the center and those at the center have been pushed aside. New enterprise is the heart of the college. But the college itself, in this latest incarnation, is displaced and downgraded. Not even first among equals, the college now is merely one of many education options in a pluralistic culture.

1

A change of this magnitude, amounting to a major relocation or dislocation, is as difficult for persons committed to the liberal arts as was the loss of the empire for British subjects. That on which the sun never set, the empire, has dwindled to a few islands where the sun seldom shines. That on which the spotlight always shone—the college—has been moved to the wings where the spotlight seldom reaches.

Some liberal arts colleges can afford to go on serenely as though nothing has changed. They have a strong tradition, a solid base of support, a constituency from which to draw students, and a supply of facilities and faculties for the work they do. For them, the old ways are still the best. Most liberal arts colleges, however, do not have this luxury. They are vulnerable to pressure for change because of variations in constituency preferences and the perils of a small endowment. They are, as we say, consumer-driven institutions. Their survival depends on an ability to provide the services deemed necessary by students and parents who, for their own reasons, patronize these colleges. Such conditions are the disquieting reality for most educators in most colleges. And they are hard on the ego, the pocketbook, and the integrity of the institution.

What are the consequences? Low faculty morale, endless belt-tightening, collective anxiety about what should be done and about whether what should be done can be done. High visibility for tough managers who can squeeze blood out of a turnip. Even higher visibility for synthetic programs that tap into consumer interests without completely disregarding institutional traditions.

When the Lost Is Found

The behavior of faculty and administrators in the colleges reveals that not only do they feel displaced or relegated, but they also have a vague sense of being lost—not lost in theological terms, not damned for sins committed, although that idea has some validity, but lost in terms of location and direction. Administrators and department heads talk a lot about getting from here to there, and they are big on process and arrangements, but the tremolo in that talk reveals uncertainty about what it means to be here and whether it would be meaningful to get there.

More substantial evidence that the colleges have lost their sense of direction after being pushed around is seen in the fact that most of them have wandered off in one of two directions. Many college leaders decided their hope for survival and significance lay in the "versity," in its several manifestations: the miniversity, the university, and the multiversity. The institutions adopting this model defined themselves as research-oriented, professional, equipped to take on the big issues and to provide global leadership. Many liberal arts colleges have tried to become miniversities, appointing faculty committed to basic research but not to teaching, hiring faculty loyal to their professional guilds but not to the college community, appointing presidents whose definition of their job transcends the traditions of the college and the interests of its constituency, hiring administrators who can program computers but cannot counsel students.

While certain of the colleges confronted their identity crisis by following the "versity" model with its massive institutional structures, another group of colleges, growing in number, is following, especially in its latest emendation, the lead of the community colleges. This strategy calls for making the college a center of education services that responds to the needs and interests of the community, right down to small groups and isolated individuals. If the "versity" represents education defined by impersonal professional standards, community college revisionism represents education defined by interest groups and personal preferences. A veritable herd of bewildered liberal arts colleges is stampeding straight into the CC corral, where they will be branded as members of the individualized education movement. And their administrators and faculty, their specialists and therapists, will be taught to ask not what the college may rightfully demand of the students but what it can do to satisfy their every desire. In this way a college becomes a center of education services—and loses any claim to being a college.

Is it necessary for liberal arts colleges at this time of dislocation to emulate the "versity"? Exemplified by the university that has become a multiversity, this model has become so attractive that many colleges have been lured in its direction, at least to the point of trying to become miniversities. Or is it better to imitate the *au courant* community colleges, a model so attractive at this time of fiscal retrenchment and individual entrepreneurship that even some versities are, as Clark Kerr said, trading down (Carnegie Council on Policy Studies in Higher Education, 1980, p. 30)?

Despite the appeal and domination of these polarities, there is another position that liberal arts colleges can take. They can find it despite this time of disarray and their identity crisis. But how?

Have you ever been lost in the mountains? The first reaction, Ernst Gellner (1974, p. 11) says, is to look for familiar signs, clues, or landmarks. But if you are really lost, you will not find recognizable guideposts. Your second response to the situation will be heightened sensitivity and sharpened attention. These can be useful but are not, in themselves, enough. Finally, if you lack connections that allow you simply to sit down and wait to be saved, the realization dawns that you must make some painful choices. You must decide on a course of action and get moving. So you follow a ridge, even though you are not certain it runs in the right direction. Or you start down a canyon, searching for a stream that might suggest a way out. Later, perhaps, a second ridge appears, you spot a cabin, the sun moves across the sky—one thing leads to another, pieces of information fit together, you use your energy judiciously, and after a while mere movement becomes real progress. The start is in some ways quite arbitrary. The course of action followed is not the only one available. You have no assurance, at least at the start, that it will prove to be the best one. But you move on it nevertheless.

The metaphor applies to education. Colleges and universities that put general and liberal education at the center of the enterprise are disoriented, lost—no longer at the center of the action. They no longer serve as the institutional standard against which everything else is measured. Second, despite the use of old, familiar terms to defend traditional categories, there is no longer a mainstream in higher education any more than there is one in religion. Ivy League colleges, like the Episcopal church, think they constitute the mainline. But at a time when nearly 50 percent of the students in higher education attend community colleges, and the numbers enrolled in nontraditional programs exceed those in traditional programs, the inescapable conclusion is that those who claim to ride the mainline really sit on the sideline.

What else characterizes those lost souls, the liberal arts colleges? Although there is no longer a single collection of colleges and universities that sets the standard for all other institutions, and although cultural pluralism has encouraged educational diversity to the extent that variety has become the only absolute, in truth most educators and institutions of higher education are pulled like filings toward the magnet of the versity or of the community college, to the pole of institutional professionalism or of individual preference. These models are recognizable guideposts, to be sure, but they draw colleges in the wrong directions. And the leaders in such schools sense that, despite the attraction of these external influences, the conscientious college cannot allow itself to be pulled along. These colleges, then, find themselves in a world neither structured by legitimate authority nor held together by persuasive tradition. Yet education, by its nature, cannot forgo either authority or tradition (Arendt, 1961, p. 195). What should be done? Accept the leadership of available models—the versity or the community college—even though these models distort the historic mission of the college and point it toward spurious functions? No. It is better to admit to being lost, and, without yielding to the spirit of resignation and with full knowledge of the risks, to take a deep breath, marshal available resources, and move out to seek a better future. This is the challenge facing colleges. Those leaders and institutions willing to follow such a course of action will find allies and resources for the journey. They will find signs along the way. Progress can be made if those educators who feel displaced and lost will get up and get cracking.

Five hundred, perhaps seven hundred, colleges in this country that look much like other institutions of higher education cannot, on the one hand, go blithely forward as though nothing has happened or, on the other hand, effect changes so dramatic that what the institutions become bears no relation to what they have been.

Many of these colleges have leaders who are committed to the notion that humane learning and career training can be companions, that it is not necessary to embrace one and abandon the other. Some colleges have leaders who, while acknowledging that their institutions no longer hold center stage in numbers or influence, know that 20 percent of the college graduates in America come from these places and that, to this day, their graduates exert an influence in public affairs out of all proportion to their numbers.

Several hundred colleges have administrators and faculty members, trustees, alumni and students, constituents and community leaders who believe that together they can find a better place in the spectrum of higher education than the peripheral positions to which these colleges have been assigned by conventional wisdom.

There must be an intermediate and mediating position for these colleges, one that will give them distinction and authority. The challenge is to find it. And the way to begin, as when lost in the mountains, is to step out daringly, using available resources, to seek a unifying educational mission and an appropriate curriculum, accumulating connections that show promise of multiplying existing resources. This is the task: to develop a college of character that will stand as a model of what a liberal arts college can be and, more importantly, to test the possibility that such a college can respond not only to moral and ethical dilemmas in higher education but to the immeasurably larger crisis in American society.

The Shallow Culture of No-Context

George W. S. Trow, Jr. (1980, 1981) has written about living as an American in a culture of no-context and a history of no-history.

Despite its need to be informed by a tradition and to have a history longer than a life span, the culture of modern Americans has been compressed into an alluring flash on a television tube even as history has been shortened to accommodate the viewers' limited attention span. Television, the eye and voice of history in the moment, presents a culture as up-to-date as your last heartbeat, and just as fleeting.

This culture of no-context and history of no-history feature what Trow calls the grid of 200 million and the grid of the unit of one. The traditional continuum of human experiences and social institutions has been broken up and relocated. Life now gravitates toward the mass scale with its huge institutions and impersonal experiences or toward what is called the "interior drama" of the solitary individual, the inner psyche or the soul.

The intermediate and mediating relationships of family and neighborhood have been scaled down and pushed to either extreme. Americans are identified by what they do on these two grids of dominance. Every experience or relationship that does not contribute to building the immense edifice or to deepening personal intimacy is strung out on a line between the polarities, like out-of-style laundry, to be air dried, sun bleached, and stored.

Intermediate and mediating institutions of society, such as the church, are welcome to participate in the largesse of the state as long as they sanction agreements reached on the grid of 200 million. Or these institutions have a future in the domain of the solitary individual, dignifying and sanctifying the special moments of life—birth, confirmation, marriage, death—and interpreting what was once called "the still small voice of the spirit" so that any messages received by the inner person are made compatible with the exterior policies of the institutional masses.

By providing these services, persons identified with what in other times would have been called intermediate and mediating professions and institutions—law and medicine, religion and education—assure themselves places of importance in the public or private domain. They join other experts (politicians, scientists, bankers) and celebrities (rock stars, media anchors, electric church lights) in transferring information back and forth, in describing agreements reached by this process. Their services are important to the general citizenry living in a civilization of no-context, and to people devoid of historical authority. Their services are questionable, too, because the process of agreement tends to become more important than any principles from which it is derived or than any of its outcomes. The reaching of an agreement becomes more important than the content of the agreement (Trow, 1980, pp. 170–171).

Everyone has a favorite enemy on the grid of 200 million. For Americans on the political right wing, it is "big government." For Americans on the left wing, it is "big business." Almost everybody would combat bigness with bigness. Even the concept of "the people" standing against "the bureaucracy" pits big against big. Voices protest giantism, fingers point at this or that form of giantism, but, apparently, it takes one to know one. Americans don't really believe in the victory of the little guy. They love the story of David and Goliath, but the orthodox interpetation is that David can't kill Goliath unless God is on his side. It takes little David plus God to dispatch Goliath, two against one. Ultimately, the story is a tale of competing giants.

In the arena of the individual, the action is not little or small in scale. Turning inward, to the deep mind, the layers of the self, the stages of interior development, is to enter a realm as vast as the universe. The experts on this grid have no less to work with than do the experts on the other. And they are no less important, no less a stabilizing influence, than are the global experts. Therapists and pastors provide direction for people who would otherwise have to make up the rules as they go along and bear the burden of improvising an ethic every day.

How impressive they are on TV, those authorities of process, those brokers of agreements. But we must not be fooled. A shallow culture a mile wide and an inch deep makes it easier for celebrities to appear to walk on water and for experts to probe its "depth."

People concerned about education in America—presidents, trustees, deans, faculty, parents—should realize that they inhabit a world of extreme distances. They are in it, and it is in them. The educated citizenry, no less than other people, are informed by shallow, momentary encounters with global events that are identified and explained by celebrities and experts.

That is not all. Many educators, by training and preference, have a short history that they may not recognize as history. They entered teaching as a job, not knowing the history of that profession as a vocation. Their loyalty is to subject-matter specializations, not to students, faculty, and administrators working together in a humane community. Yet society acknowledges them as leaders because of a legacy that grants them the right to interpret events and to put things into perspective. They are counted among the experts if not the celebrities.

Many college and university professors joined this collective of expertise—consulting here and advising there—even though they sensed that their authority was only technical and far inferior to the spiritual, wide-ranging authority once credited to their profession. Teacher-scholars had previously been respected for the range of their services—educating youth and standing as exemplars of intellectual integrity and human sensibilities—and honored because of the public notion that professors had much more to profess than narrow skills. In more recent times, however, as the mentality of professionalism captured scholarship, they were lumped with "for hire" experts and, hence, without honor in their own country. Most faculty members accepted the arrangement because they concluded, as did other professionals, that the only valid authority in these decades was individual expertise. Their conclusion also evidenced the triumph of the ideology of individualism in America.

Traditionally, in this country and in Europe, the basis of authority had been some notion of God. Contenders for this distinction were various ideas of the nation-state and one or another concept of natural law. They were often substituted for God as the supreme authority to which all authorities were accountable. Only in comparatively recent times, since the sixteenth century, has the authority of the individual successfully challenged other authorities. In the United States particularly, that challenge finally prevailed among the social and intellectual elite, filtering down to the masses, so that, in society, the authority of the individual has been given free rein to shape the culture.

A culture molded by individualism is, of course, suspicious of every other authority—natural law, nation-state, or God. Nothing can be accepted that inhibits the freedom of the individual. "Distrust authority" is a popular slogan on campus. Trust only the authority of the individual. Distrust history, except your own. Distrust spirituality, except personal insights. Distrust community, except a "community" of independent individuals. Trust yourself and that which can be perceived by your senses. Your sense of the immediate is the authority of significance. These emphases have been true to the mood and mode of many influential social and intellectual leaders. The values of a narrow cult have shaped a national culture.

Because autonomous individuals found through personal experience that persons differ in aptitudes and interests, it became necessary to equate the cult view of individual authority with a new culture of pluralism. Evident human differences of fundamental importance necessitated social flexibility and political compromise. The trade-offs would be that the individual could maintain considerable personal freedom in exchange for a little conformity, social and political, to an ideology of accommodation. Did it work? No. The notions of diversity and accommodation, stripped of limits, have been extended to include not only contending interest groups and contentious individuals but also ideas and people whose views contradict individualism, thus making possible only a coalition of opposites leading to stasis or open warfare. Under these conditions, there is insufficient unity to develop a coherent culture. At best, for the present, we have a civilization of accommodation—a culture of no-context.

It is a distressing time for educators who, whatever their basis for authority, have pledged to search for truth, beauty, and justice, even when nothing can be known for certain and nothing will stay in place. No wonder that the teacher-scholar, as he or she observes the flux in society and the downward shift in the status of standards and community, laments:

> Why is it that what we felt so deeply yesterday,
> Is so shallow now,
> That forever is not even tomorrow?

Another problem for humane educators in the present culture of no-context is that it is hard to find elements of contemporary society that are spiritually meaningful and that express "a richly varied and yet somehow unified and consistent attitude toward life" (Sapir, 1970; quoted in Arrowsmith, p. 156). This so-called culture shows the characteristics of a civilization, not a culture. In the essay "Thoughts on American Culture—and Civilization" (1976, p. 154), classicist William Arrowsmith shows how a synthetic civilization is being substituted for authentic culture: "We get compensatory 'individual culture,' style without substance . . . the semblance of pluralism unmoved by any defined norm or unity—the culture of shard . . . all the decorous and organized pretenses of a civilization which provides the paraphernalia, but not the substance, of culture. For education, training; for knowledge, sophistication; for inner necessity, a series of decorative life-styles; for morality, law or equity; for community, groupiness and collective isolation; for bread, a stone."

A culture of no-context is at best a pale imitation of an educator's understanding of culture. Whatever the teacher may do, whatever the compromise, he or she senses that one tragedy of the time is living in a civilization of no-culture.

Faculty members with a humane attitude are outnumbered now by colleagues whose orientation has been shaped by that so-called culture devoid of context as well as by that shallow history providing no sense of history. Fifty percent of college and university faculty today were born after Hitler came to power in Germany. Few of them studied history seriously, as children or adults. Few of them held the subject in high regard, either as a record of events or as an orientation toward events. Not surprisingly, therefore, the students of this younger generation of teachers have an even more limited knowledge of history and less appreciation for it. They have a chronology, as do their mentors, but the long history behind their short history is unknown to them. Yet few of these students, like their teachers, feel any sense of loss. They invest only in the history at hand, in living day by day. Theirs is a history of no-history.

A Short History of No-History

In the beginning was the war—World War II. That is when this history began. Everything before it is considered quaint and has been discarded as an old man who walks with small steps is seen as quaint and is discarded. That which came after the war became flesh, our flesh; its facts, our facts. Americans did not read history any longer: they made it. The difference between that which preceded and that which followed was not just a difference in degree but in kind. A man ages and ages, writes John Barth, changing in degree, but when he dies, he changes in kind. The old world died and a new one was born. Our history since World War II has been like a new heaven and earth: atomic bombs and nuclear power; space probes and satellite transmission; television, computers, lasers, cloning, robots, life-support systems.

Consider the effects of this transformation on one institution of American life: higher education.

Colleges before the new era were out on rural hilltops and, from a distance, could hardly be distinguished from farms. The campus culture featured *in loco parentis*, dorm mothers, cards and beer, dressing for dinner, chapel services, much singing, and at least one verse of *alma mater*. Academic life consisted of classroom seating charts, straight lectures with *ex cathedra* authority, squarely in the tradition of the liberal arts. Collegial administration enforced the provisions of a collegewide curriculum.

Universities before the new era were characterized by colleges essentially writ large; liberal arts at the center of the institution's curricular wheel, with connective spokes to cognate graduate programs and a few professional schools; teaching and research: the teacher-scholar as model, in search of new knowledge to supplement old verities; tutelary relationships with students, that is, mentors and apprentices; manageable scale, modest ambitions, tolerable pretensions—that is, still the university.

How do the college and university look today? How does the history of thirty years compare with the earlier epoch of 300 years? No comparison. A difference not in degree but in kind. Rebirth.

The university has grown so much that there are more administrators now than there were faculty then, and more faculty now than students then, at least in many places.

Systems management, lawyers and computer technicians, deputies and assistant deputies; state equalization formulas, and federal regulations are all appropriate for the university in this new age of grants, fellowships, and subsidies. The university as a business requires administrators with the corporate mentality. Collective bargaining, appeals procedures, hearings; research and scholarship dominant, teaching and service dormant; professional criteria and union loyalties; and interest groups, adversarial relationships, bruised egos, and sagging morale are among the effects of this business-oriented approach to education.

Yet, universities carry out extensive research in the service of the here and now. They have no need for history when it has nothing to say to present interests. They have good facilities, varied and numerous, with so much sophisticated activity that the college on a hill has become the university as city, with all of its problems and costs as well as its services.

What has happened to the liberal arts college? Campus rules have been transformed. Faculty and administrators are mainly of the new breed—fully professional, finely tuned, just like those at the university. As for programs, old-timers would not recognize them. General and liberal education are seen as an impediment, but as hard to shake off as wool socks when your hands are on your mate.

Emphasis is on preprofessional education and job training for skills—measurable, marketplace skills, the real stuff. Programs once peripheral are now central. Once at center stage, the college has lost the limelight.

Parents' expectations still carry an echo from across that grand canyon that separates the old from the new, a reminder of education for the whole person, not just career training. But the parents' pragmatism, their utilitarianism, is the dominant voice. Students now are attracted to the practical career programs—on the side of shallow history. Nevertheless, parents and students in moments of reflection glance back now and then, across that canyon, curious about the relics of life visible on the other side, aware of the echo, wondering about that voice with its point-counterpoint.

> *Where is the life we have lost in living?*
> *Where is the wisdom we have lost in knowledge?*
> *Where is the knowledge we have lost in information?*
>   T.S. Eliot

Consequences and Prospects

Why do parents and students, or for that matter, faculty and administrators, or all the people for whom life and history began after World War II, bother to look back if the old history has nothing to say to the new age? Why repeat the mistake of Lot's wife?

People look back because the new history, no-history, includes a commitment to *process,* sometimes called "historical process." That fact makes people curious about antecedents, especially if the record can be used to reinforce their own predilections.

Another commitment of the new age is to *evaluation* and, alas, that suggests a context for this time of no-context. When living without a history, one is tempted, even when fleeing something terrifying, to look back for a point of reference, even at the risk of being turned into a pillar of salt.

That which the people, especially younger people, fled after World War II was terrifying. There had been over forty years of peace in Europe before the war's first chapter—that introductory drama of 1914-1918—but then, after a period of rearmament, all hell broke loose between 1939 and 1945. This second chapter ended the hopes of idealists for peace in our time. And it ended for realists any hopes they may have had for peace in the hearts of men. War without and within was the lesson.

What else can be said about American life during the last thirty-five years of this history of no-history and culture of no-context?

If you do not have a history, and must always be creating it, if nothing is definite and everything is in process, then you have to decide who or what will be your basis for authority. You cannot do everything. You cannot go everywhere. If it's not in vogue to look back, to whom can you turn for help in making choices? The answer comes from the egalitarian process and the culture of pluralism: Your guides are the state and yourself. The basis for authority will no longer be some notion of a transcendent God and His church, or some notion of the natural law as interpreted by human reason. You rely on the two remaining authorities: the *polis,* in the form of 200 million, the state; and the solitary person.

The primary goal at the level of the state is agreement. The culture of pluralism is based on agreements through compromise— ultimately, at the lowest common denominator.

The ideal at the level of the individual is fulfillment, in the most personal, intimate terms. This commitment to self-realization is the biggest vote of confidence ever given to human nature.

Who negotiates differences between persons or between states? Experts—diplomats and advisers, therapists and counselors. They all rely on data, on demographics. We once thought that the data were made for man, not man for the data. No more. Now the demographers say, with the solemnity of priests quoting scripture, "Our survey indicates . . ." (Trow, 1980, p. 67). The finding becomes the conclusion. The inference becomes the absolute. We must accept it, at least for now, because we live from moment to moment.

Despite their talk of identity, people do not really have personal histories; they have characteristics. Men, like women, are their statistics. Such thinking is the contribution of sociology. Where sociology ends, psychology begins. It emphasizes self-authentication. It gives instructions: "Sit in the circle and tell us all about yourself." (Instant intimacy, please.) In the absence of the pastors and teachers of discredited history, Americans follow the advice of the therapists and social scientists who serve as the accredited agents of the history of no-history.

We are discovering, as Robert Bellah has said (1981, p. 502), a private world of great intensity, emphasizing procedures for feeling but having little or no content. "There is a vehement insistence on selfhood but it is an absolutely empty self; except for the sheer quantity of excitation there is nothing there at all." Such is the outcome of radical secular individualism.

Where are the agencies other than the media, especially television, and the experts, especially social science researchers, that are able to give direction to American life now? Could the schools and colleges bridge the two worlds and help unite them? How about the churches and synagogues? Could they, even with their encumbrances, be our guides for the relentless process? Did this generation or recent generations give away too much too soon? People sense the need for context and perspective, for history beyond personal judgments, especially because the substitutes for traditional values fill the void so poorly.

What a shock to realize that in substituting the history of mass authority and the authority of intimacy for the authority of Western culture, Americans were not able to substitute integrity for hypocrisy, fairness for inequity, freedom for bondage. They lost some of the old virtues but none of the old vices.

Americans have fewer resources for dealing with their loneliness, that is, for the problem of living in the civilization of no-context. The political, social, and personal dilemmas arise, and in sorting them out and making choices, we have recourse only to the situational ethics of a short history and shallow culture. We thought we would live above the debacle of the long history, but we are floundering in the muck of our own situation. Our lives, the life of this country, and prospects for this planet are all threatened by the magnitude of the crisis.

The most damaging development in the last fifteen years has been disintegration of a societal consensus about the nature of the good life and the best means to achieve it. During the first twenty years of the history without history, 1945–1965, there was widespread agreement about the vision or theology that should motivate the people—the American dream. In that vision, elements of the traditional ideology remain apparent—pragmatism and the work ethic, deferred gratification, role definition and class status, the primacy of the home and the authority of the state.

Education was the cornerstone on which personal ambition was expected to build, whatever the edifice envisioned. Education was as important to the post–World War II plan of salvation as the church was to the Christian plan of salvation.

In the mid-sixties, with the rise of the so-called counterculture and the war in Southeast Asia, basic articles of faith were challenged. And by the mid-seventies, for a variety of reasons, many of them had collapsed. In education, for example, expectations that the poor would achieve financial security through education, that racial and ethnic minorities would be transported by education into the mainstream, and that nearly every adult in America would want higher education and would profit from it were modified or abandoned, not in public pronouncements but in the hearts of men. Education proceeded but without a moral basis.

Since that time, for fifteen years, America's unifying ideology, motivating theology, sustaining vision, societal consensus about the most fundamental values have dripped away like brake fluid from a leaky cylinder—unable to stay in place under pressure, hence unable to carry out essential functions, with effects as dangerous as those of an automobile racing along after the hydraulic brake system has failed.

Today educators lack a coherent, morally compelling, widely accepted theology of higher education. We no longer have a persuasive rationale for a costly, inflexible system maintained for more than a decade by a legacy in which we no longer believe.

Can educators who are a part of the problem become part of the solution? Yes. Can colleges and universities transcend this civilization of no-context, even now, despite their recent history? Yes. A better future is possible if students and faculty, administrators and presidents, trustees and constituencies will face the fact that this crisis is not about technical procedures but about basic purposes. They must also realize that the problem we have is nothing less than a moral and ethical crisis and that what institutions require is not more accommodation to the characteristics of the times but development of those characteristics that make them colleges of character.

A Definition of Terms

One of the consequences of forcing everything into the polarities—the grid of 200 million or of one—was that everything in the middle distance had to be relocated. Two of the mediating institutions, the church and the college, were almost destroyed, that is, pushed out of shape or reshaped to the point that they no longer had a recognizable profile. And without definition there can be no mediation. The first task, then, is to define a college of character.

College. It is worth the trouble to define the college because no matter how the word and the concept of the college have been abused, they still have value: the people in the community, and most students, still believe that to "go to college" means something specific and significant.

Educators, not other citizens, have the most trouble in reaching agreement about what is meant by *college.* Some envision the grid of the masses: big scale, redefinitions, programs in the service of the nation and the world—the college as miniversity. Others want the college redesigned to serve the needs and interests of the individual. They picture the institution as a center of individualized educational service or of therapeutic experience—the "What do you feel? What do you want?" approach to education. Still other educators want it both ways, traditional and nontraditional: the college is whatever we want to make it.

The word *college* has as many connotations as the word *church.* Almost any place can be called a church as long as "religion" is reported to be among its activities. Similarly, almost any place can be called a college as long as "education" is among its activities.

However, if that so-called church is considered Christian, and the "faithful" say: "We are Christians, but we do not believe that Jesus is the Christ, the son of the Living God; we are Christians, but we do not believe in the doctrine of the Trinity, nor in the Apostles' Creed, nor in the Bible as the basis of authority for the church," the observer will be obliged to conclude that these people may be religious but are not Christian. Although they may congregate in a place of worship, it is not a Christian church. We do not know whether what these people believe, as compared with what they do not believe, and what they do in their place of worship, as compared with what they do not do, justifies their place being called a church. What we know is that there are categories of meaning, about which there is broad consensus concerning what is meant by the word *Christian* or the word *church,* and we cannot permit a revisionist to engage in infinite regression, going beyond the categories, and still use those words without being challenged.

So it is with the word *college* or the phase *liberal arts college.* If an educator asserts that he or she represents a liberal arts college, and then proceeds to tell an audience that colleagues in that college do not believe in teaching the arts and sciences, nor in teaching and learning by the orientation and procedures that characterize a liberal arts college, sooner or later this person's auditors have the right to question whether the institution described is truly a liberal arts college. After a further exchange of views, it will be possible to determine whether this educator represents a college of any kind. There are categories of meaning attached to *college* or *liberal arts college,* from which it is not acceptable to depart without risking neglect of essential work of a college.

In this book, *college* means the undergraduate institution that offers an education both sequential and cumulative, theoretical yet practical, specific and interrelated. Also, the *college* nourishes the mind without neglecting the needs and interests of the whole person. It offers tertiary, not to be confused with secondary, education. A true college defers to the high school for the students' instruction in basic skills.

The college as defined here is not another variation of the multiversity, miniversity, or university. It is not research-oriented, with tight specializations and narrow methodologies for producing new knowledge. In the real college, syntheses and applications are as important as discovery and definition.

Educators tend to discount the contribution of the interpreter as compared with the inventor, that is, the person whose creativity is manifested in creative synthesizing or reordering of existing knowledge rather than in the discovery of new knowledge. Both types of persons have contributions to make. In the college, that fact is recognized. The college serves as a countervailing force to the university in that it honors the skillful blending, adaptation, and application of discovery whereas the university emphasizes the analytical process of discovery. Jazz offers an analogy: the college is more like Oscar Peterson, the university like Miles Davis. Frank Conroy, writing about Oscar Peterson, said: "Peterson is not a great creator of jazz. His compositions have been few, and his improvisations more celebratory than revolutionary. He is a great executor—which is every bit as great as a creator—whose life has been spent immersed in the music of the jazz masters for whom he feels the most affinity" (1981, p. 70). Miles Davis has been on the inventive edge of jazz. He is a discoverer. Peterson swings, but from a solid center. As Conroy (p. 70) puts it, "He does not so much discover—he reveals." The college is like that: it knows its place and does its job. It is true to itself.

Society surely needs a college that *is* a college, even in a culture in which a lemonade is sold that can boast only the scrapings of the skin of a lemon, and apple or orange drinks often have no trace of apple or orange juice, and places called colleges offer educational services showing little of the content of a college. The biblical injunction applies: "By their fruits ye shall know them."

Character. In this book, *character* means disciplined, evident, enduring commitment to principle, usually to goals and purposes seen as moral or ethical, and expressed individually and institutionally.

Character requires fidelity to duty under pressure, dignity amid controversy, courage in the presence of adversity. Character is earned, not conferred. A baseball season of 162 games may or may not help *develop* character in the players. But the winning team, after the dog days of summer and the almost interminable number of games, will certainly have *demonstrated* character.

Vince Lombardi, legendary football coach of the Green Bay Packers, took a bedraggled franchise in 1959 and, by the power of his commitments, by an expression of character, transformed the team into the football powerhouse of the next decade. We do not have to accept all the extremes of Lombardi's style—for example, "Winning is the *only* thing"—to learn some lessons from him about character. The Green Bay victories were less important than what Lombardi did with his team members: he made average players extraordinary. He did it by teaching and example, persuasion and demands. Lombardi's dedication and courage inspired the development of character in his teammates. He proved character to be more important than talent.

Character conveys authority. We say, "He speaks with authority." If we refer to authority as a way of describing character, we do not mean that this person speaks by the power of his office or under the mantle of his honors or title. The pope can speak *ex cathedra* and, when so doing, expresses authority. But that is not necessarily a manifestation of character. When we say, "He speaks with authority," we mean "with power," in the service of principle; we mean "persuasively," because of the quality of the message conveyed.

Character is commonly equated with reputation. However, we must be careful about following that line of thought. A person can have character without having a public reputation even as a person can have a reputation without having personal character. It is true, however, that an individual or institution of character develops, because of the disciplined, evident, and enduring commitment to principle, a reputation—and one worth defending.

Character is sometimes confused with "presence." However, using these words interchangeably is a mistake. Teresa Stratas of the Metropolitan Opera has that mysterious quality known as *presence*—the quality that arrests one's attention the instant its possessor appears on stage. Even when Stratas stands still on stage, the eyes of the audience are riveted on her. She gives an impression of being *somebody*, of having "an extraordinary talent," "a beautiful voice" (Sargeant, 1981, p. 40). That is presence. Character, however, means more than presence or reputation.

To say that character merely means characteristics, an office, title, or style, is to emasculate a powerful word at a time when words need to have their full vitality preserved. Saying, "He is a character," makes the word a caricature: it draws a laugh but seldom motivates action. Character should not be confused with odd or peculiar behavior. It involves more than being out of step or marching to a different drummer.

Ralph Waldo Emerson said that "character is more important than intellect." His statement applies to individuals and institutions, including academics and colleges. As Franklin D. Roosevelt said that "the all-important factor in national greatness is national character," so we can say that the all-important feature in a college of consequence is institutional character.

In a time when liberal arts colleges are increasingly relegated to a marginal status, at sixes and sevens about their mission and, consequently, wandering aimlessly as though lost, leadership is needed. Out of that bewildered, frightened company of institutions must emerge colleges of character that will give other schools a sense of possibilities beyond those presented by the versity with its emphasis on massive institutional services and the new community college with its endless options for individuals.

The challenge confronting liberal arts colleges and a college of character has to do with more than survival, although that is a significant challenge; and with more than finding an educational mission that does not imitate the two dominant models, although avoiding gridlock would be a noteworthy accomplishment. The ultimate challenge for a college of character extends to the political, economic, and religious crisis that attends the polarization of American society into grids of organizational immensity and personal intimacy.

The college of character offers hope for the revival of intermediate and mediating institutions in American life, institutions that are not merely playing the game of independence—as is the case with so many institutions spewing out doctors, lawyers, businessmen, and teachers. The nation needs institutions that will stand between the poles and serve as centers of countervailing force to the culture of no-context as well as truth squads for a society that knows only a history of no-history.

American education is experiencing a moral and ethical crisis, as is American society. The college of character can respond to both even when these crises are at their worst—worse than we can imagine in our worst moments.

2

─o─o─o─o─o─o─o─o─o─o─o─

Roots of Education's Dilemmas in Government, Economy, and Religion

─o─o─o─o─o─o─o─o─o─o─o─

In democracy, capitalism, religion, and education the fact of crisis, the emergence of another crisis, is not new. Democracy has always been a matter of somehow muddling through. Yet other political systems are even more muddled. Capitalism has helped produce such an unseaworthy ship of state that most Americans would identify with Noah when he looked into the ark after thirty days on the flood tide and said, "If it wasn't for the storm outside, I couldn't stand conditions inside." Religion in America, in its organized expressions, has been riding a roller coaster of ups and downs, twists and turns, for more than one hundred years. Education's record is much the same, with memories of the late sixties reminding us that education's troubles are not always trivial.

To emphasize the notion of crisis, or another crisis, is not to imply that little that is useful to the future can be learned from the past, or that nothing from earlier crises in democracy, capitalism, religion, and education has relevance to the present crisis. What we do now and how we plan for the future are affected by the past as surely as children establish their identity in the context of their

22

families and through the contributions of their heritage. Hannah
Arendt (1975, p. 6) said: "I rather believe with Faulkner, 'The past is
never dead, it is not even past; and this for the simple reason that the
world we live in at any moment is the world of the past; it consists of
the monuments and the relics of what has been done by men for
better or worse . . .' In other words, it is quite true that the past
haunts us; it is the past's function to haunt us who are present and
wish to live in the world as it really is." Thus, emphasizing the
present crisis does not assign it a virgin birth.

That there is a crisis of major proportions seems indisputable. Governmental policies wildly oscillate as inflation and recession prove intractable. The visible distress of the urban poor
contrasts with the subtle affluence of the suburban wealthy. Thousands undertake the religious quest stretching to the East and back
to the Bible, or forward with science because nothing satisfies the
yearning of the heart.

The culture of no-context is too limited to meet human needs
that transcend the moment. Confining history to paltry no-history
devastates quality because it reduces comparisons to incestuous
strokings, devastates authority because everything that challenges
autonomy is called authoritarian, devastates morality and ethics because today the moral person is one who constructs his or her own
ethic.

A culture of pluralism that aggregates everything at the extreme of the nation-state or at the other extreme of the solitary person is devoid of the middle distance essential to art or to the middle
axioms essential to philosophy. Such a culture cannot deal properly
with traditions and experiences, with groups and institutions too
large for the unit of one and too small for the grid of 200 million.

The culture of no-context does not acknowledge human aspirations that cannot be packaged. Nor does it recognize human sensibilities that refuse to be expressed either at the pitch of a sing-along
in Central Park or through the mode of whispered confidences in
the bedroom.

The values of this ersatz society—hurried immediacy, unqualified intensity, momentary loyalties, contrived quality, blood-
less experts, survey demographics, provisional agreements, audacious distractions, scale without focus—these "values" are, as has
been said, the virulent disease for which they are the proffered cure.

The crisis arising from distorted values indiscriminately applied now ravages government, the economy, religion, and education. It is at base a moral and ethical crisis that, in this chapter, will be described first as it manifests itself in education, then, in terms of its effect on democratic government, the capitalistic economy, and the civil religion.

Ethical Dilemmas in Education

Of all the crises in higher education today, the most serious is the ethical one. The financial crisis, the management crisis, the "basic skills" crisis, the institutional mission crisis—these and other crises are secondary.

The ethical crisis is the most serious because other crises cannot be settled until this one is confronted:

1. We cannot overcome threats to institutional integrity without first dealing with our confusion about what is meant by *institutional integrity*.
2. We cannot address the problem of the loss of education quality without first overcoming our ideational disarray and agreeing on standards of excellence.
3. We describe the problems of intercollegiate athletics as a "scandal," which implies the existence of widely accepted values and purposes when, in fact, we have only conflicting norms and objectives.
4. We cannot wrestle with issues such as autonomy or accountability until we agree on the rules of the game.

Again, why is the ethical crisis the most serious and important? Without moral principles, the institutions of higher education and the teaching profession lose moral authority. Moral authority, not technical services or professional skills, is a college's most prized possession. Despite a tradition of detachment and claims to value neutrality, the institution of higher education, along with the church and synagogue, is expected by the people to be an instrumentality of idealism. Without ideals that direct and correct behavior, institutions of higher learning are like a perfectly outfitted ship without a rudder.

Historically, American colleges and universities have not only had moral authority but also have performed with comparatively high ethics—certainly no worse than those of the church and surely better than government and industry. We recall occasions when some obscure functionary tampered with an athlete's transcript (as occurred ten or twelve years ago in Texas, although it involved the University of Oklahoma). Then, too, there have been the intermittent cheating scandals. (My memory immediately locks on the Air Force Academy and West Point.) Some could point to "that grade," the so-called "gentleman's C," or to the smattering of diploma mills grinding out bogus degrees for benighted students.

Nevertheless, most of these misdeeds of the past could be considered mere peccadilloes. If the English have taken their pleasures sadly, American academics have taken to sinning poorly. American colleges and universities have been admired as bastions of traditional moral values and exemplars of institutional integrity. Individuals have sometimes faltered, but the institution seldom has (Martin, 1974, pp. 28–29).

Yet we all know that educated people and educators have no corner on the moral virtues. From the time of the Greeks, there have been warnings that to know what is right is not necessarily to do it. We need to go back only into our own century to be reminded that the educated are sometimes the frauds and fools. In a time of charges and countercharges, payoffs and bribes in corporate life, and corruption compounded in politics, this is no era for educators to be smug about their traditions or indifferent to the evidence of moral dilemmas becoming ethical crises in the institutions for which they are responsible.

What are some of the factors contributing to the ethical crisis in colleges and universities? And how did this crisis come about?

Federal and State Influence. Thirty to fifty percent of the budgets of major research universities come from federal contracts. At least one half of the undergraduates and graduates receive some federal aid. The federal government has the power, by use of its economic leverage, to shut down all but the best-endowed universities.

Granted, not everything the state and federal governments have done is wrong—the tuition equalization programs of most states have been educationally useful and politically benign. But many state and federal programs have induced faculty and administrators into dependency as dangerous as that of the robin who spends the winter in the north and becomes dependent for his daily diet on the household breadcrumbs tossed into the snow.

Between 1957 and 1972, a period during which federal programs and influence grew explosively, few leaders in higher education warned that money entailed regulation, that institutional autonomy was threatened, that the costs of accountability were rising precipitously. (In 1980, Columbia University spent $450,000 to install an accounting system for the purpose of assuring that designated funds were not used for other purposes [Fiske, 1980, p. 86].) Educators failed to see the deeper meaning of what was occurring or, seeing it, they lacked the courage to speak out. Thus, independence eroded and dependence built up. Senator Daniel Patrick Moynihan: "Clearly, the university has all but lost its institutional distinctiveness in the eyes of the state. This was the predictable development as universities became ever more dependent on the state and ever more supportive . . . of a powerful, activist, multifaceted state" (1980, p. 32).

Most private colleges are 80–90 percent dependent for their annual operating budget on income from student tuition and fees. But 30–50 percent of student tuition in almost all colleges has been coming from federal and state programs. And one sixth to one fifth of total institutional income has been generated from these same sources. The painful truth is that many so-called independent colleges are, like universities, in a locked embrace with federal and state governments. This condition contributes to the ethical dilemmas that wrack academe.

Business and Industry Connections. In summer 1981, newspapers carried reports of a $6 million grant by the DuPont Chemical Company to Harvard University for research in geriatrics, with the proviso that the company have an exclusive contract to market any patentable product or process. This news followed a similar but ten-times-larger deal between the Harvard-affiliated Massachusetts General Hospital and a West German drug and chemical conglomerate, Hoechst-Roussel Pharmaceuticals.

These grants reflect the confidence of drug and chemical companies that, by allying themselves with university genetic research labs, they will share in the new biotechnologies and resulting marketable products.

But there is anxiety in academe over these developments. The DuPont grant alone equals nearly half of the Harvard Medical School's annual tuition and endowment income. Will university labs succumb to industry's agenda? Will industry leaders expect to have their sociopolitical values accepted by the college in the same package with their dollars?

Exxon has joined MIT for basic research in combustion. Harvard has major contracts with Monsanto. Edward Fiske of the *New York Times,* noting these developments and others like them, has commented: "The practice does raise ethical questions of whether the purity of academic research can be compromised by commercial exploitation. If the paths of the pursuit of knowledge and the pursuit of profit don't always coincide, which path will be taken?" (1980, p. 84).

The problem is increasing because universities are losing contracts for research to private or independent labs and companies. Also, the sociopolitical conservatism of most businessmen is offended by the sociopolitical liberalism of many university faculty. Some industry leaders have talked openly of using their economic leverage with the universities to make those institutions more politically conservative.

Within Institutions of Higher Education. Problems and situations with ethical ramifications, issues containing moral dilemmas, include:

1. Headline topics such as sexual harassment, rape, the low status of professional women in the ranks of the profession, salary discrepancies, and other forms of exploitation
2. The intercollegiate athletics scandals (Martin, 1981b)
3. The status of racial and ethnic minorities, for example, the so-called ghettoization of minority faculty in Third World programs or Black Studies or other quasisegregated assignments

4. Student cheating—plagiarism, computer manipulation, tinkering with lab assignments

5. Faculty collusion in student cheating

6. Unethical behavior among faculty—expropriation of graduate student research; manipulation of work schedules and leave assignments and sabbaticals; intimidation of faculty by students, and of students by faculty

7. Administrative improprieties—ballooning student tuition budgets, concealing work-study violations and student loan irregularities; unethical student recruiting activities and misleading, if not dishonest, advertising

8. Fiscal opportunism contributing to the debasement of the academic currency, for example, new programs introduced because of their income potential but without much regard for the adequacy of the institution's resources for those programs

9. Cannibalism among educational institutions—for student FTE, for territory and programs, for publicity (intercollegiate athletics used as a general student recruiting tool . . . "Welcome to fun and games, and a little learning too!")

10. Failure of institutional representatives to support federal and state officials as they administer student loan programs and try to cope with loan defaults

11. Administrators, cooperating with faculty, who intentionally subvert institutional traditions by helping to move the orientation of the college toward professionalism, guild loyalties, and so on, thereby damaging institutional identity and the sense of community. The resulting professionalism of the faculty, and the organization of the institution by subject-matter specializations, puts unmanageable strain on general education and cross-disciplinary programs. Thus are institutional missions, and educational philosphies changed—without discussion and perhaps without alteration in the statements of purpose

12. Administrators, faculty, and trustees of a college that has a self-proclaimed distinctiveness, who change or add programs—an MBA, a nursing program, an external degree program—that make the historic and basic contribution no longer possible for all students

The Deepest Reason for the Crisis Among Crises. Behind the various special threats to institutional integrity—those coming from the federal "partnership" or from the business connection, or those caused by administrative centralization, professorial cronyism, and various forms of intimidation by students—and behind the problems in general and career education, nontraditional programs, in financial aid and work-study arrangements—is a more fundamental problem and threat: the presence of ideational inertia, even despair. Uncertainty about an appropriate education philosophy, disagreement about the desired outcomes of teaching and learning, in sum, confusion about the nature of the enterprise, has led to immobility and a spirit of resignation.

There may once have been general agreement on a body of knowledge that, when accepted and mastered, would give to its holder self-understanding and a role in society—the Greek Academy, the medieval trivium and quadrivium, the liberal-humanistic curriculum of the nineteenth century. But there is no agreement now on the essential intent, the best form, or the likely consequences of students' courses of study.

The present situation with its paucity of character and its infinitely complex problems can lead to two undesirable outcomes for colleges and universities. One is academic anarchy—not anarchism, that well-reasoned political philosophy that downplays governmental authority and encourages voluntary cooperation and the free association of individuals, but anarchy, a mindless denial of order and tradition, with the solitary person as the sole basis for authority, and no regard for voluntary cooperation and the free association of individuals.

As for *academic* anarchy, it is especially in the realm of standards, criteria, or guidelines for determining and evaluating the nature of the academic enterprise that educators are threatened. By insisting on the limitless creation of alternatives to established procedures and goals, we produce a condition defined only by options, in which there is nothing stable against which to measure fluidity, nothing permanent that provides a standard by which to measure change.

The second serious danger for the future is the threat of imposed probity. In legislatures, in state system offices, among our education sponsors, there are those who have already concluded that faculty and students are incapable of monitoring their own behavior, that the institution is incapable of reforming itself, and that correction of abuse requires the imposition of external authority. A hint of things to come was given several years ago when the trustees of the California State University and Colleges censured four of the nineteen presidents of the system's campuses by withholding salary raises for these persons because they had not handled various forms of trouble on their campuses in the way or with the dispatch desired by the trustees. Although the action was later modified, the incident stands as a warning of how rewards and sanctions can be used to enforce order.

Government legislators, federal and state, are becoming more and more assertive in the interests of fiscal accountability and economic efficiency, and more and more concerned about the range of professional training offered through the curriculum and about the quality of educational services. Where an ethical crisis emerges in the colleges, the threat of imposed probity cannot be far behind (Martin, 1974, p. 33).

Ideational inertia at the colleges and awareness that ethical dilemmas can cause spiritual exhaustion and moral paralysis may increase the danger that the experts and consultants will be more assertive than usual in promoting the advantages of those safe, popular models of the versity and the community college. There is no paucity of advisers oriented to the grids of dominance who presume to be able to solve the ethical crisis in education. Unfortunately, they don't invest themselves in overcoming the crises in social institutions out of which the educational problems came.

Crisis in Government, the Economy, and Religion

Education's ethical crisis, in its several manifestations, is related to ethical dilemmas now confounding other social institutions. Here are several of those issues in certain key areas.

Democratic Government. Consider one sign of crisis: There is now no coalition of interests in the nation able to devise a program of comprehensive government reform and to carry it out. Among many observers of this situation, James Reston makes the point in referring to Republicans and Democrats as well as to America's relationship with a divided world: "They [the politicians] have several things in common: They are divided among themselves in both parties and with one another, and they are facing a host of world problems, economic and political where nobody is in charge. . . . The nations of the world are spending about 600 billion a year on military weapons, while half the human race goes to bed hungry every night.

"There are now at least seven nations producing nuclear weapons and more than 20 more capable of doing so—not to mention the terrorist minorities that may get hold of nuclear wastes and hold not only hostages but whole cities for ransom" (1981, p. A31).

Here is a related sign of crisis: There are no governmental nor transgovernmental agencies that are widely supported and morally persuasive. Harlan Cleveland summarizes both signs: "The condition we now face is . . . the apparent incapacity of existing political institutions, whatever their ideological color, to manage unprecedented complexity" (1978, p. 31).

This is a time when the movement of ideas and events in America has been from uniformity to pluralism to paradox and contradiction. We are left with a situation much akin to that of the internal combustion engine, in which power generates from countervailing force or counter pressure. Through pressure and tension, our culture, like the engine, is empowered, and things move, but always with the threat that the generative condition will blow the engine apart. The academy is like that, empowered and moving, but without a sense of direction, without confidence in where it is going or how it will get there, and with anxiety that everything may soon be blown to pieces.

Economy of Capitalism. Further evidence of crisis? Americans cannot reconcile capitalism's acquisitive drives with their moral sensibilities, nor democracy's rewards for citizens with initiative and its perils for the destitute.

This nation has shown compassion and benevolence toward the needy through churches and synagogues, wealthy benefactors, state and federal programs. The people have acted as though social interdependence were as important as personal freedom. But we have also shown a commitment to individualism and entrepreneurship.

In today's struggling cities of the Midwest and Northeast, on many street corners of commercial districts there is physical evidence in the form of faded signs and old building facades of family businesses that rose and fell with market demands and industrial competition. In those cities, the streets reflect tears and laughter, success and failure—the American dream and the American nightmare.

Europeans have always been more attentive than Americans to the moral dilemmas created by civilization and democracy. Certain of the literary intelligentsia in the twenties, represented by English-speaking conservatives—Yeats, D. H. Lawrence, T. S. Eliot—flirted with fascism because they considered democracy intellectually exhausted and capitalism morally corrupt. Europeans are now dismayed by the apparent willingness of many Americans to submit the nation and the West to the working of the market, to the proposition that free enterprise and free political institutions should be the arbiters of civilization. Nor do Europeans like the notion, again common in the States, that numbers count best and count most—"money talks," "he has the numbers"—those sentiments are repulsive to an elite of conscience who know that truth is not always determined by a show of hands. But the same anxieties about the corruptions of pragmatism and democracy in this country have been shared by American intellectuals. They perceive in this nation a moral sensibility that is, to their dismay, often shielded by materialism and selfishness.

Perhaps nowhere in the United States is the discrepancy between the wealthy and the poor, or the invariable if not inevitable tendency of capitalism to divide people into the overclass and the underclass, more strikingly evident than in St. Louis, Missouri.

In this moderately proportioned city (520,000), the midtown area along Grand Avenue was in the twenties a thriving shopping center and the heart of the theater district. The city was larger then, and confident about its future. But in the fifties and sixties, Grand Avenue and other areas declined, with several large theaters and other commercial buildings closed or underutilized. One of the old theaters became the home of the St. Louis Symphony Orchestra, the glittering Powell Hall, noted for its cut glass chandeliers and abundance of gold leaf embellishments. Nearby, literally within sight of Powell Hall, was Pruitt-Igoe, a huge public-housing project, built in the fifties as a model of urban renewal, high-rise architecture, and liberal good will toward the poor. The Pruitt-Igoe project won numerous awards, but by the sixties it had become the home of the city's most wretched poor—thousands of people living in ever more deficient buildings. While music of high quality reverberated through Powell Hall, to the benefit of the affluent, the quality of life deteriorated in Pruitt-Igoe, to the distress and humiliation of the poor. This housing project by the seventies had to be totally abandoned and the entire complex of buildings blasted to the ground, obliterating what would otherwise have been a grim monument to human failures. Powell Hall, meanwhile, continued to prosper as a place for the elite to celebrate civilization through classical music. Thus did the culture and economy of St. Louis unite to produce a version of upstairs-downstairs.

Today the crisis in capitalism and the American economy is quantitatively large enough and qualitatively serious enough to warrant, to necessitate, a restructuring of the capitalistic framework. Only in this way can we avoid the desensitization of our moral sensibilities.

National Religion. Christianity in America, and the Judeo-Christian tradition, as expressed in the so-called mainline churches and Reformed Judaism, have almost from their beginnings in this country been paralleled by and, more recently, superseded by a moral and ethical development that Sidney Mead and other scholars have called "the civil religion" (see Mead, 1963, pp. 25ff., 59; also Bellah, 1970, pp. 168ff.). This "religion" has been a limited yet influential set of beliefs and practices that existed alongside, yet distinct from, sectarian Christianity or Orthodox Judaism.

The civil religion developed its own authority and leadership, both of which came to have influence with most Christians and Jews. The Declaration of Independence and the Constitution served early in our history as the holy writ of this religion. The key tenets of dogma were the sovereignty of God and America's manifest destiny. George Washington was the American Moses. The American political experiment was seen as a decisive event in the mighty acts of God, "that Sovereign to whom all governments are ultimately accountable" (Mead, 1963, p. 66). Americans were the almost–chosen people, even as Abraham Lincoln was almost a saint.

The civil religion in America was a necessary expedient because of the concept of social pluralism, which was itself dependent on the evidence of diversity in American life. Hence, tolerance came to be emphasized as a concomitant of pluralism. Martin Marty, of the University of Chicago, has commented on this rationale and the struggle that occurred before it gained preeminence: "Most pluralisms have been based on the idea that there should be a host culture and then there can be guest cultures. First, there is an official, legal establishment and then dissenters are allowed to exist in the society on some terms or other. Assent is present so that there can also be dissent; conformity is present so that there can be nonconformity. The United States . . . learned its new plot very slowly. It took a couple centuries before a true legal basis was provided, and down even into the middle of the twentieth century, it was still hard for privileged religious groups to learn that in mores and ethos they had to yield privilege and share equal space and time with groups they had once considered to be marginal" (Marty, 1977, p. 139).

Pluralism came to be seen not as a necessary expedient to be tolerated only until the truth had been revealed, but as an end in itself.

Before the nation gained independence, Benjamin Franklin sensed the need for a unifying creed but despaired of the churches ever providing it. He advocated a "Publick Religion." It would take its authority not solely from Scripture but also from the social contract, from the sensible moral and ethical guidelines that reasonable men could agree on because of their capacity for reason. Franklin offered a modified deism—one of the contributions of the Enlightenment—that would meet the need of the solitary individual and provide a collective ethos for the institutions of society; it would draw on the Judeo-Christian tradition but also provide the sanction for substantial diversity. The lion and the lamb, Christianity and humanism, would lie down together.

Over the next one hundred years, or perhaps longer, the scales tipped from the advantage of the Judeo-Christian tradition, with a growing tolerance for outsiders, to a preference for humanism and secularism, with tolerance so broad that there were no discernible outsiders, nor real insiders. Consequently, over time, as John Murray Cuddihy has shown, the American civil religion became the religion of civility or inoffensiveness (Cuddihy, 1978, pp. 191ff.; for a summary, see Gunn, 1978). Sectarianism or the belief in a singular truth became heresy. One of the civil religion's main features was incivility toward persons or ideas that did not share its dedication to civility.

Now, in the fourth quarter of the twentieth century, the religion of civility is itself under attack and is being forced to change. Reform has become necessary because the recent expression of the civil religion, the religion of civility, is putting unbearable stress on American society.

The religion of civility is too limited. It does not satisfy the human yearning for a religion that is, on the one hand, vitally personal and, on the other, awesomely transcendent. Consequently, the faithful are increasingly unfaithful. Religion should provide the basis for the ethics of a culture just as society provides the setting for the expression of the culture. The civil religion today is a derivative of the culture, not a shaper of it.

> *The bay trees in our country are all withered, and*
> *meteors fright the fixed stars of heaven.*
> *The pale-faced moon looks bloody on the earth,*
> *and lean-looked prophets whisper fearful change.*
>   Shakespeare, *Richard II*

Everywhere people talk about the need to reduce the size and influence of the federal and state government. However, given the magnitude of the nation's problems and our expectations of the government to take the lead in solving those problems, given the extent of present governmental involvement and the range of federal and state services that most people do not want to give up, the government will probably have a larger, not smaller, role in determining the social philosophy during the eighties and nineties, that is, in designing and carrying out what is meant by disciplined democracy.

Everywhere people talk about the need to restrain the growth and to contain the avarice of multinational corporations. However, given the present influence of those corporations around the world, given the fact that they seem necessary to provide the money and skills needed for tasks that are national and international in scope, given the fact that the United States, Western Europe, and Japan are outstripping the rest of the world in computer technology essential to meet the problems of all countries, multinational corporations will probably have a larger, not smaller, role to play in our changing national economy, in "planned capitalism" and its effects on the world.

Although many mainline churches in America have declined in popularity and influence, and the sects and cults attract more people every day, it is unlikely that the new evangelical revival, or the influence of Eastern religions, or the charismatic movement, will determine the civil religion of America in the next two decades. This country is too diverse to permit that to occur. The civil religion arose, in part, because of the need for a comprehensive religion that was not exclusive or sectarian, one that expressed and endorsed cultural pluralism in America. We still have that need.

This same pluralism, however, continued to erode the limited content of the old civil religion that stressed the sovereignty of God and America's manifest destiny, to the point that the civil religion became the religion of civility (Cuddihy, 1978), a religion concerned with justifying cultural differences and ideological diversity and, as necessary, softening the points of impact where people collide. That is why the so-called mainline churches and Reformed synagogues came to appear as extinct volcanoes. People need a religion that offers and demands more than mere accommodations to and rationalizations for social compromises—hence, the popularity of the sects and cults, the healers, charismatics, and televised church.

Now, precisely because the sects are sectarian while the nation is pluralistic, the old civil religion will be replaced, with the help of a theology of pluralism, by a new civil religion—an enlivened pantheism. The new religion will be promoted as free from rough edges but having a solid core, the religion for the whole person in a world culture.

The new civil religion and the new theology of pluralism must, therefore, establish moral authority: probity must be defined, its claims stated, its effects acknowledged. The good life defined in egocentric, self-indulgent terms proved ultimately shallow, even boring. The problem with permissiveness is that it requires standards against which to define and establish itself. It is like gossip, which has no zip without social norms and absolutes. Permissiveness stands only by leaning against that which it tries to tear down. To the extent that it is successful, then, it is self-defeating. The mark of an enlivened pantheism will be its ability to establish a basis for moral authority.

As Will Durant has shown, history, in its literature, arts, government, and morals, tends to alternate between liberty becoming license and authority becoming authoritarianism. Therefore, we may expect the current movement away from indulgence to continue and to found a new epoch of authority, discipline, and restraint (Durant and Durant, 1977, p. 402).

The civil religion in America, during its earlier incarnation, emphasized the sovereignty of God and America's manifest destiny. In its later form, influenced heavily by cultural pluralism, it emphasized the sovereignty of the people and America's interdependence with other nations (America being, of course, the first among equals).

Early public education in America emphasized social indoctrination and preparation for work. Recently, influenced heavily by cultural pluralism, it has emphasized egalitarianism (a form of social indoctrination) and job entitlement (an attitudinal preparation for work).

The future civil religion in America will emphasize a humane pantheism and America's interdependence with select nations (as well as the select nations' manifest destiny).

The future public education in America, affected by the excesses of cultural pluralism, will emphasize egalitarianism (a form of limited pluralism) and job security (a feature of state socialism).

Consequences for Education

How will this challenge—the crises in government, the economy, and religion, as well as the effect of the responses, disciplined democracy, planned capitalism, enlivened pantheism—affect education, particularly higher education?

No society tolerates an educational system that subverts the values of the prevailing culture. It has not happened elsewhere in the world and is not happening in America. The first task of schools and colleges has been, and remains, to inculcate youth in the values of the state, to drill the students in requisite skills and persuade them to accept the attitudes deemed important in maintaining and improving the sponsoring society.

Colleges will be expected, during the next two decades, to follow the lead of that coterie of control from the multinational corporations and the bureaucracy in training students in the various work skills and inculcating them in the prevailing social values. Colleges in the new culture will serve the social consensus through educating for disciplined democracy, planned capitalism, and the new civil religion.

To the extent that society's values are clear, the service of the educational institution will be apparent. To the extent that societal consensus is lacking, the service of the educational institution will be confused and inconsistent. An example follows:

Integration of the races and desegregation of the schools characterized American policy in the sixties. A social consensus seemed to have been achieved. Colleges and universities were expected to carry out that policy through affirmative action. Federal funding was soon tied to institutional adherence. Educational institutions accepted responsibility for implementing this policy—they had not been conspicuous leaders in affirmative action or desegregation before that time—and proceeded in their admission policies, curricular development, and statement of institutional purposes to conform college practice to social policy. This service was not provided wisely or well, rather, haltingly and fumblingly; nevertheless, it became a feature of college life for more than a decade. In such a manner institutions of higher education serve social policies developed in the centers of political and economic power.

Society at large was less clear in the sixties about its social and economic policies for war-ravaged southeast Asia than it was about civil rights. Despite political commitment to the war, there was societal disagreement. Colleges and universities reflected that uncertainty, even while they continued serving the military through contracts and ROTC and serving government through research and consultants. The antiwar movement, springing up in two or three locations, developed its fullest expression on the campuses. But contrary to popular opinion, colleges were not fully persuaded by that movement. Institutions of higher education were divided, reflecting the division in the nation. When consensus is lost, confusion reigns—on campus as elsewhere.

Can colleges be more independent despite the present movement in America, albeit with much twisting and turning, toward authoritarianism?

Perhaps. According to the speeches of academic leaders, colleges and universities are still centers of independent thinking. They serve society, to be sure, but sometimes they serve best by criticizing, refusing to go along, developing alternative models and promoting them. Alvin Gouldner of Washington University claims: "To understand modern universities and colleges we need an openness to contradiction. For universities both reproduce and subvert the larger society. We must distinguish between the functions universities publicly *promise* to perform—the social goods they are chartered to produce and certain of their actual consequences which, while commonly unintended, are no less real: the production of dissent, deviance, and the cultivation of an authority-subverting culture of critical discourse" (Gouldner, 1979, p. 45).

My claim, and another element in my thesis, is that the college, not the university, has the best potential for becoming a center of countervailing force—*if* it refuses to be a community of convenience and becomes a community of conviction, *if* it develops a coalition of support so that not one but many colleges become colleges of character.

What can be done, and what should be done? What will education's response be to the challenge of this crisis in American society?

Of the 3,000 colleges and universities in the United States, most will cooperate with the emerging national establishment and the cadre of leadership from global business that will take responsibility for creating order out of near chaos in the eighties and nineties by imposing on America disciplined democracy, planned capitalism, and a new civil religion. The majority of colleges and universities will adhere to the nation's education agenda—doing their part of the basic research, training leaders and functionaries, inculcating students in the attitudes and values appropriate for a garrison state.

The first law of life is "survival," and these institutions are hooked, for their survival, on federal and state aid.

The second law of life is "significance," but under the circumstances, most colleges and universities can be expected to define significance in terms of services dictated for them by their nation-state.

Lest all of this sound too cynical, it should be added that much of what the coterie of control can be expected to promote—for government, the economy, the social culture, religion, and education—makes good sense. Freedom can be diabolical and has frequently been carried to indefensible extremes. America's acquisitive drive and materialistic preferences have proven excessive—wasteful of natural resources destructive to human sensibilities. We need to rein in lest our wild stallions become the four horses of the Apocalypse.

Community is the word for those who would assure the survival of the species. It is the password for the future. *Individualism* is the word for those committed to creative change and the search for new experiences. It is the password of the past. In times of apparent peace and material abundance, of unlimited territory and inexhaustible resources, individualism and freedom expand. In times of war and famine, of reduced resources and social perils, the tide turns to community and order.

There are times when freedom and individualism can flourish and other times when human beings cannot afford such extravagance. These privileges are as beautiful and fragile as a field of poppies. We have known such a time. We have been in such a place. But we have left that place and have blocked out that time.

A most difficult task in the future for education will be to discriminate between the good and bad, the right and wrong elements of this culture of control and its expectations for education. Only a few institutions, usually private universities and colleges with a long tradition of independence and high endowments, will be able to withstand the pressures and remain essentially independent or autonomous. Nothing more will be said about these institutions now except that they will have awesome responsibilities in the future—if the culture of control is to be mitigated.

At the other end, the tail end of what David Riesman called the snakelike procession of academe in *Constraint and Variety in American Education* (1959), will be those institutions that are so weak, so dependent, that they must cater to every fad or whim, every innovation or opportunity, every federal funding incentive or available state subsidy. These institutions become so distorted by this pandering life-style, as with many community colleges, that even today they are not colleges by any recognizable definition: they are better called centers of educational services. And, of course, in the future, given their past, they will have no qualms about flexible definitions of accountability, even when the culture of restraint becomes the culture of repression and authoritarianism becomes tyranny. Leadership sometimes comes from the economically poor but never from the morally bewildered.

Between the institutional extremes, within that great middle range of colleges and universities, there are several hundred colleges and several thousand administrators, faculty members, trustees, and alumni who show promise of avoiding capitulation to the forces of control and of becoming, instead, resources for the creation of centers of corrective action.

More often than not, the community of conviction and the college of character will be found among the seven hundred or so liberal arts colleges in this nation and, to be even more specific, among the church-related colleges and universities. Why there more often than elsewhere?

1. Because the notion of a purposeful community, a community of conviction as compared with a community of convenience, has retained a certain vitality, at least a theoretical validity in these institutions
2. Because the idea of value-oriented higher education, or what Martin Buber called the "education of character," has survived in statements of institutional purpose, in curricular offerings, and in the education philosophy of trustees, administrators, and faculty at such places
3. Because these colleges provide the best opportunity for linkages with other appropriate institutions of society, especially with

churches and synagogues, at a time when the forces of domination can only be withstood by coalitions of like-minded people
4. Because these colleges are usually somewhat more homogene-
ous than the public, larger, more heterogeneous places; and
more malleable, more responsive to leadership, than the impersonal, fully bureaucratized institutions.

Also noteworthy is the prospect that liberal arts colleges, particularly those with church affiliation, are best positioned to begin a
job that is always best begun "at home"; that is, they are capable of
attacking the ethical crisis on their own campuses as a way not only
of setting their own house in order but of gaining experience and
getting ready to contribute to the infinitely bigger task of dealing
with the ethical crisis in the nation at large.

In the new culture approaching there will be a place for that
old institution called a college. The college for that culture will be
recognizable to traditionalists. But there will be noticeable differences as a result of changes compelled by the crisis. The tasks that the
new culture will assign to the college for the nineties and beyond
cannot be carried out easily. They will exact a price. The college
should not accept those assignments and pay that price. There is no
doubt, however, that the new culture will have a place for an old-
new college.

The Royal Palace in Holland, begun in 1648, is supported by
13,659 wooden pilings. Indeed, the entire city of Amsterdam is built
on wooden or concrete pilings. Major institutions of Western life—
political, economic, religious, and educational—are built on thousands of supports, not short posts as could be expected in a history of
no-history, but deep foundations that are centuries old, as enduring
and basic as those pilings under the Royal Palace and the city of
Amsterdam.

The present culture of no-context has been brought to prom-
inence by people who would be pleased, for good and bad reasons, to
see the supports for institutions, such as those symbolized by the
Royal Palace of Holland, rot out. Let the Palace and everything
associated with it collapse into the mire of a stinking tradition.

But the new builders have not replaced the old foundations. They have covered them over with the grid of 200 million and the grid of one. On these planes contemporary life has been concentrated. Everything is happening atop supports that are still in place—even though ignored. The civilization of no-culture has been jerry-built on old piers and hidden pilings that are not being maintained. With further neglect, those supports will finally collapse, taking all surface manifestations of prosperity with them.

The House of Intellect in America today is no better built, no better positioned, no more secure or enduring than the other institutions of this culture. Unwilling to shore up sagging foundations, education's landlords make temporary repairs, patching and painting over structural deficiencies as well as surface flaws. Consider what is called general or liberal education: In most colleges this form of education is neither general nor liberal, but a product of faculty trade-offs or market demands. When finally assembled, liberal education looks like a California tool shed—all chicken wire and rough plaster, having neither external beauty nor internal coherence. The question is not, does this "product" have integrity, but did it ever have any.

Could the managers of the House of Intellect do better than they have done? Could trustees and presidents, working with faculty and students, discard the confrontational mentality suggested by terms such as *landlords* and *tenants* and, together, as interested parties if not as a true community, do something special with those institutions of higher education called liberal arts colleges? How could these colleges be improved to meet the threat of the ethical crisis on campus and in the society at large?

3

‱0‱0‱0‱0‱0‱0‱0‱0‱0‱0‱0‱

Qualities of a
College of Character

‱0‱0‱0‱0‱0‱0‱0‱0‱0‱0‱0‱

William James (1928, pp. 49–50) said that differences in one place make a difference elsewhere. Stung by the implication of his assertion for too many liberal arts colleges, we must ask, What distinguishes a college *in* but not *of* the new culture; an institution with service to society among its purposes, indeed, one that functions *for* the society and the good of the nation, an institution that is no longer content simply to have characteristics and, instead, that sets out deliberately to become a college of character? Following are several hallmarks of such a college.

The Synoptic Function

The basic rationale for that college committed to relevance as well as distinction is none of the institutional justifications most often heard. It is said, for example, that 60–70 percent of the basic research in America is done in institutions of higher education or under university contracts. The labs, equipment, experts—all the necessary resources are there. The nation has tremendous equity in the research university. However, is that argument the keystone in the university's defense? Basic research is not confined to the university, and there is no reason to foster a university monopoly on that enterprise. Basic research can be done, is more and more often done, in corporate or independent labs, with corporate, state, and federal funding.

Another rationale used to support all modern universities, and most liberal arts colleges, is that they train Americans for the major professions. Education for careers is the proper business of institutions of higher education. But again, does this function justify, better than any other, society's support of colleges and universities? Training, whether for research or job skills, can be done outside the university and beyond the college by the corporations, the military, special federal and state programs. And it can be carried out more cheaply, faster, perhaps better. Furthermore, many schools of law, medicine, and business administration chafe against the constraints of the traditional university, even as nontraditional undergraduate training programs find the environment of the college restrictive. Is job training the keystone of higher education's defense?

What about general education and instruction in reading, writing, composition, and other basic skills? These services are prominent in the rationale for today's colleges and universities. General education is hard to define, especially in the university, but if it is meant to be more than survey courses and introductions to disciplinary specializations that lead to careers in teaching, then general education is the responsibilty of the entire community inside and outside the college. It is the task of family and home, churches and synagogues, museums, libraries, and the media—especially television. Formal education is only one approach to general education. As for basic skills, these are best learned early in life, at home and in the grammar schools. Why should the colleges try to do the work of the grammar schools when, aside from the absurdity of this waste of the resources of colleges and universities, high schools can finish that work? Can the nation afford the extravagance of such triplication? Do we use basic skills instruction to justify colleges and universities because of some vague hope that, as the saying goes, "The third time is the charm?"

The best rationale for universities and colleges, for colleges particularly, is none of the aforementioned. The true rationale is that the university and college are places best suited for what can be called the synoptic function. It is in institutions of higher education that many tasks such as basic research, which should be among the tasks done there; and job training or professional education, which should also be among the work done there; and general education plus instruction in basic skills, which are facts of life there, are brought into contact with each other so that the social, political, moral, and ethical ramifications can be held up for sustained investigation. This synoptic function, with its cross-fertilization of ideas and methodologies, is the crucial rationale for the college because this system yields answers to the questions of meaning and ends, of significance and effects.

> *The capacity to judge rightly in a choice of both means and ends cuts across the specialties and the technologies, and it is, I dare say, the hallmark of a liberal, as distinguished from a utilitarian or vocational education.*
>
> Walter Lippmann

A Comprehensive College. The words *liberal* and *arts* or *liberal arts* as used today, are dysfunctional as well as inaccurate. They should be downplayed, if employed at all.

Liberal no longer has the classical definition employed by the Greeks and Romans. Aristotle's and Cicero's use of *liberal* was as an antonym for *servile.* Nor is the word used today in its modern political sense, as with a decreasing number of Democrats called liberals who are politically liberal.

The use of the word *arts* is just as inappropriate. Currently, it has neither a practical connotation nor a generally understood technical meaning. It incorporates no body of knowledge, at least none that is a trademark of a college.

The words *general education* are better but do not adequately define the college. General education is properly a part of that education offered in the college, particularly that defined by Ernest Boyer and Arthur Levine in their 1981 monograph as the education all people should have in common. But "general education" as usually offered is not general—it is "basic skills" with introduction to the various disciplines; or it is not general enough—it does not integrate subject-matter specializations and their applications; or it is too general—that is, loose and ill-defined, with too many electives and broad distribution requirements set up more to protect faculty than to educate students.

In a college having the synoptic function as its first priority, programs of study are comprehensive in that they are broadly educational, meeting the needs and interests of the whole person, but also narrowly academic, theoretical, and intellectually rigorous. The curriculum includes general education and the subject matter of the arts and sciences, but professional education and career training have equal importance.

The mission of the comprehensive college is not to promote the study of subjects that have no evident application any more than it is to shelter faculty or students in separate, elite functions. This college does not require the students to choose between theoretical studies and applied skills, or between academic and educational functions, or between traditional and nontraditional studies, or between the liberal arts and professional education. Hence, the word *comprehensive* applies to programs of study, the types and ages of students served, the methodological approaches used in the various fields of study, and the institution's larger relationships—with churches and synagogues, with business and industry, with museums and libraries, social service agencies, secondary schools, and other educational centers such as vocational, proprietary schools.

Not all social orientations, philosophies of education, and teaching methodologies can be accommodated. The college will not be comprehensive in this sense. Nor can the college take up every professional training assignment, or each graduate school specialization, or most of the job-related training that business and industry may propose. The college will not be comprehensive in these dimensions.

Comprehensive is herein a synonym for *synoptic* and is used in a limited and relative sense: The college is more comprehensive in its subject matter and its specializations than the traditional "liberal arts" college. The college may be more comprehensive in the composition of its student body, welcoming older as well as younger students. It may be more comprehensive in the location of its programs, with most of them on campus but with some at sites in the institution's catchment basin and, if supervision can be assured, across the nation and around the world.

I do not hesitate to use the term *comprehensive college* even though former teacher's colleges that have broadened their mission, adding programs in professional fields and graduate studies or training in a variety of careers, have come to be called "comprehensive universities." The emphasis for the college here designated a *comprehensive college* lies in its blending of themes and subject matter from general and humane studies with those of professional or vocational programs so often substituted for general and liberal education.

Because of the familiarity of the phrase *liberal arts college* and the equity in that designation, it is not likely that the expression *comprehensive college* will take hold and be widely used. What is at stake is something more important than phrases, descriptors, code words. What matters is that the concept expressed by the word *comprehensive* be understood, accepted, and fearlessly endorsed— education for, quaintly phrased, "body, mind, and spirit." The college is not comprehensive in trying to be all things to all people but, rather, in the sense of offering each student a complete education, that is, education for—say it without embarrassment—"head, heart, and hands." That emphasis is not optional.

The realization of this concept of service seldom occurs in the typical university. That institution is too specialized, too inflexible; the orientation is wrong, the training of faculty and administrators wrong, the probable outcomes wrong. Society needs cross-disciplinary research and teaching concerning the social psychology of medicine, the esthetics of engineering, the social responsibility of business corporations. But the typical university rarely responds to this need. A course here and there, in remedial ethics or whatever, exhausts the effort to meet the challenge of moral integration.

The modern college is not much better than the university, given its tendency to imitate. It, too, features professional functions narrowly defined. Failing that, the college will often substitute junior college activities, catering to individual preferences and vocal interest groups. But the comprehensive college, despite these dangers, has a better prospect for reform and for the assumption of essential functions.

The college of character is not only a place where trained people do science—that work can be done elsewhere—but a place where trained people explore the implications and applications of science and its basic assumptions. No other place does what the college can do with science. And nothing is more important for science and society.

The college is not merely a place where trained people design new technologies, or refine existing technologies, and train other people for the management of technologies. That work can be done elsewhere. Rather, the college is a place where the effects of technology are examined and the future of technology charted. No other place does what the college can do with technology. And nothing is more important for technology and society.

What we say about the college's special relationship with science and technology can also be said about its relationship with the humanities and arts. Although there are writers and artists, dancers and actors, historians and classicists practicing their professions, developing their skills, and producing works of art or novels or historical studies within the college, it is not these activities that make the institution's relationship with the humanities and arts something special. Again, if people want only to do history or write novels or stage plays, they can arrange for all that elsewhere. What is unique about the college's relationship with the humanities and arts is that the faculty and students insist on mixing disciplines, getting into the history of art, the social significance of the theater, and so on. The college is the place where studies count most when they relate to one another, where skills are acquired and applied not as mere techniques but with concern for their meaning and their effects.

The college's special relationship with the humanities and arts, or with science and technology, bringing diverse specializations together, never develops easily and is always done imperfectly. It is a struggle involving the most serious people in the institution working out the most consequential problems. Perhaps that is the best reason for supporting the college.

According to the perturbational theory of learning, creativity and growth are encouraged by the tension of differences. This theory is put into practice almost every time self-confident academic professionals organize a panel discussion on a controversial topic: The first speaker's point of view will be contradicted by the second speaker, whose introductory words emphasize the dialectic, "I disagree with almost everything our first speaker said." Then comes the third speaker with an intermediate position, usually beginning by saying, "I find myself somewhere between our first and second speakers." Indeed. It was the assumption of the meeting's planners that truth would be found or, at least, the session would be lively, if the program was based on the Hegelian or perturbational theory of learning. Good educators structure struggle: they factor it into their equation and rely on diversity of opinion to benefit everybody.

The well-being and advancement of society, educated people believe, require a place where basic assumptions are examined, alternatives are created, trained minds weigh options; a place where schools of thought are developed, where the social, political, and moral ramifications of that thought are tested. This is the work of the college of character.

Science and the Humanities. Today, in American society, important struggles are under way. In the college these struggles should achieve their highest expression. Here is one example: In the college there is a struggle between science and technology on the one hand and the humanities and arts on the other. This dialectic reflects a monumental tension in our society expressed in a variety of ways: science versus religion, head versus heart, objective analysis versus experiential learning, technology versus humanity.

John Hersey (1980, p. 78), writing in *Atlantic,* reminds us that it has been more than twenty years since C. P. Snow gave his famous lecture on "The Two Cultures and the Scientific Revolution." In that lecture, Snow said: "There have been plenty of days when I have spent the working hours with scientists and then gone off at night with some literary colleagues. . . . Constantly I felt I was moving among two groups—comparable in intelligence, identical in race, not grossly different in social origin, earning about the same incomes, who had almost ceased to communicate at all, who in intellectual, moral, and psychological climate had so little in common that instead of going from Burlington House or South Kensington to Chelsea, one might have crossed an ocean." With these words Snow identified a condition easily recognized once it is pointed out: the two cultures of science and the humanities, separate entities, coming together like two wrestlers, each one determined to gain supremacy. These combatants seem to forget their interdependency and the fact that they can grapple with each other and hope to win only as long as each participant is acknowledged and the match proceeds within the rules. This is what the Greeks saw, and it is what we must see.

This is not an idle issue or a squabble over irrelevancies, but a profound struggle with important values at stake: whether American society will be dominated by science and technology, without a sense of history, without social sensitivity, without a spiritual nature; or, on the other hand, dominated by the humanities and arts without the methods and tools of science and technology.

In the eighties we may see the emergence of machine intelligence and the death of the popular but mistaken idea that a computer can never become anything beyond what is specifically programmed into it. "A computer with a sufficiently large memory can be a self-organizing machine, in the sense that it can take in vast quantities of information . . . assemble that information into tentative structures which it can then test for correctness as time passes and provides more data. This process would be strikingly similar to the development of the mental ability of a child" (Geilker, 1979; see also "And Man Created the Chip," 1980).

Science and technology have the capability of blurring traditional distinctions between the machine and the human being. Hence, the humanities and arts struggle to keep the human side dominant. They do so by pointing out the limits of method, the exceptions to law, the importance of intuition. Humanists say that the mysteries of what Yeats called "the foul rag and bone shop of the heart" are as profound and significant as the mysteries of outer space or of scientific discoveries in the natural world. And the methods of the humanities are as useful as, albeit different from, those of science. John Hersey writes: "In the arts, the interest lies in more or less controlled departures from the norm. Here it is inexactitude that fascinates us. As Itzhak Perlman or Isaac Stern draw the hairs of a horse's tail across a string taken from the gut of a cat attached to a box known as a violin, a lovely sound comes forth, the interest in which is not in the perfect pitch of any given note; the interest, the soul of the sound, is in that trembling of personality we call vibrato—a rapidly pulsing series of departures from the correct pitch" (1980, p. 80).

In the physical sciences and engineering, laws hold sway. Or so it seems. Scientists move step by step toward something that has

forever been there waiting to be discovered. Lewis Thomas has reminded us, however, that science is not particularly orderly and
sequential:

> The great body of science, built, like a vast hill
> over the past three hundred years, is a mobile, unsteady
> structure, made up of solid-enough single bits of infor-
> mation, but with all the bits always moving about, fitting
> together in different ways, adding new bits to themselves
> with flourishes of adornment as though consulting a
> mirror.
> This is how we fell into the way of science. The
> endeavor is not, as is sometimes thought, a way of build-
> ing a solid, indestructible body of immutable truth, fact
> laid precisely upon fact in the manner of twigs in an ant
> hill. Science is not like this at all: it keeps changing,
> shifting, revising, discovering that it was wrong and then
> heaving itself explosively apart to redesign everything. It
> is a living thing, a celebration of human fallibility. At its
> very best, it is rather like an embryo [1980, p. 21].

In the humanities, the Heisenberg principle of indeterminacy
is carried to its extreme expression—every attempt to know for certain disrupts that which would be known for certain, leading to the
flip comment among humanists who work with contingencies and
exceptions and departures from the pitch that the only thing that
can be known for certain is that nothing can be known for certain.
The life as well as the spirit of the humanities and arts seems anti-
thetical to science and technology. But is that really true?

We are finding through the Promethean struggles of science
and the humanities that the lines between them cannot be sharply
drawn. C. P. Snow said, "There is a moral component right in the
grain of science, and almost all scientists form their own judgments
of the moral life" (Hersey, 1980, pp. 80–81). And as science and
scientists tend to slip over into the territory of the humanities, over
toward history, philosophy, religion, morality, and ethics, so the
scholars and practitioners of the humanities and arts have found
uses for the methods and technology of science. Nevertheless, in the
university and college, as elsewhere in modern society, there is a
tendency for faculty and students to embrace one culture and scorn
another. Yet, in the college, more than elsewhere, a colossal strug-

gle rightly continues between these contenders. And the college is at its best, and contributes most, when this struggle is dealt with directly. The future of the nation and the Western world, of the citizenry and each individual, depends on our ability to reconcile those cultures and their forces, those ways of running the world and assessing human life. The college's aim is to contribute to understanding and reconciliation.

Reason and Faith. There is an epochal struggle going on between faith and reason in American society, in homes and businesses and political offices.

Here are two illustrations, one historical and one modern, one outside the college and one within it. The first, provided by Renford Bambrough (1969, pp. 29-30), is of faith in action. Suppose that we, as educated persons, are walking with the Homer of ancient Greece along a beach beside a stormy sea. Watching the thrashing water and churning waves, Homer might say, "Poseidon is angry today." And to that we might smile and say, "Yes, Poseidon is very angry today." Notice that all participants in this exchange use the same words. Yet it is clear that there is a vast difference between what Homer means by those words and what we modern persons, with our greater knowledge of meteorology and oceanography, mean by those words. When Homer says Poseidon is angry, he is offering an explanation for the lashing of the waves. But when we speak, using those words, we are giving only a picturesque description of the lashing of the waves. We sense that Homer speaks out of his faith in Poseidon's authority over nature. Meanwhile, we speak out of a rational grasp of nature's laws, even though we couch this comment in picturesque terms. To us, Homer represents faith. We represent reason.

Now here is a second encounter. Our companion is Seymour Papert of the Massachusetts Institute of Technology. He is telling us how computers affect the way children learn and about his plan to use this powerful new technology not to "improve" the schools we have always known but to replace them with something better. Nor is Papert referring to "computer-assisted instruction." He is describing, actually projecting, the emergence of a new "computer culture" in which the presence of computers will have been so integrated into new ways to think about human life and about the subject matter people learn that the nature of teaching and learning will be literally transformed (Papert, 1980, pp. 230–240). Again, on hearing his grand design, we smile. We have heard this sort of thing before. That was what movies and TV were said to be able to do for education. But the surge of interest in audiovisual education quickly faded, and now schools and colleges have millions of dollars of hardware sitting in closets and gathering dust. So, courteously, we say "yes" to Papert, but it is a figurative, not literal, assent. Deep down, we note that a man of science is speaking beyond science, beyond facts, beyond reason's safe reach, into a vision of technology's ability to create a new culture.

Was Homer wrong? We think he was. Poseidon, defined in Homer's terms, does not stir the waves, and Zeus does not live on Mt. Olympus. Homer's explanation was not fact but faith. Is Papert wrong? We are skeptical of his vision because he is moving beyond fact into faith. Yet, his explanation seems to project reasonably events to come.

These two examples show how complicated life gets when persons of faith use their reasoning ability to defend a position more relevant to faith than fact. So it was with Homer. The same is true for persons of rationality and science who use modern technology to develop a position that carries them beyond what is known into what is speculation, beyond reason to faith. So it was with Papert.

And so it is with all of us. The businessperson has faith in competitive capitalism or the American economy, in management systems, in the loyalty and productivity of employees, in their product's value for consumers. The college professor has faith in the capacity of students to learn the lessons of the classroom by using reason. In all institutions, among all professionals, everywhere, faith and reason blend and contend. Faith and reason are as interdependent as science and the humanities. Therefore, we should support that institution—the college—in which this struggle in all of its dimensions occurs and in which the resources necessary to encourage reconciliation can be assembled.

What does a college of character do well that is less likely to be done well, if at all, elsewhere? What distinguishes it from other institutions? The college's chief reason for being is this task of grappling with relationships—between science and the humanities, between reason and faith. The college is especially concerned about the effects of methods and procedures, the meanings of established processes, impact. The college's main function is synoptic—searching for the relationship between sources and outcomes, searching for comprehensiveness.

History in a Time of No-History

What else does a college of character do well that is less likely to be done well, if at all, elsewhere?

A college of distinction emphasizes history in a time of no-history. I refer here not to history as a subject-matter specialization found in the training of historians, nor to the rote memorization of historical details, the majority of which are promptly forgotten (although the boredom of such exercises is long remembered). The emphasis is, rather, on giving the student a sense of living within a historical tradition, and of a certain continuity to life—for good and ill. In this era of immediacy or no-history, when students at too many educational institutions are lucky if they are able to identify leaders and events of the last thirty years, the college of character makes them aware that behind the thirty years of their personal history are three hundred years of Western social and political history that affect them directly, and behind that, three thousand years of history that add perspective and substance to their lives.

There is a historical context for the civilization of no-culture. A college student's wisdom begins in learning some of the details, some of the historical hinges, on which this culture turns. And it is more than the beginning of wisdom: it is real progress for that student to develop an *attitude* toward history, to get, as educators say, "a feel for history."

Frances FitzGerald, in her book *America Revised,* reminds us that at all levels of education so much of what we retain from classroom encounters is in the form of an attitude, a mood, or an orientation toward the subject:

> A wholly unscientific survey of my own would show that few American adults can remember as much as the name of the history textbook they "had" in secondary

school. And the sight of an old textbook is much less likely to bring back the sequence of Presidents or the significance of the Hawley-Smoot Tariff Act than it is to evoke the scene of an eighth-grade classroom; the sight of, say, Peggy, one long leg wrapped around the other, leaning forward on the scarred green bench, or Stevie talking a mile a minute and excitedly twirling his persistent cowlick. Rabbits, it is said, cannot remember pain or fear for more than sixty seconds. Perhaps human beings cannot remember things that bored them. Memory has its own antidotes. On the other hand, the fact that one cannot remember the order of the Presidents does not mean that all is lost. Amid the telephone numbers, nursery rhymes, and advertising jingles that we carry around in our heads, there are often snatches of textbook history. My own snatches consist of visual images detached from their context: Balboa on his peak in Darien; the supporters of Andrew Jackson celebrating his first election by tromping over the White House furniture in their muddy boots. Other people have more literary memories. "I had Muzzey," one friend told me recently. "Wonderful book. I'll never forget the scene of Lincoln after the Battle of Gettysburg looking over the graves in the cemetery and a voice crying out to him, 'Calhooon! Calhoooon!'" The memory of my friend was not, as it turned out, perfectly accurate, for in David Saville Muzzey's *American History* William Lloyd Garrison is speaking at a banquet in Charleston after the war, and about him Muzzey asks rhetorically, "Did the echoes of his voice reach a grave over which stood a marble stone engraved with the single word 'Calhoun'?" Still, my friend had remembered the dramatic irony, and that was surely the essence of this particular passage.

In some general sense, this may be the truth of the matter: what sticks to the memory from those textbooks is not any particular series of facts but an atmosphere, an impression, a tone. And this impression may be all the more influential just because one cannot remember the facts and arguments that created it [FitzGerald, 1979, pp. 17-18].

An atmosphere, impression, attitude—these endure whether one is thinking about American history in the schools or about general and liberal education in the colleges. What educators give students, ultimately, is an orientation toward learning, a perspective on history, a feeling about literature, a representation of the teacher's sense of things important and not important.

The climate of an institution is as essential to vitality as the subject matter taught therein. That climate will influence what is taught as well as how it is taught, what is learned as well as how it is applied by the learner. In the college of consequence, history is not dismissed with a shrug of the shoulder and a curled lip nor revered with eyes closed and hands folded. Through the study of history and the climate of the school, American attitudes and behavior are shown to be rooted in deep history—mainly Jewish, Greek, and Christian. To act as though contemporary civilization and the history of the moment had no obligation to those roots is like substituting a potted plant for a real tree. The culture of no-context, like the potted plant, has immediate utility and maximum portability. But, like the plant, it can be easily toppled by a breeze and will probably be replaced by the next interior decorator.

For some time now, even when we least expected it, there has been evidence of a yearning among educated persons for the security of a defined context, for historical milestones by which to measure progress, for a culture that is contemporary but also an expression of continuity. We need the attitude captured by the word *querencia*— that place called home which, despite its problems and weaknesses, provides a special environment for us. The richness, and complexity, and importance of querencia, and that sense of belonging that gives context and history to a world too often devoid of these distinctions, was beautifully stated in a *New Yorker* editorial: "'Querencia' is a Spanish word that means affection for the place one calls home and the sense of well-being given by that place. It means being nourished by that to which you belong. Normally defined, it means the immediate environment in which the person lives, but one can apply it to home in a larger sense without vitiating its meaning. One could say, for example, that T. S. Eliot moved to England because he found his 'querencia' there. Solzhenitsyn, despite his hostility toward the Soviet government, remains cold in his attitude toward the West at least partly because his querencia is in Russia. We live in a world awash with people torn from their querencia. Or people who have forsaken it and find that its lack is a kind of starvation. Querencia nourishes" ("Notes and Comments," 1977, pp. 27-28).

One thing that a college of character does well that is not likely to be done as well elsewhere is to give students and faculty a sense of history that provides a querencia, which in turn gives a perspective by which to assess a culture in which the only history of record is the history of no-history.

The Borders of the Known Contexts

Another mission of the college of character is to lure, seduce, or compel students to venture out to the borders of known contexts, to experience life "at the edge of history."

Carl Schorske, professor of history at Princeton University, has written persuasively about the characteristics of two creative communities: Vienna and Basel. In his book *Fin-de-Siècle Vienna,* Schorske describes a creative explosion in Vienna in the late nineteenth century, when an innovative culture arose out of a liberal social and political environment. That explosion sparked exploration in every direction—in architecture and city planning, in literature and art, in politics, science, and education (Schorske, 1981; see also Schorske, 1980, p. 30).

In liberal Vienna, the history and context of public life were changed by young people who investigated the edges of received truth and established experience. Informed by their history and provoked by the liberal context inherited from their fathers, these young leaders proceeded to expand what scholars have come to call the growing edge of knowledge.

What happened in Switzerland as compared with Austria, in Basel as compared with Vienna, was even more impressive because, contrary to conventional wisdom, the creativity and criticism in Basel sprang from a conservative rather than liberal environment. According to Schorske, Basel was unique in that its brand of conservatism took pride in conserving the right of individuals to work at the edge of history for the purpose of reforming that tradition in order to improve the future of the community. Consequently, in the Basel of the mid-nineteenth century, the most successful innovations were those with the strongest fidelity to the values of the city's

tradition—community, order, intellectual persuasion, faith in man
and God (Schorske, 1980, 1981). The action at the edge, the creativity
and criticism of Basel's best minds, was community-centered; directed
against all changes that divide and rupture that community, the
ground of being in which the roots that nourished the reformers
were deeply positioned. This city encouraged controversy within a
tradition—and it worked.

A college of character is distinguished at this time of cultural
and historical disintegration, when the culture of immediacy and
the history of the short span give most Americans such organizing
principles as they have, by its emphasis on deep culture and long
history. Yet, the college of character combines this emphasis with a
second: the thrust of life at the growing edge of culture and history.
Thus the type of criticism that led to the creation of the tradition
revered in the college is reapplied, this time to that tradition itself in
order for creativity and life to reemerge.

Encouraging students and faculty to venture out to the limits
of the established context does not require that each adventurer discover virgin land. Most of us, in fact, find that what Frederick Jackson Turner reported in the late nineteenth century, concerning the
American frontier, is also true in the realm of ideas: the frontiers are
closed. The college community cannot produce new knowledge: its
creativity is not of that kind. What it can do, out there on the borders
of the known, where the familiar and the unusual meet, is to use its
critical and analytical skills to reformulate and synthesize useful but
previously disparate ideas.

The college of consequence encourages its members to move
to where fresh perspectives are possible, where the community's center
can be assessed from the limits of its context, out where criticism and
reconfigurations are likely to occur. It is a truism that ideas are
channeled in concentric circles, with those on the fringe sometimes
acting as the cutting edge. The college of character dares to encourage movement to the outer limits, not because the center should be
abandoned, but because this is a way to overcome the constraints of
automatic responses and to find new support for a revitalized center.

More specifically, coaxing students to chart new territory entails guiding them in study from the Jewish and Christian sources of
the dominant Western tradition into other religions and philoso-

phies of non-Western traditions. It means moving beyond the social, political, and economic absolutes of the developed nations in the Northern Hemisphere into the aspirations and contributions of the developing nations most often located in the Southern Hemisphere. It means moving closer in attitude and knowledge to the heretofore underrepresented citizens of the United States, to the so-called underclass of American cities, to racial minorities living in rural as well as urban poverty in this country.

The Librarian of Congress, Daniel Boorstin, argues in an essay that American creativity has always flourished on what he calls the "fertile verge": "America was a land of verges—all sorts of verges, between kinds of landscape and seascape, between stages of civilization, between ways of thought and ways of life. During our first centuries we experienced more different kinds of verges, and more extension and more vivid verges, than any other great modern nation" (1981, p. 3). Boorstin goes on to describe geographic, political, technological, cultural, and generational verges. Wherever creativity occurs in America, regardless of context, the verge or edge where the action happens always has three characteristics: "First, there is our exaggerated self-awareness. On the verge we notice more poignantly who we are, how we are thinking, what we are doing. Second, there is a special openness to novelty and change. When we encounter something different we become aware that things can be different, our appetite is whetted for novelty and its charms. Third, there is a strong community consciousness. In the face of the different and the unfamiliar, we, the similars, lean on one another. We seek to reassure one another as we organize our new communities and new forms of community" (pp. 5–6).

If the college of character is to help defuse the crisis in education as well as in the nation, it dare not allow the first of Boorstin's characteristics of the fertile verge to remain dominant. Our nation has had enough "exaggerated self-awareness." So have our colleges. This mood leads to preoccupation with life on the grid of 200 million, mass characteristics, surface realities; or to life on the grid of the unit of one, with its incessant preoccupation with the questions of Who am I? and How am I doing?

Neither the nation nor our colleges can any longer tolerate the luxury of that second characteristic that Boorstin finds in the history of American verges: "openness to novelty and change." An appetite whetted by novelty and its charms has made us gluttons for gimmicks and overindulgence. We end up getting elaborate, bloated, costly education systems.

A Growing Center

Boorstin's third characteristic, the commitment to community, is important to the nation as well as to a college seeking to respond to cultural and educational crises. If a college is going to tap the creativity at the edge of knowledge, that is, if its members are going to channel the energy generated by the friction between criticism and creativity, there must be a vital center in which the entire endeavor is founded. The community stands on that foundation, takes confidence from it, and is enabled thereby to grapple with life on the frontier.

Suzanne Langer (1964) wrote an essay with the wonderful title "The Growing Center of Knowledge." In it, this philosopher argues that Americans tend to emphasize the importance of the growing edge of knowledge while ignoring the fact that development is possible only as long as there is a vital, or growing, center of knowledge. The hollow tree that has stopped growing at its core falls into decay, loses its leaves, and eventually topples.

Educators must distinguish between what goes on at the circumference of academic life and what goes on at the center. Out there, on the growing edge, are miscellaneous discoveries, with every new fact suggesting others, one discovery leading to another. We salute the contributions of research and scholarship on the frontiers of inquiry, making possible that growing edge of knowledge. However, too little attention has been given to the health and vitality of the center, the heart of the enterprise. We need vigorous, sustained concentration there to assure that the frontiers of knowledge relate to a growing center of knowledge. We need to think more about institutional purposes, coherence and character in the educational experience, the meaning of this enterprise, and all those ways to assure that our community, at its center, is growing and healthy. Martin Buber clinched the point: "The real essence of community is to be found in the fact—manifest or otherwise—that it has a centre. . . . The circle is described by the radii, not by the points along its circumference" (quoted in Koch, 1960, p. 181).

The college of character has a center where its education philosophy, its theology, its metaphysics are found. In the statement of institutional mission or the statement of educational purposes these central assumptions are expressed. Professional development programs for faculty members and administrators, orientation programs for support personnel, and all other forms of instruction for the nonstudent members of the community will be affected by the radiating influence of the center. Student services and student activities, alumni and trustees' activities will be equally influenced. The total community is energized by its center.

Much authority can be given to this central nervous system as long as it continues to grow—to understand, utilize, and criticize the discoveries made on the growing edge. In Chapter One, reference was made to Oscar Peterson, who improvises jazz within a tradition, reaching out to the borders of the known occasionally but always from a solid center: his accomplishments arise from an emotional and technical affinity with Art Tatum and other players for whom the beat sets the limits within which the artist works. There is another view, more modern, favored by many jazz musicians, a view ably represented in the following statement by Frank Conroy (1981, p. 70): "The modern view is to treat time rather like a loose web—a freer, less metronomic condition. This allows a much larger canvas, as it were, upon which to play. Players can swing when appropriate, and they can also drift back and forth through the web, together, without getting lost and without loosening tension. They pay attention not so much to the beat as to the pulse."

The beat and the pulse, the loose web and the growing center—these are representations of essentials that, in a college of character, define the arena within which creativity and criticism function. Deviations from the theme are possible only after the theme has been stated; playing before or after the beat is possible only when the beat is steady; the circumference can be explored only after the center has been located. The circle is described by the radius.

What does a college of character do well that is done less well, if at all, elsewhere? It refuses to mimic the versity's self-serving professionalism defined by guilds and too often expressed through pinched research. The true college refuses to follow the example of the community college in its extreme populist or egalitarian expression, the new subcollege committed to the proposition that all colleges are created equal. The college of character, rather, emphasizes the synoptic function, sharing concern for cause and effect, for relationships, for a more integrated and comprehensive approach to teaching and learning. It carries out its commitment to the synoptic function in three principal ways: by respecting the deep history in an epoch of no-history, by extending teaching and learning to the edges of the circumstance, and by keeping its ideational core a growing center.

The commitment is evident at the departmental level, in which every faculty member tries to show in her or his teaching how the subject matter or discipline has a history relevant to the growing edge of knowledge. These activities at the edges of known contexts are nourished by a growing center—basic assumptions, purposes, ideals—to the end that findings on the frontiers of knowledge are brought back to foster new growth at the center. Parenthetically, it is when the professor works with students in that second category of concern—the growing edge of knowledge—that the methodology of the discipline should be emphasized. When new knowledge is brought home, that is, related to established points of emphasis not only in the subject-matter specializations but also to basic institutional purposes, opportunities for cross-disciplinary teaching will be greatest.

The commitment of the college to the synoptic function is equally evident when candidates for faculty positions are interviewed. Effort will be made to determine each candidate's willingness to teach with a sense of history, to investigate new developments in his or her field of study, and to weave the basic values of the college throughout all activities. Not every faculty member will be equally skilled in each component of this endeavor. Some will be more research-oriented, and they can be expected to emphasize what is happening at the edges and beyond the edges of established knowledge. But they will also know the historical antecedents and will try to bring the substance as well as the spirit of new knowledge into service to the community at its center. (Other faculty colleagues will emphasize historical developments or assumptions and theory.)

Administrators, department chairpersons, and senior faculty will join together to assure that the rewards and sanctions of the institution serve these commitments, for only then will the differences really make a difference. These leaders will also emphasize the synoptic approach to teaching and learning and those three means to its achievement, in the literature and public pronouncements of this community. What a difference it will make if students know that whatever their field of study, whomever their instructors, wherever they find themselves as they proceed with their college education, the connections between historical antecedents and the methodologies involved in the quest for new knowledge, and the meanings of it all for the integration of life and learning in their community, will be sought after always and frequently found.

4

Educational Philosophy and Institutional Commitment: The Search for Coherence

---

The idea of a college having a growing center of knowledge, from which members of the community go out and to which they return, is disquieting for many academics. They remember a time when the axis around which everything revolved was church doctrine as interpreted by bishops and pastors. Loyalty oaths and heresy trials were accoutrements in some centered institutions, especially in church-dominated, god-intoxicated environments. Education suffered. When the college is an arm of the church, it cannot be true to the full body of knowledge. So goes the criticism.

The danger is real and can only be overcome when the assumptions and purposes of the college include emphasis on vitality and growth at the center encouraged by creativity and criticism from the edges of the known context, and when the long history of the tradition is made a deep and fertile history through attention to that history's meaning for and effects on the present and future. The synoptic function balances the obligation to history.

Educators who have thrown off stultifying doctrine, perhaps with great effort and scars to prove it, should be made to see that they haven't necessarily bettered their situation. In truth, although the old center may no longer hold, a center of something or someone always exists. Mistakes and disasters in a doctrinaire past, plus conceptual confusion in more recent years, led many younger academics to conclude that history and authority predating World War II were at best "a fable agreed upon." They thought they could live in the moment, up to the minute, with only short and provisional connections. They have made their presence known; hence, this epoch is characterized by the history of no-history and the culture of no-context.

Everybody else, whether older academics or church leaders, who still thought that history is more than "the tricks the living play on the dead" (Voltaire), and that a culture ought to be more than mere civilization, were pitied and ignored or held up to ridicule. The young breed proclaimed tolerance while practicing intolerance.

Because the new deal for academe did not escape the old needs—for a history and culture, for a synoptic vision and a fixed center—today, as before, assumptions and purposes undergird the daily life of academics as surely as wooden and cement pilings support Amsterdam. When they took up pluralism, moderns may have thought they were discarding every expression of monism as a core or center for the college. They supposedly rejected the single life, but they have in fact been living with the concept of pluralism to the exclusion of all else. These moderns scorned dogma dogmatically, even while supporting certain basic assumptions that, in other times, would have been called dogma. Is this what it means for the sins of the fathers to be extended to the second and third generations?

We live . . . under the spell of ideas, good or bad, true or false. We may think that we are responding directly to events and changes in the histories of institutions, but we aren't; we are responding to these events and changes as they are made real or assimilable to us by ideas already in our heads.

Robert Nisbet

Assumptions and Purposes

It was William Butler Yeats (1959, p. 184) who said, "The centre cannot hold." But despite continuous changes and evidence that values once central are now out of favor, some point of ideology is invariably the central organizing principle for individual and institutional life. The basis of authority has historically been some notion of God, natural law, the nation-state, or, recently, the solitary individual. In the present and for the foreseeable future, the basis of authority will be a combination of authorities—the authority of 200 million, the state, dramatized by the celebrities; coupled with the authority of the person, standing alone, defined by the experts. Today, then, this form of pluralism occupies center stage.

Again, something is always at the center—a notion of monism, that effort to discover and proclaim the one truth; or some form of skepticism, ranging from a commitment to universal doubt to a lack of confidence in any single belief (except, of course, belief in the validity of skepticism); or a variation on the theme of eclecticism, which after all is pluralism in little pieces—a slice of this position and a snip of that one.

Again, yet again, there is always a center, even if it changes. In Western civilization, God was credited with being the basis for authority, but the church became the repository of God's will. And, for Protestants, the tragedy was that the church became an end in itself; it took over the center. In the language of Paul Tillich (1957, p. 212): the conditional usurped the unconditional.

When George Steiner reviewed Alexander Solzhenitsyn's third volume of the Gulag series, *The Gulag Archipelago Three*, he provided a valuable perspective on Solzhenitsyn as a moral prophet whose pronouncements are as irritating as they are insightful. Solzhenitsyn is, said Steiner, "a searcher out, a harrier of man's debilities, and an embarrassment to the world" (1978, p. 97). He exposes the moral flabbiness of our Western culture, the improvisational norms, the fads and momentary allegiances. He calls our gods by their name—idols.

Reason and reasoners provide important services, according to Solzhenitsyn, when functioning according to moral norms or, more specifically, within the moral standards of the Judeo-Christian tradition as represented by the Russian Orthodox Church. When Western intellectuals turned to secular ideals and material hopes, however, they severed Western civilization and culture from its history and motive force. These substitutions at our center have proven to be radical and embarrassing—"degenerate hedonism," "materialistic secularism." Most Western intellectuals have been exposed as leaders of a "substitutionary radical libertarianism," which restlessly, shamelessly, has culminated in Marxism and utopian socialism (Steiner, p. 98). These ideational themes, according to Solzhenitsyn, have taken over the center that belongs to Christ and His church.

It is current dogma in America—to mention one of the operational assumptions of academics and colleges—that cultural pluralism is mandated by the fact of our nation's social diversity, and that only a fool would question its validity. What is needed, leaders say, is the further extension of cultural pluralism. "Let the voices multiply; the more voices we have, the more truth will finally emerge." That statement is Wayne Booth's, from his book *Critical Understanding: The Powers and Limits of Pluralism* (1979, p. 4). "In most matters of complex judgment we in fact must distrust uniformity of opinion; it surely results not from reason but from coercion, idolatry, or laziness" (Booth, p. 4). The reader gets the impression, confirmed by the remaining text, that Professor Booth, like most of us, is attracted more to pluralism's powers than to its limits.

In the modern university it has been popular to claim that the basic trait academic institutions have in common is real differences. Indeed, we are told, let us celebrate the fact that our differences are our commonalities. An expression of this orientation has been proposed for the curriculum at the University of Chicago, where a student under this plan could choose a course in Western civilization, or one in Eastern civilization; or a course with a noncivilization emphasis—the study of tribes and prehistory; or again, an anti-Western civilization course, for persons persuaded that Western civilization is male-dominated and mainly political history. A development such as these proposed curricular options at Chicago shows that these vaunted differences arise from a basic commitment—cultural pluralism. It stands at the center.

Institutions of education, including colleges and universities, are subject no less than other institutions of society to the ideas, the dogmas, of the prevailing culture of pluralism. Colleges live not by physics but metaphysics; by ideas of value that can be described and never totally suppressed. Here are some examples, provided by E. F. Schumacher, British economist and author of *Small Is Beautiful,* of unifying or centering ideas from the nineteenth century that, he said, still dominate the thinking of most educated people, and most educators:

> There is the idea of evolution—that higher forms continually develop out of lower forms, as a kind of natural and automatic process.
>
> There is the idea of competition, natural selection, and the survival of the fittest, which purports to explain the natural and automatic process of evolution and development.
>
> There is the idea that all the higher manifestations of human life, such as religion, philosophy, etc.—what Marx calls "the phantasmagorias in the brains of men"—are nothing but "necessary process," a superstructure erected to disguise and promote economic interests, the whole of human history being the history of class struggles.
>
> . . . There is, fourthly, the Freudian interpretation which attributes [all higher manifestations of human life] to dark stirrings of a subconscious mind. . . .
>
> There is the general idea of relativism, denying all absolutes, dissolving all norms and standards, to the total undermining of the idea of truth [as found] in pragmatism.
>
> . . . There is the triumphant idea of positivism, that valid knowledge can be attained only through the methods of the natural sciences and hence that no knowledge is genuine unless it is based on generally observable facts. Positivism, in other words, is solely interested in "know-how"—and denies the possibility of objective

knowledge about meaning and purpose of any kind
[1973, pp. 88-89].

To Schumacher, the success of these shared ideas and their
extensive influence is no reason for celebration: "The leading ideas
of the nineteenth century, which claimed to do away with metaphysics, are themselves a bad, vicious, life-destroying type of metaphysics" (pp. 91-92). However, this economist does endorse the emphasis
on the importance of metaphysics: "Education cannot help us so
long as it accords no place to metaphysics. Whether the subjects
taught are subjects of science or of other humanities, if the teaching
does not lead to a clarification of metaphysics, that is to say, of the
fundamental curriculum, it cannot educate a man and, consequently, cannot be of real value to society" (p. 93).

It has been possible, even during recent decades when conscious attention to a society's metaphysics was frowned upon, to
ferret out the ethical and intellectual values favored by most political, social, and educational leaders. The Harvard "Redbook" said:
"Our society, like any society, rests on common beliefs and a major
task of education is to perpetuate them" (Committee on the Objectives of a General Education in a Free Society, 1945, p. 46). For the
Harvard committee members, at least during the preparation
of their report (1943-44), certain themes deserved the support of
education—the dignity of man, trust in the scientific method, the
centrality of the test of reason and experience, and the mutual obligation of human beings.

In *The Crisis of the University,* Sir Walter Moberly said that
the following items were among the "absolutes" of Western society:

> Democracy is meaningful and right as a form of
> government.
> Ordered liberty and self-discipline are essential to
> self-realization and social security.
> The individual has rights and responsibilities.
> There is at once the dignity of man and his duty
> toward his fellow man. There needs to be a balance be-
> tween continuity and change.
> A certain activism is favored—a sense that it is
> normal to be up and busy.
> The cardinal virtues remain unchanged—wisdom,
> temperance, courage, justice [1949, pp. 130-131].

An educational institution will have commonly held purposes, certain organizing principles, explicit or implicit, usually drawn from an ideational blend of Jewish and Christian history, elements of classical humanism, and scientific humanism, with traces of existentialism, libertarianism, egalitarianism, and Marxism. The life of the college or university cannot be all process and method. Nor can institutional policy give equal weight to every ideological contender. There will be limits, even to pluralism. Pluralism, too, must have a center.

Monism is discredited in a society as diverse as America because it insists that while the search for supreme truth may not be literally rewarded, the vision of truth standing over truths is still our best organizing principle. I am among those persons who believe that there is truth behind our partial understanding and fuzzy perception of truth. I have argued, in this book, that there is truth for the church behind the manifestations of that truth in the churches.

When most Christians speak of the church, they are not referring to churches. They have in mind an ideal. The church is not to be confused with buildings and budgets, the clergy and parishioners, the programs, activities, and investments. The substance of the church is not the same as its forms: the essence transcends its expression. Otherwise, the church would be little more than a club or a business—as is the case with too many churches.

So it is when people speak of a college. Their notion of a college is not limited to its land and buildings, or even to its curriculum and faculty. The character of a college is more than people with Ph.D.'s, more than courses of study and institutional procedures, more than bricks and mortar.

The church is an ideal, the idealized expression of religion, the religion of Christianity. Some believers trace its beginnings to Jesus Christ and His apostles, who gave the church its distinction. Other Christians regard the church as a human response to divine initiative, as the earthen vessel that carries this treasure. Yet they, too, with the other believers, know that the church is something more than the sum of its parts.

The college is ultimately an ideal, an idealized expression of higher education. The notion of a college transcends its day-to-day life. Although few citizens would assign transcendent authority to education or the idea of a college, most people believe that there should be ideals for the college determined by the social, economic, and moral goals of the state.

As the stuff of the church is religion, so the stuff of the college is education. As the authority for the church is the religion of Christianity, so the authority for the college is the education of the state.

That which goes on in churches relates more or less to religion. That which goes on in colleges relates more or less to education. When things are right, in the church or the college, what you see is only part of what you get.

Unfortunately, things have been going wrong, not right, for religion and education. Both have lost their basis for belief or vision of the ideal. Both have turned to that which they can see: facilities and programs, budgets and job descriptions. Given this loss of the ideal and this preoccupation with details, what goes on in most churches and most colleges has little to do with religion and education. What you see is, alas, all you get.

Fully recognizing how hard it is to generate faith in any ideal, educators must address the issue of ideals and the claims of faith. The crisis of our time is one of faith, and the need now is for faith in worthy ideals.

Accepting that we cannot escape belief, but knowing, too, that some beliefs educators have held in the past discourage faith in the future, we must struggle with assumptions and goals. Experientially we live by our certitudes, in the absence of certainty. Yet it makes all the difference to believe that these certitudes relate to the certainty that eludes us, that behind the realities of our lives are ideals such as truth, beauty, and justice—ideals that penetrate the realities of institutional forms and become favorable influences. Such a faith is the beginning point for overcoming the crisis of faith. That faith is the cornerstone of colleges equal to the challenge of the civilization of no-context, the cornerstone of colleges that deserve to be called colleges of character.

Basic Convictions for a Purposeful College. Having reviewed some of the assumptions of democratic society and of education in America, and having argued that there is no alternative to commitment to ideas that have the weight of dogmas—education in the service of cultural pluralism, for example—and having admitted a preference for monism or a fixed base, I now address other pivotal assumptions of the college of character. But first a few caveats and qualifications.

Certain ideas that give purpose and direction to the college are, in fact, shared with most colleges and universities. However, the college of character is more likely to be conscious of its commitments and more likely to keep them under constant evaluation than is the case in other colleges and universities. So often elsewhere, basic values are imposed without inquiry and retained without examination.

Granted, not every college of consequence will have the same set of assumptions and goals. The purposes listed here seem to me to be especially appropriate, given the moral and ethical crisis in higher education and in the nation. Other observers will emphasize variations on these themes, or alternatives to them. But every purposeful college will have reasonably coherent metaphysics in place, operating daily, yet under continuing assessment.

Not every college worthy of notice will have a theology of education based on the Jewish and Christian traditions. Some schools will be more humanistic and secular, more attracted to classical Athens than to historic Jerusalem. But most will be Christian in orientation. Haverford College has character, as does Earlham— both affected by the Quaker spirit. William Jewell College and St. Olaf College have character, in part because of the influence of an evangelical Protestant tradition. St. Mary's College (California) and the University of Notre Dame have character and characteristics shaped by the sponsoring religious orders of the Roman Catholic Church. Centre College represents liberal arts institutions that have maintained vital connections with theologically liberal Protestant denominations. On the other hand, Reed College, Washington University, and St. John's College are examples of institutions whose distinctiveness results more from secular thought and the humanistic tradition than so-called Judeo-Christianity. A college of character may have a church affiliation or none at all, a creed based on Christian metaphysics or on other beliefs. But all such colleges will be rooted in something other than the politics of the faculty senate. Their stability will depend on something more important than the school's endowment. They will honor a tradition other than the vapid civilization of no-culture.

The college of consequence accepts responsibility as an institution of higher education chartered by the government to educate students in those skills and attitudes essential to the continuation and improvement of the state. This is an assumption of the college regarding its relationship to government. But the college dares, in fear and trembling, not in the arrogance of power, to insist on its right to participate in the determination of that which will assure the "continuation and improvement of the state."

Another central responsibility of college leaders is attention to the definition of key terms—not always the technical terms of education, but terms such as religion, values, morality, and ethics. I suggest that *religion* should be understood as the formal and normative expression of religious faith which, in turn, is concern for the mystery of the "ought." The word *values*, often used synonymously with *religion*, represents a concept based on religion and religious traditions but is not to be confused with religion. *Values* should be defined as religiously based standards held with conviction.

Ethics, like values, flow from religion but are not religion. *Ethics* is the formal and normative expression of morality. We sometimes speak of ethical systems and ethical standards of morality, and we are correct in doing so. Another way of thinking about these terms, a popular way, is to consider *morality* the word for the behavioral expression of moral norms. Morality is the moral norm in action, and, given the human condition, morality usually falls short of that norm. *Ethics*, meanwhile, is defined as disciplined reflection on moral norms culminating in ethical systems or the codification of moral ideals. A moral and ethical crisis means, then, a crisis in both norms (ethics) and behavior (morals).

Among convictions in the heart of a college of character, as stated earlier, is the centrality of the synoptic function. Teachers in this college help students put the civilization of no-context into the perspective of the long history. Every person in the college is challenged to move out to the edge of history, to the limits of the established context. Persons in the college can feel secure because they are members of a purposeful community; that is, they have not only a circumference but a center, a growing center of knowledge.

The Scope of Reason. What else is basic to a college of character? Commitment to the scope and authority of reason. The capacity of human beings to think and reflect, in a disciplined, orderly way, the importance of reason and reasoning, the life of the mind and its traditions and accomplishments are all fundamental values in a college of character.

Here are two metaphysical assertions about the scope of reason, given human capabilities: "There are no unanswerable questions." "For every question, there is a right answer." These statements are cornerstones in the metaphysics of Renford Bambrough at St. John's College, Cambridge. He also believes that "between the unity and variety there is no essential conflict" (1969, p. 157; also see pp. 50ff.), that reason is our best tool for defining the unity and the variety, and for working through apparent conflicts—until we discover that in many cases there is no conflict. We can't find the answer to every question, and not every answer we give is the right one. There are things we know, and there are things we will know, and even for those questions about which we know nothing, or have wrong answers, there are—according to Bambrough's metaphysics—right answers. Some things we know, for example, the date of the death of Abraham Lincoln, April 15, 1865. Some things we do not know but may someday know, for example, the full extent of the collusion between the British and Israelis at the time of the 1956 Suez invasion. Finally there are things we do not know and probably will never know, for example, the date when the last dinosaur died.

Professor Bambrough wrote a book called *Reason, Truth and God* (1969). By the time the reader finishes it, and grasps the extent of the author's confidence in reason, the conclusion wells up that the book could have been more accurately titled "Reason Is Truth and God." However, to the extent that this philosopher extols the services and authority of reason without depreciating the singularity of the transcendent One, we can join with him in this affirmation: "To insist that God cannot be beyond reason and above truth is not to ask that God be narrowed and lowered but to ask that reason and truth be seen in their full breadth and height and depth" (1969, p. 157).

Are educators prepared to move away from a currently stylish depreciation of the human capacity for reason? Are we ready to affirm the importance of the authority and scope of reason? Between the unity and the variety there is serious conflict, but not as much as we have been inclined to claim. Must we give unqualified support to those persons who insist that all reasons behind human reasoning are nonrational? Todd Andrews, in John Barth's *Floating Opera* (1956, pp. 170–171), offers a proposition that hounds Barth's heroes and many educators: "The reasons for which people assign value to things are always ultimately (not necessarily immediately) arbitrary, irrational. In short, there is no ultimate reason for calling anything important or valuable, no ultimate reason for preferring one thing to another." If this position anchors a person's metaphysics, one is soon led to ask: If there are no assurances about better or worse, good or bad, transcendence and essence; given no procedure for sorting out the options and establishing a hierarchy of values, why should a man's reach exceed his grasp?

> *Two extravagances: to exclude Reason,*
> *to admit only Reason.*
>
> Blaise Pascal

The Tragic Sense of Life. People in a college of character are unwilling to be poisoned by capriciousness and irrationality. Yet they will not assert that the authority of reason is unqualified. Our basic convictions are deeper and broader than the scope of reason.

Miguel Unamuno stressed an important concept in a single phrase—"the tragic sense of life"—meaning that principles tend to follow personalities, that people determine practices, and that practices are decided more by what people feel, by their attitudes, than by their ideals (Unamuno, 1954; see also Ferrater, 1962, pp. 32–33).

Unamuno's emphasis is akin to the point made by Oliver Wendell Holmes: Law is not based on logic, but on life. J. R. Pole's (1978) examination of the efforts of the courts, including the Supreme Court, to interpret and guide the search for racial equality in America shows how limited has been the independent reasoning of our judiciary system and how extensive its dependence on emotions and passions, attitudes and values. The behavior of that allegedly dispassionate body of rational experts, the justices of the nation's highest court, reinforces the view that although the scope of reason may be epistemologically unlimited, our ability as human beings to reason is experientially limited, not only by the finite nature of our rational powers but by the intrusion of passion and emotion.

To believe that human beings can always act logically is illogical and contradicts history and human experience. Reason often serves emotion. Human reasons are passion's rationalizations. Reasoning is one of passion's favorite modes of expression.

The word *passion* is used here not in its most popular connotation, sexual passion, but, rather, to denote deep emotional drives, strong positive or negative feelings, as in the case of a person who has a passion for music. When Jefferson Davis announced to the United States Congress in 1861 that he would leave the Union and return to Mississippi, even if the doctrine of nullification and states' rights was shown to be wrong, and would do so because of his spiritual commitment to that state, Davis was exemplifying the power of passion to override reason's case for law and logic.

Whatever we may think of the philosophical position attributed to David Hume that human beings cannot proceed from an *is* to an *ought* by logic—a position probably unfair to Hume and certainly wrong—most of us agree that men and women are more likely to be motivated by passion than by any other mode of persuasion. We know from personal experience that however our core values may be determined, whatever their source—body chemistry, genes, family influences, social and cultural forces—they are channeled or employed not so much by philosophy as by passion, not so much by reason as by emotion.

It is precisely because we have experienced the power of deep feelings, and quake with memories of excesses to which we have been driven by passion, that we are eager to find ways to contain and direct those noncognitive forces. Thus, we acknowledge reason's restraints as well as reason's power and acknowledge reason's limits as well as its reach.

We have an ally in this quest for control: what intellectual leaders in the nineteenth century called *will*—the human capacity to use both passion and reason judiciously. It is to this resource that we should turn individually, even as it is this resource toward which a college of character has turned institutionally. This old-fashioned word *will* still stands for the conviction that men and women are capable of making a controlled response to most stimuli. It is will that disciplines human judgment. Hence we speak of "a man of strong will." The word also implies determination: "Where there's a will, there's a way." And it usually suggests enthusiasm: "To work with a will."

What we say about an individual's will power can be extended to institutional life, to convey, for example, a community's social resolution—"the will of the people." To recognize the collective as well as the individual will allows us to apply Abraham Lincoln's admonition to a college community as well as to an individual: "Nothing is more important to success than your own resolution to succeed."

In a day when it is assumed that the solitary person can do whatever he or she wants to do, or that the individual has no will and can do only what social forces dictate, the college of character defends an intellectual tradition arguing that individuals have will power sufficient to balance the reasons of the heart and the mind.

Here, then, is another difference that makes a difference in the metaphysics of a college of character: This college and its leadership have seen enough of the effects of ignorance and sloppy thinking and irrationality to know that such a mentality cannot provide a basis for a viable college or culture. This college community has also seen the effects of intellectual arrogance: that cock-eyed cocksureness that fosters community but stifles creativity. This college has among its deep commitments strong support for the human faculty of reason. However, it also acknowledges the limitations of reason and accepts the invariable if not inevitable presence of passion, will, and spirit.

The scope of reason, the limitations of reason; the hopeful signs of life, the tragic sense of life; "man the measure of all things" and "What is man that thou art mindful of him?"—these are levels of awareness, dimensions of faith and learning, and challenges and perils in a college of character. Individual perspectives will differ, emphases may change, but the community will never forsake the responsibility and the privilege of working back through history, moving out to the edge of understanding, and coming home to the living center.

Addressing issues of this magnitude, which shake the foundations of modern life, can tear a community apart. But that risk should be taken. Great religious movements have shown that the best way to arouse a sluggish institution, or to motivate apathetic people, or give directions to wanderers, is to attract a community's allegiance and abilities to problems, to ideas, and to ideals that speak not only to needs of the moment and the place but to the future and the larger human community. All of us need to be drawn out of ourselves. We can be saved, as the preachers used to say, by the power of a new affection.

This new affection, expressed through a purposeful community, embraces complexity as opposed to simplicity. It is, therefore, unlike the simplistic affectations promoted by most religious, social, and political movements. It praises historical antecedents that can be applied without cant, and the growing edge of knowledge that revitalizes rather than destroys tradition. This new affection accepts the reasons of the heart as well as of the mind: both can be persuasive.

When heart and mind conflict, it is the college as a community that has the power to resolve the issues, without lessening the community's affection for either head or heart. The college of character has the power to lift our spirits and focus our abilities, to exemplify true character so strongly that students will always have their experiences in the college as a point of reference, to unify a community and make it a model for society.

Mission Statement

During 1980–81, I collected college and university catalogues for leisure reading. To add a little spice to the assignment, I read student handbooks. My interest was primarily in historical statements and institutional statements of purpose. I wanted to trace the way missions and traditions were transmitted to readers through these old-fashioned but honorable media.

I found that most American universities do not have a historical statement more than a paragraph or two in length, nor do they have a substantial statement on their mission. There were notable exceptions: Washington University in St. Louis has a splendid catalogue statement on its history. Miami University in Ohio has three paragraphs on the mission of the university. St. Lawrence University is another exception: it provides both history and mission. However, most universities, like the University of Denver, offer only a passing reference in the student handbook to their history, with no explanation, and an equally light touch regarding the church connection or earlier conceptualization of institutional purposes.

Church-related universities, whether they have a residual or more definite affiliation, usually seem embarrassed by their history and aggressively explain that the student body as well as student activities are characterized by diversity and opportunities for individual choice or no choice at all. In most religious and social matters, the institution shows a hands-off attitude. Although this condition was more common among public universities, particularly the large systems such as the State University of New York, private universities, too, were subject to the syndrome. Both types of institutions, public and private, communicate with students about drugs and alcoholic beverages—usually speaking against use of the former and favoring controlled use of the latter—and about plagiarism, firearms, and so on, but little effort is made to communicate the rationale for any regulations. Again, there are exceptions—Georgetown University and the University of Notre Dame are unapologetic about their histories (Notre Dame was downright euphoric), and both spell out some of the differences that their traditions make in the life of these universities. Valparaiso University gives its religious orientation a prominent place in its literature. Brigham Young University is quite specific about the effects of its religious commitments on academic and social life. One BYU brochure is entitled "A Style of Our Own."

The inadequate communication of history and mission by most universities also prevailed in most colleges. In both types of institutions, the closest thing to a firm declaration of institutional policy is the nondiscrimination statement and the statement of student rights and responsibilities. These are prominently displayed and presented in a forthright manner using explicit language. We all know the financial and legal factors that prompt these statements, and most of us share the concern for access and equity that these statements express. However, the visibility given to policies of nondiscrimination and affirmative action, or statements of student rights and responsibilities, proves that important changes can be effected at even the stodgiest of institutions and can become policy in ten years, not one hundred years. Also, putting things in writing, giving them formal expression in official publications, may be considered important even today—not something that can be dismissed as a ritualistic observance having no significance (a frequent criticism of catalogue statements on institutional purpose).

What is lacking in the literature of most colleges and universities, even in those booklets giving some space to history and mission, is a statement that lifts history and mission out of isolation and integrates them with the ongoing life of the institution. Too little attention is paid to the importance or lack of importance of a college's history in its present. No purpose is served by simply depositing a cold, disembodied history on the back page of the student handbook.

The same point should be made about the institutional mission statement. Its relevance to the curriculum, governance, and social policies should be stated. The objectives and means to those ends ought to be made explicit. Mills College has a two-page catalogue statement on history and mission that at least partially meets this challenge, by stating characteristics of the college, their role in the school's history, and their relationship to current programs and goals.

Eckard College, St. Petersburg, Florida, opened in 1960 as Florida Presbyterian College, an educational subsidiary of two Presbyterian denominations. Over a decade later, in 1972, the name of the college was changed to honor Jack Eckard, whose gifts and financial commitments became influential. Over the last twenty years, there have been other changes, the most important being the evolution from an institution best known for certain highly visible innovations that gave it a national reputation to a somewhat more conventional college confronting an array of financial problems from a regional base of operations.

However, amid every turn of events, Eckard examined its mission and objectives in the light of its ideals as well as its resources. It never abandoned the search for institutional distinctiveness and never ignored its commitments. The 1982 Eckard catalogue states current commitments—some familiar, some less common—to individual development, Christian values, students, general education,

the integration of liberal arts and career preparation, human relationships, and being a pace-setting institution.

The point is that the Eckard College community, with some
twisting and turning, amid changes internal and external, has kept
its assumptions and purposes and educational programs under constant assessment—in the name of and for the benefit of that
community.

Administrators and faculty members, community representatives, trustees, and alumni leaders who have an interest in living not
only in the moment but beyond it, and who would build their college on a solid foundation in order to assure its usefulness in the
future, must be willing to inspect institutional underpinnings regu-
larly. These deep beliefs are the pilings in bedrock upon which
everything should be constructed. Failure to attend to the ideational
basics leads to a college of expediency. Success in getting down to
bedrock is the first step in building a college of character.

A second step, an easier yet important one, is to examine what
is called these days "the institutional mission statement." That
statement expresses, or should express, college objectives, just as
campus daily activities show, or should show, evidence that the
college objectives in the mission statement are at work in the life of
the community.

In the late seventies, the only people in higher education who
were not working on institutional mission statements were those
who had just finished the job. It had been a preoccupation for administration and faculty. Too often, however, that exercise was carried out for the wrong reasons and with negative effects.

Managers wanted a mission statement in order to direct and
assess procedures. Management was supposed to be "management
by objectives." Without a statement of objectives, leaders said, there
could be no sense of direction and no way to distinguish progress
from mere movement. Management systems were being installed,
and criteria had to be set up by which to measure the success of the
systems managed—hence, the mission statement. What that statement contained was, for managers, less important than the fact of its
existence—as long as the stated objectives were within the reach of
the managers' acquired skills. Why hang up a dart board unless you
can hit it?

An example: A mission statement has provided on some campuses the general terms within which collective bargaining took place, the conceptual tent under which managers and union representatives worked out their contracts. Collective bargaining, to be sure, mainly concerns salary schedules, job benefits, work rules, procedures for hiring and firing. But for every rule there must be a reason, even as each reason can be used to justify another rule. Taken together, rules and reasons serve a larger purpose. They will often mold what once was a true college into an educational factory. They may occasionally shape what had become an educational supermarket into a true college. Too often, however, the people at the negotiating table have not cared whether the mission statement was consistent with the traditions of the institution, or whether the institution as defined would meet a real need: they simply wanted boundaries for their maneuvering so that conclusions would be, as we say, within the ballpark.

There were other and better reasons for that flurry of interest in mission statements a few years ago. It is important to have a statement of principles and standards that grant the power to block policy infractions. In football, that no-nonsense game, there is a penalty for something called unsportsmanlike conduct. It is a difficult penalty to assess because it often involves a judgment about intentions—not only those of the player at a given time but also those of society in decreeing that certain forms of behavior reflect good sportsmanship while others do not. The conduct that is likely in football to be called unsportsmanlike can be identified—kicking, gouging, tripping—but it cannot be fully defined. Yet fans and players generally agree about forms of behavior that are appropriate to the sport, in part because that behavior conforms to a kind of social consensus about "fair play" that in a general yet definable way sets the limits of propriety and guides the game official who must judge player conduct. Social ideals influence behavior just as there are behaviors that, even in this day of situational ethics and moral relativism, society condemns.

Judgment calls are often complicated, as every player knows. Consequently, most educators have of late preferred to sidestep the difficult decisions that would set their institution apart from others and, instead, have taken refuge in expedient mission statements in the middle of the playing field, where they can make decisions that are easy, imitative, familiar, and compromising. This escapism has given education critics a field day: what should not be said of redwoods, they point out, can be said of mission statements—"When you've seen one, you've seen them all."

Mission statements are usually full of platitudes and generalizations far removed from institutional realities. The statement of mission may promise a coherent curriculum and a set of unifying education principles, but the day-to-day life of students and faculty shows that they are marching to a different drummer, with the beat set by professional guilds, not by their own values nor the character of the college or university.

In the recent past, faculty and administrators were not equipped to develop successful mission statements. Faculty had never been encouraged, let alone trained, to think relationally and comprehensively. They were subject-matter specialists—theoreticians perhaps, but not in educational matters. (Some faculty assumed that all academics were education authorities just as all teaching was thought to be adequate.) Administrators were usually managers, lawyers, or politicians surrounded by specialists and technicians. These experts had the skill to call an off-side penalty but not to judge unsportsmanlike conduct. The former infraction is visible to the eye, but the latter, involving intention as well as action, requires quick movement from the eye through the head to the heart.

Because of the superficiality of so many mission statements and the ineptitude of persons charged with designing such statements, American colleges and universities require, more than ever, a reconciliation of mission and management. Attention needs to be concentrated on this question: Are management systems determining mission statements, or should management serve mission? Effort should be made to develop the skills required to produce a coherent and influential mission statement. Otherwise, immediate urgencies push aside long-range planning; what is being done determines what will be done—that is, present actions dictate future policies; and technique becomes the terminal skill.

Why spend time on the statement of an idea, as in a mission statement, when we can predict that practice will fall short of it?

Because actual practice, procedures, arrangements, settings, and appearances must always be measured against an ideal. A statement of institutional mission, at its best, formally represents assumptions and purposes that will guide the planning as well as the activities of a college or university. Despite flights of rhetoric, sweeping generalizations, and other evidence that the reach exceeds the grasp, a good mission statement informs behavior and helps members of the community decide when to say no and when to say yes. It is a statement of intention that affects practice. It is informed by tradition and experience and yet transcends both. It relates to reality but is basically an ideal. And we need ideas and ideals even more than technique and dollars.

When, during 1943 and 1944, the committee at Harvard produced the so-called Redbook on general education in a free society, team members used a single phrase informally to describe their intentions: "a few deep wells in a few selected places." They would not try to be all-encompassing. They would discriminate between *general education*, a term they favored, and *liberal education*, a term so abused as to be useless. They would eschew general survey courses and emphasize specific areas of study for deeper investigation. They would approach general education in a disciplined way and seek to legitimize it without succumbing to the temptation to stress global education at the expense of specialization and professional preparation.

So it is with a college of conviction. There will be a mission statement that expresses as accurately as possible the educational assumptions and purposes of the institution. The commitments will have a rationale based more on principle than expediency. Therefore, some things will be favored and other things not done. The college will put its wells deep in places carefully selected.

5

~~~~~~~~~~~~~~~~~~~~~~~~~~~~~~~~~~~

Leadership: Beyond Survival to Significance

~~~~~~~~~~~~~~~~~~~~~~~~~~~~~~~~~~~

What chance is there for a college to provide a statement of institutional mission that will be noteworthy for something more than being honored in the breach? Will every attempt to unify a college with institutional purposes widely shared and deeply felt be as difficult as trying to push a stalled car when one's feet are on ice and the brake has been set?

Academics are accomplished nay-sayers. Murphy's law is the first law of faculty dynamics. Consequently, this or that may go wrong because we will it so; that is, we conclude that it must go wrong because it can go wrong. And so it does. Faculty are also accomplished dissenters. Thorstein Veblen claimed that these dissenters offered only "feigned dissent," but what was said of John Lilbourne, a seventeenth-century dissenter—"If all the world were cleared of all save John Lilbourne, John would argue with Lilbourne and Lilbourne with John"—can be said of our colleagues. They are not only "on the other side" of many arguments, but their ideas tend to show up "on the other hand."

This argumentative tendency of academics must be resisted now because its effects have been destructive: laymen conclude that faculty are always cynical; students fear to speak up lest their views be ridiculed; people wonder whether faculty believe in anything other than their right to be debunkers. The need now is for leadership in reconstruction and reformation. Although criticism and skepticism are useful, they are not sufficient. Cynicism is devastating. It is time to examine, once again, what educators have in common with which they can build a community of conviction, and what characteristics of leadership would be appropriate for such a community.

Common Ground

Most of us have some knowledge of the "commons," or the common ground that usually occupied a site near the center of a colonial New England village. The parish church and sometimes the town meeting hall were located on or near the commons. Parades, rewards, trials, and punishments were carried out there. The commons was the turf belonging to all citizens where the town conducted much of its business.

Is there a common ground today? Not a parcel of land, a park, a place, but some shared set of values, concerns, and objectives that are commonly held? On what do we agree?*

In the society at large, according to conventional thinking, about the only commitment shared by nearly everybody is the commitment to pluralism. As the means to achieving this end, people agree to disagree—and to make a space for every disputant. Leadership can only arbitrate differences and negotiate compromises.

There are, of course, values other than pluralism that characterize the lives of most persons in our society: materialism, pragmatism, individualism, nationalism. These themes are omnipresent, albeit not promoted to the same degree as is pluralism. Yet the consensus seems to be that there is no social consensus, that the yearning for community about which we hear so much is a yearning

*Parts of this section are adapted from an essay written by Warren Martin, printed by the Danforth Foundation, with the title *Common Ground*, 1979.

for something out of the past that has no future because there is so little about which Americans can agree.

Must the same thing be said about those of us who care about liberal arts colleges, church-related colleges, and other focused educational communities? Many critics impress on us the difficulties in achieving agreement on education purposes and values. In fact, they bombard us with questions about every assertion until, exhausted, we are expected to say that the only thing we know for certain is that nothing can be known for certain.

Leadership for a college of character is not so easily intimidated. It is both determined and resilient. That there are difficulties in staking out the common ground is indisputable, but that fact has never been sufficient reason to throw up one's hands in despair or to wave the white flag of undifferentiated pluralism.

Although we may not know anything with absolute certainty, we know that in order to live we must operate under provisional certitudes. That our basic beliefs are certitudes gives us something on which to stand, some criteria with which to sort out options and to measure accomplishments. That these certitudes are provisional reminds us of our humanity, keeps us humble, and enables us to change.

Another group of "advisers," including many colleagues, tell us that the agreements possible now, given social heterogeneity, are those relating to procedures—those accommodations that people work out in order to avoid bumping into each other. In these terms, *community* means only a community of convenience, not a community of conviction. The modern university, these persons contend, is a good example of a community of convenience: a place of labs and libraries, facilities and parking lots; a place used by professors and students who have differing reasons for being there, but who all consider the university a convenient place to go about their business.

Is that all there is to it? Are there not various procedures in the service of certain principles, especially in the university? Is it not also true that university people have only a slightly less difficult time agreeing on those procedures than they do on the principles? Yet, despite the difficulties, under the principles of fair play and free speech, they set up procedures to guide human interaction—to encourage civility, for example.

It is not hard to detect convictions that hold the community of convenience together. One is that it not be inconvenienced in the use of its conveniences. More seriously, I repeat the point that despite the difficulties, there is no escaping the responsibility of trying to determine those things central and those things marginal; those means that are ends in the process of becoming and those ends that should be ended or extended.

A college of character provides a varied fellowship; it is both a community of convenience and a community of conviction. Its fellowship has substantial diversity yet is always matched by a unity of purpose that is unusually substantial and ultimately controlling. The purpose of the college is to stand between the professionally oriented university and the service-oriented community college, a position that not only improves prospects for institutional survival but also allows the college to mediate between those influences that shape American life on the grid of 200 million as well as those that shape life on the grid of the solitary person.

And what does the college do, for individuals rather than for itself as an institution, while occupying this middle ground? It offers students, faculty, and administrators the opportunity to belong to a coherent educational community that integrates knowledge from many disciplines through the synoptic function. This is a community informed by its history but not limited by it: it has a growing edge as well as a living center. This community defines its terms, and states its mission, and keeps its assumptions under constant assessment (whether the assumption deals with the scope of human reason or the meaning of the tragic sense of life). This college stands on common ground that educates younger and older members for purposeful leadership in the community and the world at large.

> *To compose our character is our duty.*
> Montaigne

Leadership: Beyond Survival to Significance

What more can be said about leadership for a college of character?

In the college as elsewhere, it is as hard to talk about leadership as it is to talk about creativity. We are not sure of the sources of either even though we observe manifestations of both. We see that educational institutions may inhibit the expression of creativity and that the most creative people are not content to stay there, even as we see that educational institutions can frustrate leadership and may drive the most creative leaders away. Yet creative leadership is often reported by the social scientists to be the most important variable in case studies of institutional change. Furthermore, educators are confident that they can educate for leadership as well as for character. Or, more modestly, we assert that as educators we set up an environment that improves prospects for the expression of creativity. And we relieve institutional constraints that might otherwise defeat leadership. We claim to help free the leader to lead.

Because educators know so little about the true sources of leadership but see so clearly its necessity, they readily conclude that the best thing to do is work on social and structural settings, particularly through techniques of institutional manipulation developed by sociologists. Then they light a candle and step back, waiting for those persons in positions of leadership to actually become leaders. But the transformation seldom occurs. The manipulation is ineffective, and the miracle never happens.

What is required is precisely what the college of character features: relational thinking on the interconnectedness of individuals and institutions, with as much attention to the significance of the individual for the institution as to the reverse. The college emphasizes the leader who will lead despite obstacles to leadership, one who can overcome institutional obstacles as well as popular but counterproductive styles of leadership.

Limitations of Professionalism. One obstacle to creative leadership is the currently fashionable form of professionalism that encourages an ever-tighter specialization of duties and the resultant compartmentalization of public life. On most college and university campuses, for example, this emphasis on professionalism means that the president is in charge of outside connections—fund raising, alumni relations—while, inside, the faculty control the curriculum and the students manage their own affairs. The president is surrounded by his managerial and legal experts, the students have student personnel services, and the faculty rely on the singularity of their own skills.

This distribution of responsibilities and the emergence of ever more specialized job descriptions have resulted not only from regent professionalism but also from the societal need for various professional skills. In the late sixties, to return to that example, turmoil on campus caused by challenges to authority created a demand for the skills of legal professionals. No wonder lawyers became administrators, indeed, presidents. Similarly, during the seventies, financial retrenchment affecting colleges and universities increased the need for effective management. Managers were named presidents.

The training that people get and the professional experiences they have as a result of that training obviously influence their style of leadership. If the education of the leader is ever more specialized and the rewards and sanctions supported by his profession ever more focused on performance in that specialization, we can expect expressions of leadership to comply: the leader will follow the leader, actions will conform to training.

In colleges and communities, as elsewhere, the emphasis on professionalism and the various needs on campus have united to influence styles of leadership, indeed, to determine the preferred style of leadership: analytic, data-based; specific, task-oriented; realistic, pragmatic; law-honest, businesslike. The leader today is not the guy who persuades some other chump, *à la* Tom Sawyer, to do his chore and paint the fence. He is, rather, the guy who pays to have that job done after checking on liability insurance for the worker and figuring out that a painted fence will enhance the value of his property as well as spare him the charge of deferred maintenance.

President. Much has been said about changes in the style of presidential leadership, from charismatic to bureaucratic, from ideational to managerial, from comprehensive to technical, from seat-of-the-pants to the computer-style professional. Less has been said about what has been lost in the new leadership, about what is needed to flesh out the professional as well as to keep skills in perspective, about how to balance specific competencies with broader purposes. We are beginning to sense the limits to technique, the rigidities that attend the managerial mentality, the boredom of life bolted to bureaucratic fixtures. Meanwhile, educators still believe in education for leadership, and to this end we dedicate programs in the arts and sciences as well as graduate education and training in the professional schools. Yet we sense that there are aspects of leadership that are spiritual, attitudinal, subjective, and intuitive, aspects that cannot be quantified or reduced to formulas but remain unquestionably important. These evident yet poorly defined, idiosyncratic yet influential factors may be our greatest need, given the recent emphasis on the kind of production-oriented leadership that was about as impressive as painting-by-numbers or a German band playing American jazz.

The problems confronting colleges require not only legal and managerial aptitude but also skill in the synoptic function, in thinking comprehensively and in representing the college as an educational institution with programs of importance to students. A president who concentrates as much of his or her time on the quality of education offered by the college as on the growth of the endowment, and is sufficiently skillful in representing the college that, say, two new students are persuaded to attend the institution for four years, paying their tuition along the way, will bring in tuition dollars equivalent to the interest on a gift of $400,000 to $500,000. A president who draws students through effective interpretation of the educational program may make a financial contribution to the college greater than most fund raisers.

There are special qualities—integrative, synergistic, and interpretive—that are the leader's pearls of great price. The president need not be a lawyer: legal expertise is available to the college. The president need not be a businessperson: management skills and advanced technology will serve the office. The president's distinction should be a mind that integrates or synthesizes. He or she thinks inclusively, transcends the categories, brings ideas together. The president, more than others, moves from the specific to the general and from big issues, like the enduring nature of the enterprise, to the opportunities of the moment.

In an essay entitled "To Err is Human," from his book *The Medusa and the Snail*, Lewis Thomas points out that the fallibility so much a part of the human condition should be seen as an opportunity for creativity. When something goes wrong, we have a chance not only to make it right, that is, to put it back on the tracks, but to make it better. Here is Thomas's example: "A good laboratory, like a good bank or a corporation or government, has to run like a computer. Almost everything is done flawlessly, by the book, and all the numbers add up to the predicted sums. The days go by. And then . . . somebody makes a mistake: the wrong buffer, something in one of the blanks, a decimal misplaced in reading counts, the warm room off by a degree and one-half, the mouse out of his box, or just a misreading of the day's protocol. . . . The misreading is not the important error; it opens the way. The next step is the crucial one. If the investigator can bring himself to say, 'But even so, look at that!' then the new finding, whatever it is, is ready for snatching. What is needed, for progress to be made, is the move based on the error" (1974, p. 38). Here is an opportunity for leadership—to make the move informed by an error, a move that transfigures the error itself.

Presidential leadership of the quality most needed now has the sensitivity and flexibility, the resiliency and daring to think and act this way in the presence of adversity. We should do what we can to remove institutional obstacles and other forms of obstruction, but we should not encourage persons with authority to think that they cannot move until the obstacles have been taken away. Abraham Lincoln had characteristics of the leader who, amid difficulties, transcends the formulas, categories, and response biases by which most moderns are confined. Jefferson Davis, on the other hand, lived by an old and absolute standard handed down by Christianity and the American Constitution, wherein the responsibilities of states and individuals were precisely defined. Davis, inflexible, could not adapt to changing circumstances. Lincoln was not without standards, but he was more responsive to individual needs; he would search for the opportunity in error; he also showed humility, humor, and compassion. Lincoln had the courage to declare a point of interdiction and, then, to confound his own declaration with an occasional "Even so." Yet few persons doubted that Lincoln knew where he was going.

The college president—as interpreter of the educational functions to various elements of the school's constituency, as orchestrator of the special professional skills represented by faculty members and administrators, as the leader who sees opportunities even in errors, as a person who lives with both convictions and compromises but never confuses the two domains—is the balanced professional with the skills and spirit appropriate to institutional and societal leadership in our time.

Like the captain at the tiller of the sailboat, the president of a college works within a tradition, using a technical language and special training to utilize the capabilities of the boat under his command. He has resources—compass, rudder, sails, crew—and makes effective use of them. The captain has a long-range goal, a port. He also has an array of intermediate objectives—a point of land, the timely use of an appropriate current. The skipper tacks, comes about, moving in a more or less straight or a more or less zigzag course, using wind and tide, sail and hull, skills and insights, to make progress toward the goal.

The quaintness and familiarity of this metaphor should not dissuade us of its appropriateness. The captain of a sailboat, more than, say, the pilot of an airplane, is like the leader, the president of a college or university, that we need. He makes full use of science and technology—oceanography to astronomy, aerodynamics to fabric tolerance. He also becomes one with his vessel. And the skipper marries the vessel to the water, wind, and tide even as those natural forces drive the craft. In sailing, there is an opportunity for sensibilities as well as technical skills to be used. And the effect can be a spiritual experience. So it is with presidential leadership when the president who is freed to lead dares to free himself for the privileges and responsibilities of inclusive leadership in a college of character.

Faculty and Administrators. The education offered students in colleges of character—historically connected, contextual, centered; integrative, cross-disciplinary; responsive to moral and ethical issues—is education for leadership. It works. The fact that leaders for America have come in exceptional numbers from liberal arts colleges, despite faulty and limited realization of the goals of these colleges in actual programs, is one evidence of their influence on students. Another bit of evidence is in the numbers of teachers at liberal arts colleges who, themselves often graduates of this type of educational institution, come back to teach there with a style and substance that set them apart from prevailing professional norms and the behavior of most professional colleagues.

My confidence that like-minded persons are out there, in many locations, is partly based on personal experience with members of the Danforth Graduate Fellowship Program. These Fellows are leaders, and there are other persons in American colleges with the same qualities.

For six years I was director of the Graduate Fellowship Program and, in that capacity, had scores of opportunities to meet with the Fellows at conferences and on their campuses. We shared hopes and fears, plans and experiences. Also, because the Fellows wrote copiously for the Foundation (answers to application questions, personal statements, reports for conferences and program assessment), I have had access to thousands of pages of relevant information from which the values of the Fellows can be, in some cases, pinpointed and, in others, inferred.

One implicit assumption of the program has been that the Fellow's metal is refined in the blast furnace of graduate school. There has been the conviction that graduate education is an appropriate way to train college teachers. A second assumption of the program has been that a Fellow should have a subject-matter specialization but that, additionally, he or she should traverse the disciplinary boundaries in order to enrich the specialization. The program has also encouraged the Fellow to put his or her life into a larger sociopolitical context as a way to give it moral and ethical significance. The Fellow should not strive to be just another teacher, nor just another scholar, but a teacher-scholar of a special excellence—one with the skills of comprehension, interpretation, and application. The Fellow's goal, finally, is to apply technical expertise to human needs. By so doing, essential services are provided and the commitment to service is honored; the work expresses vocation.

Other commitments in the Graduate Fellowship Program include emphasis on the life of the mind, on reason and rationality, joined to respect for the whole person, including the noncognitive aspects of that person. Although the program featured the development of human sensibilities that go beyond cognitive rationality, the emphasis has been more on the mind than on the body, and especially on the value of reasoning.

The data show that Fellows in this community believe in discipline of the self, in the use of time, and in the use of language. They also have a preference for order—social order, orderly thought, organizational discipline—and for work. Although Fellows may be disorderly in their work habits, and criticize the Protestant work ethic, they insist on stable conditions within which to carry out their business. The work of a teacher-scholar is the organizing principle of their lives.

What else can be said about this pool of 3,500 persons who are in college and university teaching from which leadership for colleges of character might be drawn? Fellows usually attended elite universities for their graduate education (see Martin, 1981a). They are good teachers (traditionally defined). Most of them are employed in liberal arts colleges or in the smaller universities (Kirkwood and Uchitelle, 1976). And in these places, they win the prizes for teaching effectiveness. They are often more effective than the prizes suggest and deserve more honor than the prizes confer. Fellows are less well trained, however, for teaching in nontraditional settings. Some have the aptitude, but few have the skills. Their competence for nontraditional education does not equal their curiosity about it.

Most of the Fellows have led sheltered lives. They are among the socially privileged citizens. Consequently, they take much for granted. They have had a lot done for them, and for some it has become a way of life. This may explain why so many Fellows are easily derailed by life crises: a death in the family, a divorce, a professional affront, a defeat major or minor. Such a development can knock them off the track for a month or a year. The qualities that the Danforth community encouraged—sensitivity, responsiveness, concern—also make Fellows vulnerable in a crisis and especially subject to its debilitating effects. Yet the vulnerability, the availability of these people, has been part of their effectiveness (see Rice, 1980, pp. 3-5).

Danforth Fellows look like conventional academics in physical appearance, in terms of job categories, in the organization of their day. They differ, however, in that they are likely to teach more than the people who do mainly research and they are likely to do more research than the people who mainly teach. They are different, too, in their involvement in cross-disciplinary teaching. They work at it more often than do their colleagues. And they are different in their expression of that third element in the trinity of faculty commitments: service, as compared with teaching and research. They are often involved in services—out in the community as well as on campus.

The similarities of the Fellows to conventional academics are, on the surface, greater than the differences. Critics of the program have argued that the Fellows have not shown the audacity of spirit, the critical acumen, and the creative skills needed to transform higher education. However, the critics do not recognize that the program never had among its goals the transformation of colleges and universities. The leaders of the fellowship always assumed that there was more good than bad in academia, more to protect and extend than to assault and curtail. Although the Fellows should not be taken for granted—they are capable of surprises—they are basically peaceful citizens of the academy. They are more likely to stress continuities than contradictions, that which endures as compared to that which is problematic, the permanencies rather than paradoxes. They support incremental and evolutional changes that produce reformation, not revolution.

The Danforth Fellows are not so different from thee and me. They are, as stated, political centrists or maybe marginal centrists. They carry out the regular duties of their profession and their employment. They are familiar with compromise and walk most comfortably in the middle way. The Fellows will start a fire with a match but not a blowtorch. Their touch is light more often than heavy.

Similar yet different—this is my assertion about the Fellows. They are close enough to their colleagues to make contact, far enough ahead to provide leadership; members of the academic community, yet eager to see it develop a strong character; a part of the problem, but even more a part of the solution.

The reforms that Fellows will promote are likely to be those within reach of established colleges and universities. The Fellows learned from the period of experimentation in the late sixties and early seventies. And they have also learned from earlier decades because they respect history and tradition. Fellows are likely to conclude that the institution of higher education should have a more limited function—educational—and therefore they will not try, given this institution's traditions and capabilities, to make it a center for any and all community activities.

Yet these educational leaders for the next two decades will work more closely and purposefully with the community at large and with local, state, and federal governments than was the case with guild-oriented academics of the recent past. They are not wild-eyed radicals nor muddle-headed theoreticians proposing impossible schemes. They have their feet on the ground. The business executive, the politician, the community leader will be able to relate to these campus leaders and to trust them and employ their abilities.

Are Danforth Fellows the only persons who can adequately respond to the inordinate cultural challenge we face? Thousands of other faculty and administrators—former Woodrow Wilson Fellows, for example, and the so-called near misses of the Danforth competitions—share the same values and have similar abilities. The pool of concerned persons from which leadership can be drawn is larger than we might think. And the commonly held ground is more important, more significant than we expected.

This section on the Danforth Fellows, in which they are presented as concerned faculty members and administrators who have what it takes to be leaders in a college of character, has been included to counteract the persistent opinion that no such leadership exists in American colleges and universities. But these leaders are there, visibly, as documented in the records of the Danforth Foundation. They have spoken through their lives, and the foundation's files contain the evidence of their attitudes and accomplishments. And there must be at least an equal number of faculty members and administrators, trained elsewhere, teaching elsewhere, who share education commitments that transcend us all and provide an agenda to which we can bring our skills. There are individuals of character teaching in ideationally disturbed environments, leading lives of quiet dedication, who can contribute to the fountain of ideas needed to generate a powerful reform movement, and for whom the knowledge of the existence of equally dedicated persons working in more advantageous contexts will mean not discouragement but inspiration. There are faculty and administrators in sufficient numbers to make a difference—if they can be drawn together into a movement and, together, go forward.

Student Personnel Services. Because they are an additional resource, one other group of campus leaders should be recognized here: the men and women in student personnel services. It is an adage among educators that students learn more outside the classroom than within it. There is only slightly less agreement among educators that residential students learn and retain more than do commuting students—if for no other reason than that they spend more time in the formal environment of learning. What students learn outside the classroom but inside the college community—in the residential hall, on the athletic field, with students and faculty members in meetings other than structured academic encounters— can enhance the intellectual and academic orientation of the college. Or student activities can become part of an anti-intellectual force on campus, depending on the attitudes toward teaching and learning shown by campus leaders, including upper-division students who work in the residence halls and the officers of student services who set the time and shape the intent of out-of-class activities.

The climate of the campus, to which these informal educators contribute so much, can penetrate the attitudinal life of a student to the point that, in later years, he or she will recall elements of those effects and will be influenced by them in professional as well as personal choices. One mark of a college of vitality is its ability to extend its influence through the lives of alumni as they become parents, citizens, workers, and community leaders.

Because the nonacademic side of campus life is so important, a college of character will give as much attention to student life—to cultural programs, counseling services, intramural athletics, art, music, and dance—as to any academic dimensions of campus life. And the staff professionals who work in student personnel services will have the respect of faculty members and will be considered full members of the enterprise because they contribute so significantly to the education purposes of the institution. They, in turn, must demonstrate in their lives that they are not only therapists and pastors, activities coordinators and "hail fellows well met," but education leaders who appreciate the kind of teaching and learning that occurs in a college with a clear sense of purpose.

Perspective on the Context

Most Americans are living with the consequences of their emancipation from traditional forms of authority. Ancestral order, historical tradition, ecclesiastical doctrine, communal cohesion, high culture have all been dismissed or relegated to the background of the so-called open society.

Among the consequences of this emancipation has been an extension of individualism or personal freedom, with its invigorating sense of new potentialities unknown to the old closed society. Also, as an institutional rather than individual consequence of emancipation, class barriers have been lowered, racism blunted, ignorance and disease and other obstacles to equality at least partially overcome—as confidence fed by hope has energized collective experience.

There have been, however, other consequences of emancipation, negative ones, a few of which were stated by Walter Lippmann, as reported by Ernest Boyer in his foreword to this book—the feeling of living within a void, on the one hand, while feeling the elation of freedom, on the other, seeing the decline of organized religion offset by the ascendence of science and technology—these consequences cause many Americans to conclude that in times such as these, colleges and universities should accept a special responsibility—to evaluate all contenders to the throne of authority, to help produce new knowledge so that the void is filled with something better than a mere reordering of those dogmas from which we were emancipated, and to educate leaders who will show wisdom defined as "the capacity of judging rightly in matters relating to life and conduct" (*Oxford English Dictionary*).

The company of teachers and scholars in colleges and universities has been given this responsibility because, first, these institutions and their leaders profess to seek truth. At a time when many people celebrate their emancipation from traditional authority that claims to have the truth, and live instead in the presence of contending truths, it is still deemed necessary to promote institutions where disciplined inquiry into multitudinous truths will be carried out as part of an ongoing search for truth. To be emancipated from old forms of control is to be delivered into a search for new forms of authority.

In a civilization emphasizing process and change yet requiring citizens to have a sense of right and wrong, as well as ways to recognize that which is good in order to avoid that which is bad, society relies on colleges and universities to help students who will become the nation's leaders develop a capacity to judge rightly.

The responsibility given scholars and teachers is not only the search for new knowledge or, as we say, the search for truth, but, additionally, to shape knowledge in its immensity to fit the details of life, to apply truth to conduct. Colleges and universities are intended to be somewhat like hydroelectric dams where water is channeled through generators to create electric power for various specific uses.

One problem with this metaphor is that it suggests that success, for the educational institution as for the hydroelectric station, is a forced outcome and a matter of machinery and technology. Tragically, too many educators have thought of education in mechanical ways, when, actually, there is a kind of alchemy involved in which knowledge is recognized as truth and applied with such skill that it is eventually recognized as wisdom.

But the alchemists of academe have not been able to change baser metals into gold, to effect a transmutation of truths into wisdom. These leaders have not met society's challenge to educate a leadership with the capacity to judge rightly. They have helped reorder social priorities, but they have not filled the void caused by America's emancipation from old-fashioned forms of authority. Faculty and administrators have enjoyed the privileges that attend their position of special responsibility without carrying out the responsibilities that are inherent in their position of special privilege.

Should Americans proceed, therefore, as an additional consequence of emancipation from traditional forms of authority, to push colleges and universities still further from the center toward the outer margins of contemporary life? Perhaps the failure of faculty to transmute knowledge to wisdom, and the failure of administrators to keep their skills in the service of education purposes, means that scholars and administrators in institutions of higher education must join priests, pastors, and rabbis, bureaucrats and commissars, in sheltered retirement communities for exhausted leadership and threadbare ideas. Given the doubts of the people about the intellectual value and practicality of education at many colleges, coupled with the abdication of education leadership by too many so-called leaders of education, the people can hardly be faulted if they look elsewhere for leadership to restore social stability to American life.

In the final years of this century, Americans are likely to accept more authoritarian government because the threat of social chaos has made centralized control the assurance of security. During this time, education institutions will be expected to serve the nation-state by inculcating students in the values deemed essential to order and control. Clark Kerr and his colleagues in the Carnegie Council on Policy Studies in Higher Education (1980, p. 3) warned in their final report that during the next twenty years, "public authorities will penetrate even further into the internal life of institutions, increasingly determining what shall and shall not be done. They will undertake to manage . . . by direct intervention, both quantitatively and, more ominously, qualitatively."

Under the circumstances of expanding authoritarianism, the state will summon teachers and colleges to advance the values of disciplined democracy, planned capitalism, and the new civil religion. But the state will need not mandarins, nor transmitters of current doctrine, nor time servers, nor docile conformists. What the state will need is leadership showing moral character, capable of criticizing established policy and formulating creative alternatives. The idea of the university as a center for independent thinking, that ideal promoted so vigorously by Robert Hutchins in his books, *The University of Utopia* and others (Hutchins, 1944, 1953), may be less attainable now than earlier, given federal mobilization, nationalization, or cooptation of the university, plus the university's eager cooperation in this seduction, given the fact that colleges are willing wards of the state. Nevertheless, despite the difficulties, there are educators and citizens who see the need for institutional centers of independence and for individuals of character; people who will dare, even in the context of imposed order and heavy-handed control and questionable state authority, to point out how easily authoritarianism can become tyranny. We must have these leaders in higher education. We must stand with them and they with us. Only then can a movement emerge that will transform institutions as well as individuals and affect society as well as colleges and universities.

The history of the humanistic ideal, as Lewis Lapham (1982, p. 27) reminds us, "is a magnificent and often tragic drama, played out across the infinite reaches of the imagination against intellectual as well as political despotisms, against the ancient enemies of fear and superstition, against the wish to make time stand still. The adventurous spirit implicit in humanism has more to do with the cunning of Ulysses, great-hearted and wide-wandering, than with the intrigues of the English department at Yale or the art endowment in Washington."

The liberal or liberating arts, properly understood, relate to their present manifestations in most colleges as the Chicago Symphony relates to a kazoo band. The humanities and arts and sciences in today's colleges are coarse imitations of the real thing. Far from being waxen-faced robots serving careerism, or pious virgins drawing their skirts back from the dust of the marketplace, the subject matter of a liberal arts college and the proper leadership of this institution connote human pride and character, the spirit of courage and irony, the search for truth and wisdom—to the end that mankind will have the capacity to judge rightly.

The college of character is as central to the world of higher education and a humane society as the sun in our solar system. To adopt a familiar simile: the true liberal arts college is like a radiant sun that, from time to time, throws off portions of itself; these masses, when cooled, acquire independent careers as recognizable planets; but the sun continues on its path and does not seem to diminish in mass or radiance (Berlin, 1981, p. 146). So it is with the liberal arts college at its best, throwing off intellectual and spiritual energy that contributes to the quality and conscience of business and industry, the arts, government, health services, science, schools, and universities.

We need faith, hope, and love, especially for the human resources that can turn an organizational force waiting to be channeled into an activated, purposeful movement. What is needed can be found. This contention is not a mere theoretical assertion or a claim without documentation in the lives of individuals and institutions. It is a statement experientially confirmed. There is evidence of a movement emerging for which leadership is available. Leaders of character can build colleges of character. And the momentum of that movement can energize and guide a society trying to outrun disaster.

6

≈○≈○≈○≈○≈○≈○≈○≈○≈○≈○≈

Strengthening
Faculty Commitment
to Teaching

≈○≈○≈○≈○≈○≈○≈○≈○≈○≈○≈

Although nothing is more practical than good theory, it is also true that theory must lead to practice. Otherwise, it is not good theory, and working with it is like trying to hatch sterile eggs.

This chapter and the one to follow emphasize putting theory into practice. Having discussed definitions, assumptions, purposes, and prospects for leadership in a college of character, I would now like to relate all of that to the actual condition of administrators and faculty. What effect would the themes and emphases of a purposeful community have, first, on a college professional development program?

Delight and Meaning

St. Augustine, an ancient authority on the human condition, once said: "Who can welcome in his mind something which does not give him delight? . . . The will itself can have no motive unless something presents itself to delight and stir the mind" (from *ad Simplicianum*, q 2.21, q 2.22).

Bruno Bettelheim, a contemporary authority on the human

104

condition, has said: "If we do not live just from moment to moment but try to be conscious of our existence, then our greatest need and most difficult achievement is to find meaning in life. It is well known that many people lose the will to live because such meaning evades them" (1975, p. 50; also see Bettelheim, 1979, pp. 3-18).

Delight and meaning are basic human needs. And they are needs that are not being satisfied in the world of academe. Have they ever been in such short supply?

Administrators. It is common now for administrators in colleges and universities to report that the joy has gone out of their jobs. A university president said recently that he had been serving for six years and had just tabulated the time robbed by his work from weekends, nights, and vacations. This tabulation led him to conclude that he had squeezed nine years of work into six. And that was only the overrun on time. He dramatized the emotional investment by saying, as he came out of budget hearings with legislators, "I served a year last week." This president has now resigned "I was once willing to pay the price in time and energy," he said, "but it no longer makes sense."

That which had once made sense, for this administrator as for others, was the opportunity to influence the development of an educational institution. Development was defined in terms of growth—larger enrollments, new facilities, expanding budgets, more programs—quantitative, not qualitative, growth. Today, administrators have lost these satisfactions. To those persons who equate mental health with the growth mentality, there is not much satisfaction in a steady state.

Administrators have been motivated by more than the notion of material, quantitative growth. They have sometimes measured success in qualitative terms—seeing themselves as managing an essential service to society. The institution of higher education was not merely one among many social institutions but was the penultimate one, second only to the state. For how could democracy prosper without an educated citizenry? And how would the citizenry be educated except through the services of professional educators? The case could be made, of course, for the significance of other institutions, such as the churches, social agencies, and health services, but surely everyone understood that the institution of education was the first among equals. Today, this confidence, or arrogance, has crumbled. There is much less surety about the relative position of the institution of higher education vis-à-vis other social institutions as well as less confidence about the relative importance of the services provided.

However much the behavior and attitude of administrators reveal a waning of delight and loss of purpose or meaning, the condition of faculty is even more disquieting. And the reasons for this disquietude have to do with much more than salaries, mobility, and recognition.

Faculty. No profession is more troubled than the teaching profession.

Law and medicine seem to be untroubled professions although evidence accumulates that the nation suffers from a glut of lawyers as well as from gluttonous doctors. The rise in the cost of medical services is exceeded only by growth in the number of lawyers. Psychiatry and psychology are popular professions. Eighty thousand persons in Washington, D.C., consult psychologists. But orthodox Freudian psychiatry is called "the impossible profession" because treatment is excruciatingly slow and cures are hard to document. Politicians are in the world's second-oldest profession and seem to have learned nothing other than the secret of longevity from that oldest profession—or from any profession. However successful the major professions appear to be, they all have troubles. But no profession has troubles to equal those of teaching.

Consider how a medical doctor would feel if patients came into his office day after day with symptoms that were easily identified, and as deadly as they were obvious. Yet, despite what the doctor knew of the disease causing those symptoms, and the effects to which it led, he could do little or nothing to cure the ailment. He could, at best, help patients cope with their condition by providing "survival skills." Should a doctor be content with a profession that can do nothing more than keep patients just out of the reach of the spirit of resignation? Is this level of accomplishment enough to keep the doctor motivated? Would not this doctor and his profession be deeply troubled in the presence of such limitations?

That medical doctor's situation is precisely the situation of today's teacher—most of the time, with most students. The students' symptoms are transparently clear: a paucity of motivation and self-discipline, an absence of what sociologists call "behavior supports," little encouragement, less training, few successes. In the presence of a lot of ignorance and only limited knowledge, the best that the teacher can do is to give such students "survival skills." It is a service to help people stay one jump ahead of disaster. But if this is the environment in which the teacher must work, and if the level of his accomplishments are so limited, can this teacher feel good about his profession?

In America, success is more important than sex or anything else. But success eludes teachers. Precollegiate and collegiate-level teachers, viewed nationally, have not shown that they can succeed with students who are unskilled and undermotivated, especially when these students come from social conditions that do not support the aims and procedures of formal education. Medical doctors have generally had successes sufficient to satisfy social expectations. Law is seen as a necessary evil. Business is business. But teaching?

The troubled profession of teaching may not be a profession. A true profession involves skills not easily acquired, skills that can provide an important service to society. There is no agreement about the skills required to be a successful teacher or about how best to acquire them. Much of what teachers do—lectures, for example—could be done by actors performing on videotapes. And some of the best university teaching is done by teaching assistants who know enough subject matter to meet student needs and yet are near enough to the students' ages to relieve student anxieties. Given libraries, films, and records, motivated students could teach themselves and each other.

Professors, like prophets, are without honor in their own country, particularly when they try to base their claim to professional standing on teaching. No one is more cynical about teaching than professors who have dedicated their lives to teaching, research, and service. The teaching profession is in trouble because, quite apart from pay and "perks"—and teachers have not competed successfully for money and status compared with other professionals—faculty who teach are considered the least professional of the many professionals in the major occupations. Teachers who base their reputation on teaching are not often in the more rigorous disciplines and are not often tough-minded. The Ed.D., that degree held by many teachers and administrators, is perceived by scholars as a second-rate degree awarded to third-rate graduate students.

The profession of teaching is in trouble because teachers have claimed too much for their profession. They urged parents to turn over the education of youth to professional educators, never realizing that schools work best when linked to education in the home, that educators excel only when the students have been prepared at home for the tasks of the schools. Educators argued that everybody should have a college education, forgetting that most of the jobs in American society do not require the advanced intellectual skills that college teaching allegedly confers. Also, the big claims of the education professionals ignored the fact that not everybody has either the aptitude for or the interest in what those professionals teach. It was the *hubris* of educators that people would want whatever educators taught or, conversely, that whatever the people wanted, the teachers could teach. Thus, educational professionals have tried to attract all people to themselves and to be all things to all people.

When the question "What is the nation going to do with the unskilled and unemployed?" has been raised, college and university educators felt obliged to answer the question. But college teachers can no more answer that question than they can answer this one: "How do we deal with inflation and recession?" The only segment of higher education that has anything to offer the so-called hard-core unskilled and unemployed is the community college. But the extent to which it offers the basic education and basic skills needed by the people from the underclass who are in the worst educational condition is the extent to which a community college is no more a college even as the education it offers is no longer higher education. Furthermore, the community college cannot compete with the proprietary school in teaching basic communication skills and basic career skills, in keeping costs down and the success rate high.

Faculty and administrators have claimed too much for institutionalized education, and they have not proved their claims. Consequently, some people have concluded that schools and colleges are, for the most part, giant detention centers, and that teachers are, for the most part, babysitters, hall monitors, and playground supervisors; hucksters of off-the-shelf ideas sold as "loss leaders" to students who feel cheated by the transaction.

The teaching profession is in trouble because, despite aforementioned conditions, its practitioners have taken on airs, wanting less teaching and more leisure. Some members of this profession, particularly those in higher education, have the audacity to claim their right to all of the pleasures of a society that they traditionally scorned: boats on the bay, cabins in the mountains, golf and tennis and club memberships. The notion of this profession as a vocation has been replaced by a distorted conception of teaching as a routine job. The appeal of the extended vacation has strengthened as the ideal of vocation has weakened.

Teachers have in the past delighted in debunking administration, and they didn't change until administrators, who used to say modestly, "We grease the wheels and get out of the way," quietly collected the formulas and procedures for controlling computerized budgets. When faculty realized that administrators had their hands on the power buttons, faculty reacted by following trade unions and starting collective bargaining, which further weakened their claim to being professionals rather than hired hands.

The teaching profession is in trouble because of internal inconsistencies, even contradictions. Faculty who espouse diversity, pluralism, and academic freedom are intolerant and rigid in departmental procedures. A scholar in phenomenological existentialism has a limited chance for a tenured appointment in any philosophy department—at the University of California, Berkeley, for example—that is oriented to analytic philosophy. No academic freedom there.

This troubled profession has been able to create some trouble by feigning dissent and other forms of behavior that show chronic aggrievement; by agitating students to engage in social and political actions that few teachers would dare attempt; by repeatedly demonstrating that while a little learning is a dangerous thing, a lot of learning can be still more dangerous.

The teaching profession is in trouble because so little can be done about incompetent or unnecessary teachers:

- There is not much that can be done about the fact that most colleges and universities are tenured in. The grim reaper cuts out the dead wood—but that job takes time. Meanwhile, colleges are experiencing gridlock, with the old teachers safely on track and the young teachers locked out.

- There is not much that can be done about the fact that retraining redundant college faculty for nonacademic professional positions—in industries, libraries, and museums—is expensive and often demeaning. It is perceived by faculty to be like trying to turn a silk purse into a sow's ear.

- There is not much that can be done about the fact that America has thousands of overlapping educational programs in hundreds of duplicative institutions, complete with self-serving bureaucracies, all of which proves to be unjustifiably expensive and leads to crazy institutional cannibalism. Too many towns, politicians, benefactors, and educators have a vested interest in the perpetuation of this extravagance to permit personnel and facility reductions in the range of 10 to 20 percent—the range of diminution required for a return to sanity.

- There is not much that can be done about the fact that college faculty who try to teach were trained to do research; that they want to teach in their specialization rather than do the introductory, remedial, or developmental teaching that is most often needed. The influence of guild-oriented graduate programs on the self-image of faculty, compromised by institutional and classroom realities, has a skewing effect as bizarre as that of the distortion mirrors at an amusement park. For example, community college teachers are required by the skill and motivational deficiencies of their students to revert to the level of high school teaching—that level from which the community college emerged and from which many senior community college faculty escaped.

The teaching profession is in trouble because too many teachers, younger ones usually, seem to forget that just as life is not a continuous chain of happy events—most of us, in fact, live for occasional moments of happiness—so teaching is rarely a scintillating exchange of ideas with bright-eyed students, but more often like a slog through basic training with sleepy recruits. Routine, repetition, perseverance characterize the fatiguing realities of teachers. Teaching the introductory and remedial courses again and again, hearing the same questions, seeing familiar mistakes, is disheartening. No wonder many college teachers flock to subject-matter specializations. The students and the department curriculum make instruction more interesting. Unfortunately, the teaching most needed is mostly boring.

The trouble with that second element in the trilogy of faculty responsibilities—research—is that most teachers do not do research. Only 20 percent of college and university faculties carry on research of any consequence; yet all faculty members are judged by standards of research and scholarship. The guild-star to which they have tied their wagon makes precisely the same demands. Thus most faculty are subject to the sanctions but not the rewards of the guild system. And most faculty live professional lives that do not even faintly approximate the ideals of their occupation.

It would be better for faculty to find meaning and delight in teaching of the type promoted in this essay. But the kind of teaching favored at most colleges is that which prepares students to move into specializations and into the very research and publications cycle that most faculty have found to be a treadmill. Faculty are, again, constantly reminded of their own failure.

Another way to help faculty would be to encourage them to show, in their teaching as well as their own lives, the social, moral, and political significance of their specializations. Faculty need such encouragement because many disciplines as now conceived and represented are about as important to the lives of the people as a gold toothpick is to oral hygiene. However, the "service concept," under which faculty members could find a professional justification for seeking out and developing the sociopolitical and moral significance of their specializations, is least favored among the formal responsibilities of faculty.

Another trouble with that traditional commitment to service is that service implies giving and, alas, in America today it is not better to give than to receive—except, perhaps, a virus or a cold. Furthermore, most faculty do not receive enough pay or honor to feel spontaneously generous or to practice distinterested benevolence.

Big-league faculty members who spend one day a week consulting for corporations and advising politicians tend to define service narrowly. They say it means using their research to serve industry and government. Those faculty members who are not in demand, and are considered by their elite and distant colleagues to be bush league, tend to define service broadly. They say it means teaching a Sunday School class or making a speech at the local Rotary Club. Their numbers are legion, and never have so many talked so much about so little.

Effective undergraduate teaching today, given the realities of this troubled profession, requires the following characteristics, stated here with only a dash of irony:

- Be an intellectual dilettante. Read widely, emphasize relational thinking, synthesize.
- Do not be too bright, or, if bright, hide your light under a facade of egalitarianism. Otherwise, you will unsettle your peers and incur their wrath. You may not suffer fools gladly, but if you want to succeed, you will somehow learn to suffer them.
- Be a ham actor. Learn timing, use surprise, develop stage presence. Everything's fair in love, war, and teaching. Know your subject, but know your audience better.
- Enjoy people—including their small talk and human foibles.
- Be an amateur psychologist. Be willing to be a personal counselor. Kleenex is important equipment in your office.
- Practice situational ethics—flexibility, adaptability, immediacy. Plagiarism, tardiness, incompletes, absences from class are chronic problems for which students have creative "solutions." The only way to stand tall in these situations is to keep on your toes.
- Ring all the current "word chimes" of the teaching profession, about being overworked and underpaid—"exploited," "abused"— and dress the part. The old VW beetle has given way to the battered Volvo station wagon, but the jeans, corduroy jacket, turtleneck shirt, and desert boots are still *de rigueur*.
- Distance yourself from administrators, but answer your mail. This is the way to become a dean.

Is it any wonder that faculty lack zest for their work? The reasons for this condition, I repeat, are not merely the recent cutbacks in supplies and services, reduced salary increments, and weakened job security. As troublesome as these problems are, they do not explain faculty flatness.

In times of war or other social crises, people tolerate all sorts of inconvenience and displacement if they have a compelling purpose in which they believe, a clear sense of direction. Faculty today are still doing their jobs but are not happy in their work. Duty still motivates them. Yet few delight in the profession; few find it vital and relevant. Evidence abounds that the delight in and meaning of vocation in many faculty lives have waned.

There are two ways for faculty in liberal arts colleges to progress in finding meaning and experiencing delight, ways that cost little or no money and do not require awaiting the initiative of immutable forces. One strategy advances college faculty along the road to professional development while the other fosters personal development. And it is possible for these to be parallel tracks, interdependent, mutually useful, like two lanes of a turnpike going in the same direction.

In the following, I assume that delight and meaning must be defined and measured first in terms of self-interest, that is, in terms of what an experience means to me, personally; then, what it means for my profession; and, finally, what it means for the institution with which I am affiliated. There is no alternative to beginning with the self and selfishness, but as we shall see, there is no need to end there.

Another reason for concentrating on individuals rather than on institutions is that by beginning with ourselves, our personal and professional lives, we can prepare to deal with institutional specifics, with curriculum and governance issues. We must find ways to revitalize ourselves before we can do much to help educational institutions of a culture in crisis.

From Job to Vocation

Progress on the road to professional development will be noteworthy to the extent that administrators and faculty in the college become not merely employees but mature professionals.

Men and women who started teaching within the last twenty years learned too little about the requirements of true professionalism. This is not to say that a person who develops skill in a subject-matter specialization, or seeks status in a disciplinary guild, or joins a union and engages in collective bargaining, cannot be an academic professional. This is not a defense of Mr. Chips or faculty who sit on logs. The point is that the faculty member who thinks of his or her specialization in narrow terms and has no interest in the sociopolitical ramifications of that discipline, or who allows loyalty to guild or union to displace concern for the home institution, or the faculty member who permits the methodology of the discipline or some pretense to objectivity to preclude involvement in the moral and ethical struggles of the citizenry and the needs and interests of students, is not professional.

True professionals have a skill not normally acquired without special and complicated training. True professionals use their skill to provide a social service that shows not only technical expertise but social commitment. The government of the People's Republic of China has had the motto "Serve the people." For academic professionals in that country, this vow means applying expertise to issues. In some cases that application will be theoretical, as in physics; in other cases more applied or specific, as in sociology. In all cases the work must be relevant to the needs of the people.

Of course there is a possibility of abuse and of peril to academic freedom or institutional independence. It is likely that the Chinese experience has only limited usefulness in America. On the other hand, academics in this country abuse their privileges by being too far removed from the people, especially from nonacademic professionals. And the notion of service, as a feature of a profession properly called a vocation, needs revival and improvement.

Today faculty should demonstrate their service to society if for no other reason than that this is the best way for colleges and universities to compete for funds with entitlement programs and health services. Along the way faculty should try to persuade the people that the institution of higher education is unique in that it is the place where reflection is as prized as action, where the most important form of action may be to provide a theoretical basis for action. This institution is a place where, in the interests of creativity and criticism, the professionals will sometimes bite the hand that feeds them and will deny that he who pays the piper must always call the tune. One way or the other, however, educators must see their profession as a form of service. They serve because it is part of their tradition, because to do so is to fulfill the calling of a professional. They perform service also to bring meaning into their personal lives and to experience the motive force of delight.

There is tension now between educators and legislators across the nation in part because of the haughty superiority that has been shown by academics and "campus types." Legislators see education making the largest claim on state budgets. The best of these legislators freely acknowledge their need, as they allocate limited resources, to better understand the services of the educational enterprise. If they are to do so, they need the help of educators. These legislators are ready and eager for help but too often find themselves rebuffed by professors who feed off the society to which they are willing to be only distantly related.

Other persons, not often faculty, most often administrators, are excited by the prospect of having attention drawn to service as an important duty of educators. In some cases, this interest reflects a desire to increase and extend institutional productivity, or to assure social responsibility and accountability. In most cases, there is a desire to get faculty out of the ivory tower, away from abstraction and theory, and into the practical and urgent concerns of the people. In a few cases, the interest of administrators in the duty of service reveals their conviction that the teaching enterprise needs reorganization, that faculty in particular have lost enthusiasm for their work, and that the best way to meet this need for revitalization would be to redefine the professional life of the teacher so that the notion of vocation—purposeful service—would again be integral to a proper definition of this profession.

It may be that, ultimately, the principal service of the true academic professional will be to persuade the people of the need for critical intelligence. Perhaps, as Susan Sontag (1976, p. 36) has said, our culture is collapsing because critical intelligence—dialectical, skeptical, desimplifying—is so often denied relevance to social realities. Hopefully, educators will not only assert the importance of such intelligence but will show its value in action.

From Part to Whole

If defining and redefining what it means to have a sense of the dignity, authority, and relevance of teaching is one way to make life more meaningful for a faculty member in a college of character, a second component has to do with development along the road to becoming a whole person.

Administrators and faculty members will know that they are on this path when they have learned to organize and assess their lives not only in professional terms but also in religious ones.

Religious faith may be defined as concern for the mystery of the *ought,* and religion's task is to sort out what is from what ought to be. Religious faith has sometimes taken the form of religious philosophy, as in classical Hellenism. It is sometimes expressed in the form of a philosophical religion, as in ancient Judaism and Christianity. In the West, concern for the *ought,* historically, has been expressed through a unitary church—the Roman Catholic Church—or through reform movements such as the Protestant Reformation. It has been interpreted and applied by intellectuals and academics, poets and artists, architects and engineers. The Renaissance was a reformulation of the religious impulse, as were the Enlightenment, the Romantic movement, and an array of more recent philosophical and theological movements. Modern science built on and in part restructured the essential components of traditional religion until it nearly became a surrogate religion. For much of this century, psychology, particularly Freudian and neo-Freudian psychology, has provided categories and terms—id, ego, superego—to deal with human nature, man and nature, social organization, the immediate and the transcendent, the "is" and "ought"—the religious issues. Bettelheim has said that psychoanalysis was created to help us accept life's problematic nature. Freud said that only by struggling courageously against odds can we succeed in wringing meaning out of human existence.

Very recently, the West has been affected by the orientation of the East, by insights, attitudes, practices, terminology, perspectives on ideals and reality that to us are no less religious albeit less traditional. Some observers see a coming together of East and West. Others minimize the contribution of the East, claiming that its emphasis is much too passive to be compelling in the West.

Certain Latin American countries, Argentina for example, are guided by ideologues who believe that the superpowers of the Northern Hemisphere—Britain, France, the Soviet Union, the United States—are decadent and in decline. Very soon, according to these authorities, leadership will pass to emerging nations, most of them in the Southern Hemisphere, where corruption has been thrown off and a holy mission taken up with religous fervor.

In the United States, there are numerous observers of contemporary life—Joyce Carol Oates has been among them—who believe that there are not only signs everywhere of the death of old values but there are even more signs of the birth of new ones. An evolution into a higher humanism, perhaps an intelligent pantheism, is occurring. It is a transformation so profound that the only experience with which it can be compared is that of a religious conversion.

A religious conversion of this magnitude is needed whether or not it involves a blending of East and West or the triumph of the Southern Hemisphere over the Northern. The power of a new affection is the only force capable of turning people around and setting them on a better course. Remember this proof-test: "The will itself can have no motive unless something presents itself to delight and stir the mind." The challenge is not to move from dreams to actualities but to move from actualities to dreams.

What is offered here is not puff paste. As meekness is not weakness, so to be delighted is not to lose the capacity for discrimination. To retain one's delight in wildflowers, it is necessary to remember that the thistle will bloom among them.

Nor is this a pitch for institutional religion, although the religion or ethical movement of which we speak may take institutional form. It is a claim for the importance of "oughtness." It is a claim for the importance of *why,* not just *how.* It is a claim for the primacy of the search for meaning. As Einstein put it, "The man who regards his own life and that of his fellow-creatures as meaningless is not merely unfortunate but almost disqualified for life" (1949, p. 1).

Why is it important to grapple with "the meaning of life," with the "oughtness" of life? with religion, morality, and ethics? It is important because most decisions in judicial cases are ethical decisions put in legal terms. It is important because a large percen-

tage of the decisions made by doctors are more in the realm of ethics
and morality than in science and technology. It is important because a teacher is never merely a teacher of subject matter but is
always involved in choices and moral judgments. The religious
impulse points attention to standards and values—values defined as
standards held with conviction.

To develop the religious consciousness offers another benefit: it helps assure an understanding of tragedy, the ironic presence of the inertia of history and the human being's resistance to
change. Robert Heilbroner in *The Future as History* noted that
reformers deplore the tenacity with which the privileged cling to
their prerogatives. What is even more remarkable, wrote Heilbroner,
is the way that the masses cling to their past. Revolutions are hallmarks of history not because of their frequency but because of their
rarity (1961, p. 194).

If the religious and moral sensibility makes college faculty
members aware of the viscosity or resiliency of the past, it also makes
them cautious about relying too much on quick change. The future,
history shows, is not benign, malleable, like putty in our hands.
This is not to say that human beings are only the result of intractable forces. We are the product of history, but we also produce it.
History has an unfathomable quality and is characterized by paradox and contradiction. Habit, for example, hinders change. Yet the
persistence of habit is a source of stabilization and protection. The
old ways are not only the most familiar but sometimes the best. This
is why so-called folk wisdom must be taken seriously and why there
is an enduring relevance in some of the old cliches.

To "get religion," in the sense suggested by the definition
given earlier, is to accept mystery and awe. Western civilization,
particularly in its manifestation called scientific rationality, has
measured its success by an ability to reduce the unknown. The presence of mystery and awe has been a source of embarrassment, a sign
of failure. The university has been the place where, as Theodore
Roszak has shown, this commitment to know rather than to wonder
has been carried forward most vigorously. The emphasis has been
on objective analysis, with the terms defined by reason and the
procedures fixed by scientific methodology. Experiential involvement has been steadily reduced to that which can be controlled.

Transcendental vision has come to be considered unworthy; at best a viewpoint, at worst a cruel distortion.

Spiritual sensibilities have, to be sure, been twisted and manipulated throughout history into instruments of control. But the alternative is not "single vision," the narrow scientism against which William Blake raged, but rather the "multiple vision" that Blake himself exemplified, that multiple vision which is another gift of the religious mind (see Roszak, 1972, pp. 296ff.). This should be a distinguishing feature of a college of character, particularly its faculty leadership.

The religious person has a means of understanding the humanistic tradition as well as humane learning, the need for standards in an era of egalitarian permissiveness, the value of history understood as tragedy, and the role of mystery and awe in human experience. Religion reminds us that factual knowledge profits the total personality only when it is turned into personal knowledge.

The full professional knows how to bring the resources of the whole person into professional service. If teachers in the college are to avoid false pretensions and become true professionals, they must:

- Be unapologetic about the primacy of the synoptic function—synthesis and interpretation in scholarship for teaching at the undergraduate level. Relational thinking is the best specialization.
- Return to the notion of teaching as a vocation, not a job.
- Revive concern for the education of the whole person—body, mind, and spirit—and apply that concern to teachers as well as students.
- Emphasize the social/political and the moral/ethical dimensions of all teaching and learning.
- Acknowledge that this is a time for reassessment of what professors have to profess. Modesty and courage must go everywhere together.
- Love people with their troubles even more than they love their troubled profession.

Technical Skills and Human Sensibilities

Most faculty and administrative development programs are flawed, even doomed, because they feature procedures and arrangements—teaching strategies and management tools—that serious faculty members consider to be gimmicks, passing fads, and superficial remedies. Professional development programs that are all technique match in futility those catering to familiar faculty activities, such as sending teachers off to guild-oriented national meetings where, perhaps, there will be one session on teaching techniques with a standard bag of tricks on the table, and another session on professional assessment, that is, teacher evaluation by students and administration.

Another reason for failure in conventional professional development programs is that too many program planners assume there will be no changes in established values and arrangements. Programs are geared to accommodation and adjustment, individual adaptation to predictable institutional constraints. Day-by-day realities cannot be ignored, but too many development programs deal with them exclusively.

Finally, as evidence of another unbalanced or partial approach, some professional development programs put emphasis entirely on personal growth, with much of that growth defined by leaders using the literature on "stages of human development." The exercises of these programs build up resources for entering into that "interior drama," too often at the sacrifice of attention to the external world. When self-realization becomes a preoccupation, the professor teaches only himself.

Professional development programs in a college of consequence must deal with the most substantial issues, including those that help the person to think relationally about himself as well as the profession. The conceptualization of the teaching profession as a vocation rather than a job is equally important. Also needed are faculty development programs that grapple with complexities such as the authority of the profession of teaching in society, and the teacher's authority with students.

College teachers must have clout. I am not promoting a rigid imposition of discipline in the classroom, which compels students to treat teachers with formal deference if not deep respect. Of course, establishing the authority of teachers can, as a benefit, help with classroom discipline and provide a basis for student respect. I am not promoting the authority of teachers in departmental negotiations, with administrators, or in collective bargaining sessions. I do claim that restoring the authority of the teaching profession bears all sorts of practical, even monetary, implications. To have authority is to gain a fistful of bargaining chips.

What is meant when we say that a person such as a pitcher on a baseball team, a golfer, a politician, or a chef does something "with authority"? We refer, obviously, to skills. But we are also, very often, referring to an attitude, a style, a touch or presence. He has, we say, a certain bearing that commands respect. She has an unmistakable way about her. The person is not only professionally competent but personally appealing.

Having authority in academe has a lot to do with possessing technical skills and applying them successfully. We honor the researcher or the scholar who stands tall in his or her field. However, authority in academe also stems from developed human sensibilities. We say that a certain teacher has an uncanny ability to comprehend the situation. Or, she senses what is needed. He understands. Showing these qualities helps one to gain authority.

Charisma, like character or creativity, is more often caught than taught. It is not something that schools of education or even the most stimulating teachers can give students. But teachers can help students acquire, and a college community can help its faculty develop, confidence in the dignity and authority of the profession of teaching. The true professional demonstrates, remember, skills not easily acquired and necessary in providing an essential, not optional, social service. Once these skills are established, and their usefulness verified, that spirit of confidence arises and can be demonstrated. The confidence of authority is better, more enduring and influential, than flashy charisma.

One way for teachers and administrators, individuals and the institution to demonstrate confidence in the profession is to show in practice the distinction between authority and authoritarianism. Authoritarianism means age masquerading as maturity, titles substituting for competence, roles played without good reason. Authority, however, shows itself in technical competence combined with human sensibility. It means knowing a subject or skill quite well and also knowing how to apply it to the needs of the people and relate it to the contributions of others. Authority invites respect, loyalty, and sustained cooperation. Authoritarianism draws conformity—eventually, reaction and rebellion.

This question of authority has always been a most difficult one for Americans. Ancestral order, ecclesiastical and civil authority, as previously mentioned, have all had their day in this country. Within the last century or so, they have diminished beside the growing authority of the individual. There is an accompanying awareness, however, that strident individualism is bringing disaster to the nation and the world. Some notion of community, one that greatly qualifies individualism, a community with earned authority, is necessary as a corrective force.

If a college expects faculty members to limit their external involvements with, say, professional associations, consulting services, and adjunct teaching assignments and, instead, to increase their involvement in the life of the institution, then that college must be a community of such high quality that faculty members will find delight and meaning in their work there. Furthermore, the faculty as teachers and as community members must be made full partners in the most substantive deliberations, such as the formulation and evaluation of basic policies.

To suggest a substantial faculty development program, I will point to a couple of deep wells in selected places where faculty should be involved in digging and tasting.

Members of the intentional community will concentrate on the issue of pluralism and its concomitant, freedom. In these days, their point of focus will not be on how to extend diversity and pluralism but on how to set appropriate limits to pluralism. We must decide, together, in these times and for the impending future, when we must say no. What is the point of interdiction? On what will the interdicts be based, or what values will define the point of interdiction? Also, what is a proper form of remission? If we must say no, when do we say, "Even so" (Rieff, 1972, pp. 45–49)?

If we are to forgive, we must have some notion of transgression. This means that freedom cannot be unqualified. What are its limitations? Pluralism has negative as well as positive implications for freedom. Surely pluralism is not to be confused with egalitarianism. Can we differentiate?

A college or university must have education standards. The House of Intellect may have many rooms, but it must also have a floor. If athletic coaches and faculty committees at the University of New Mexico, at Oregon, at the University of Southern California, had shown more commitment to education standards and more concern for the limits to diversity in their institutions, sports fans would not have had to endure the scandals that rocked these campuses in 1980. One of the features of human sensibility at its best is the ability to say yes and no for reasons that are not merely expedient, or improvisational, or rooted only in the impulse of the moment or in the imperative of success.

If one characteristic of a community of character is a willingness to *discriminate* (that word's legitimate meaning must be recalled to use), a second characteristic is an ability to see things from the other side. In his essays "Education" and "Education of Character," Martin Buber emphasizes the spirit of inclusion. He offers two illustrations: "A man belabours another, who remains quite still. Then let us assume that the striker receives in his soul the blow that he strikes . . . for the space of a moment he experiences the situation from the other side. . . . A man caresses a woman, who lets herself be caressed. Then let us assume that he feels the contact from two sides—with the palm of his hand still, but also with the woman's skin too. The two-fold nature of the gesture, as one that takes place between two persons, thrills through the depths of enjoyment in his heart and stirs it" (1955, p. 96). Buber's second illustration best merits a metaphorical rather than literal application. Yet the image of the caress is helpful, especially the notion of sensing the caress from the other side. It reminds us that the first hallmark of character, expressed by words such as *exclusion, standards, interdiction, limits,* can quickly lead to abuse unless it is accompanied by that second characteristic, the one best represented by such words as *inclusion, remission, understanding, forgiveness.*

What else will the faculty, as part of a vital community, talk about in their professional development program? How about the issue of quality and its concomitant, standards?

Albert J. Nock, writing in the 1930s, warned that the majority of people is neither capable of nor interested in the academic requirements of higher education. Therefore, he argued, America should devise a variety of educational and training programs. Failure to do so would weaken existing colleges and universities to the point that the essential nature of higher education institutions would be changed, making them into something they were never intended to be, thereby threatening the existence of the best services they have supplied (Nock, 1969). Nock's successors assert that, today, we have changed the nature of the game and, correspondingly, its rules. We once played a game in academe that necessitated winners and losers. Now we've changed the rules in an effort to make everybody winners.

The English used to say, "More means worse." Put the emphasis on quantity, on numbers, they said, and quality will suffer. The American rejoinder has been "But does less mean better?" Or, as we are wont to add, "Perhaps more means different." What American colleges have come to offer is not necessarily worse or better but, as it were, a new deal for students, particularly those who have been heretofore un- or underrepresented. Now, however, confidence in these arrangements is shaken, and America's educational leaders must ask, What constitutes quality *now?* What are appropriate standards *now* (Martin, 1978/1979)? Everyone who cares about a college of character should address these questions. And a high-quality professional development program incorporates issues of this importance and complexity.

> *Character teaches over our heads.*
> Emerson

More attention needs to be given to these deeper levels of faculty development precisely because many of the issues on campus are not procedural but substantive. Consider, for example, how important it is for faculty to be personal exemplars of the best values of the educated person. Faculty probably teach most through what they do—certainly more than by what they say. Telling a student to read is not nearly as persuasive as showing the student, through one's own attitudes and actions, the power, beauty, and usefulness of a life informed by books and reading.

It has been popular to argue that a professional's service is distinct or separate from his or her personal life and character. To be sure, we care more about what the surgeon does in the operating room than about what he or she did the night before. But to stop at that distinction is simplistic. The doctor's personal qualities affect his or her professional skills. The "answers" that a psychotherapist finds to questions in his or her personal life influence the questions put to patients. Likewise, the teacher's life affects his teaching and the lives of students.

It is a worthy goal, then, to encourage faculty to embody the values of education, to be role models of the educated person. Faculty should remember that the institution of higher education has always sought to stand slightly apart from society, to be in some measure a center of independent thinking, a place characterized by creativity and criticism. They should also be reminded, at a time when the pressures to become mere functionaries and time-servers are great, that they are professionals who as individuals should embody that which they envision for the institution and that which they would encourage in students: the attitude of curiosity and inquisitiveness, the capacity for perspective and compassion, the ability to think rationally and contextually.

Few sights are sadder or more damaging to students than the spectacle of a senior faculty member or top-level administrator who has allowed his intellectual and spiritual commitments to become mere abstractions, who has applied a professional veneer to the bureaucratic structure where he goes through the motions of his work. Sheed (1982, p. E19) warns that overly ardent professionalism will squeeze from a human being all his vital juices: "The professional world becomes a kind of Franz Kafka mansion where the rooms get spiritually smaller and grayer the farther up the stairs you go. . . . Since this is the exact opposite of the way it looks, because the offices actually seem to get bigger, many people sometimes go right to the top without knowing what's happening to them. (And when they do, they claim the pressure of work is walling them in.) But the best people make time for books and ideas and it's the second-raters who don't. Time isn't the real problem. The real problem is character."

Above all else, the educator with professional skills and human sensibilities will serve the college and the students with the sobering realization that the chief characteristic of this age is the crisis in our culture. We lack a shared motivating ideology, as evidenced by the confusion between pluralism and egalitarianism;

we possess a sophisticated technology, but it is used to widen the gap between the haves and have-nots; we talk about morality and ethics, but social permissiveness usurps our right to define propriety; older people emulate the young, but the example of the imitative elders repels the youth.

What does it mean to be an educator, and to educate, in a time of social crisis? To educate during a slight disruption or a momentary interruption, not even during a serious war or other external threat, but to educate in a time of fundamental ideational dislocation, a time when the foundations are being shaken and are, some say, actually collapsing? What is meant by general education then? If education is partly a process of socialization, what would be the features of the socializing process for a culture in crisis? There has traditionally been something called citizenship education. What are the characteristics of the ideal citizen when there is no ideal state? A college community was presumed to encourage humane learning. What does it mean now to be humane? By what standard is this quality measured? Does one continue to rely on the so-called humanistic tradition when the outcomes are so often inhuman? If there is no tradition on which to depend—not the Jewish and Christian heritage, not the Hellenic or humanistic tradition, not science and technology—on what do you depend? Feeling the need for continuity, but having no experience that seems trustworthy, how do you start a new tradition? Can anything but the past be the basis for the future?

E. F. Schumacher offers a straightforward explanation for a basic element in the national crisis: Economics is a pseudoscience in the service of a pseudophilosophy—materialism—in which greed and envy are justified through the uncritical worship of unqualified growth. He wrote: "We shrink back from the truth if we believe that the destructive forces of the modern world can be 'brought under control' simply by mobilizing more resources—of wealth, education, and research—to fight pollution, to preserve wildlife, to discover new sources of energy, and to arrive at more effective agreements on peaceful coexistence. Needless to say, wealth, education, research, and many other things are needed for any civilization, but what is most needed today is a revision of the ends which means are meant to serve" (1973, p. 294).

Schumacher would have us take up afresh the search for truth. And where should we look for clues?

> It is hardly likely that twentieth-century man is called upon to discover truth that has never been discovered before. In the Christian tradition, as in all genuine traditions of mankind, the truth has been stated in religious terms, a language which has become well-nigh incomprehensible to the majority of modern men. The language can be revised, and there are contemporary writers who have done so, while leaving the truth inviolate. Out of the whole Christian tradition, there is perhaps no body of teaching which is more relevant and appropriate to the modern predicament than the marvelously subtle and realistic doctrines of the Four Cardinal Virtues— *prudentia, justitia, fortitudo, and temperantia.* . . .
> . . . Everywhere people ask: "What can I actually *do?*" The answer is as simple as it is disconcerting: we can, each of us, work to put our own inner house in order. The guidance we need for this work cannot be found in science or technology, the value of which utterly depends on the ends they serve; but it can still be found in the traditional wisdom of mankind [pp. 296–297].

To draw on traditional wisdom, in order to put our inner house in order, is to give meaning to human life as well as purpose to our employment. And meaning lends delight at a time when the flesh is willing but the spirit is weak.

7

~~~~~~

Curriculum:
Education for Character,
Career, and Society

~~~~~~

Benjamin Franklin said to George Whitefield that "people fear
being out of style more than they fear hell." Such an attitude, now as
well as then, is evidenced by the struggle of college leaders to design
career-oriented curricula at a time when being out of style leads to
the hell of flaccid enrollments and truculent budgets.

The current fashion features professional education and careerism. John Henry Newman, and others with a classical bent, held
the idea that liberal education and the work of the mind were to be
done for their own sake, as the proper functions of a human being,
and not because they served any practical end. However, this idea
seems to have dried up, to use Langston Hughes's phrase, like a
raisin in the sun.

There is, of course, some resistance to the expanding emphasis on careerism from faculty who still hold to the notion that learning is for learning's sake, from administrators in those colleges
fueled by a strong tradition in liberal education, from trustees who
equate the college with the liberal arts and for whom giving up the
equity in that phrase *liberal arts college* would be as confusing as

Coca-Cola giving up its signature logo. There are wide-awake educators, fully informed about trends and pressures, who believe that the liberal arts will survive the present challenge, shake off the corrupting influence of compromises made by persons whose expediency is exceeded only by their opportunism, and will resume its rightful place at the center of higher education.

Career Education and Liberal Education

Even in the halcyon days of liberal arts colleges, however, the end of the educational experience to which everything else was a means—second only to the goals of marriage and social status—was career training. Colleges offered preprofessional education leading to the professions of medicine and law and college teaching. Colleges offered professional education and career training for students interested in teaching at the secondary and elementary levels. There was usually a program for business majors. Liberal education as preparation for citizenship and self-fulfillment, with an introduction to professional training, evolved and revolved until it had reversed its emphasis. In most colleges, however, the curriculum has shown a persistent tendency to include the theoretical and the applied, the learning for learning's sake and learning for life—emphases that turn out to be two sides of the same coin. That which was general has been made specific, even as that which was specific leads on to generalizations.

William J. Bouwsma, Professor of History, University of California, Berkeley, in an article entitled "Models of the Educated Man," made the point that attempts to sharply divide general and more specialized studies, viewed historically, are "less than absolute":

> The earliest hints of a general education ideal were the products of professionalism. Particular occupational groups, notably warriors and scribes, developed high standards of competence; and, in doing so, they exhibited a tendency to idealization that seems regularly to accompany the formation of a professional ethos. Indeed, only at the stage of idealization have these groups first come to our attention: warriors through the competitive heroism of the Homeric epics, scribes through the Old Testament book of Proverbs. This idealization may be partly under-

stood as a response to social need. Warriors were more effective if their brutality was restrained and if they were not only good fighters but also loyal and congenial comrades; scribes, if they were honest, fair, and consistent in their administrative duties. But a more personal impulse was also at work, a profound aspiration to personal excellence and social respect, a desire for recognition as the most admirable warrior or scribe. In this way, professional roles were elevated into ideal human types, with implications extending far beyond the professional group [1976, p. 195–196].

What is sought after in our colleges is an undergraduate education that demonstrates, in its organization and manifestations, the legitimacy of learning that is particular as well as general, that prepares the student for a career as well as for citizenship. Furthermore, as Bouwsma hints, the teacher and student may come to general and liberal education from the base of specialized education, not just the reverse sequence. The market place and the ivory tower are symbiotic.

No one has made the case for theory and application in the college curriculum, or for abstraction and utility, for discrete units of learning piled up like building blocks to serve as a foundation for actual life and daily living, better than Alfred North Whitehead: "The antithesis between a technical and a liberal education is fallacious. There can be no adequate technical education which is not liberal, and no liberal education which is not technical: that is, no education which does not impart both technique and intellectual vision. In simpler language, education should turn out the pupil with something he knows well and something he can do well. This intimate union of practice and theory aids both" (1959, p. 74).

The gradation of responses by educators to this challenge of achieving balance in the curriculum, at a time when pressures mount in liberal arts colleges to accommodate professionalism or even capitulate to it, led me to devise a tongue-in-cheek taxonomy of the most conspicuous response models:

The No-Additive Model. No compromise, a total rejection of a poisonous agent: professionalism. Here the curriculum in the liberal arts is left intact at the undergraduate level, with no preprofessional specialization, no specific effort at career applications. The liberal ideal unsullied. No additives. Teach students how to think and give them the conceptual tools. They can then proceed on their own or, after other and later educational programs, to apply what they have learned.

The Layer Cake Model. This model is based on the most familiar recipe: general education at the lower division capped by upper-division specialization—a conventional two-layer cake. Pre-professional education in the junior and senior years will give the disciplines, the upper layers, a nicely marbled effect. The real blending of flavor or mutual penetration of the elements occurs in the eating, or it can happen over time, if some ingredients are juicy enough and the cake stands long enough.

The Garlic Model. Here the arts and humanities are expected to penetrate or infiltrate career education and professional training. A cook seldom uses a whole garlic in cooking; rather, the garlic clove is crushed, shredded, cut up, cooked into and along with the main dish. Without being separate, it is distinct; while unobtrusive in appearance, it is apparent in flavor. Its aroma and taste pervades the meal.

The emphasis in this model is on the dominance of career-ism. The best that can be hoped for is that, like garlic, the arts and sciences will permeate and have civilizing effects.

The Blueberry Muffin Model. Here, the professional or career program of study accommodates specific courses from the arts and humanities—the ethics of law, the social psychology of medicine, the esthetics of engineering, the moral dimension of business—as in blueberry muffins, where the berries are distinct or noticeable albeit with some blurring or melting around the edges, even as they affect the flavor and texture of the entire production.

Perhaps this model's image would be improved by using raisin bran cereal or the raisin bran muffin. The raisins in the bran muffin are conspicuously present; however, in raisin bran cereal, the raisins usually sink to the bottom, as so often happens when courses in arts and humanities are thrown into the professional curriculum.

The Peppermint Stick Model. The twist in this plan is the emphasis on a braiding of general studies and career education so that, as it were, the various elements are distinct to the eye as well as the tongue, but during consumption and digestion, the flavors or themes blend so that between the variety and the unity there is no essential conflict.

The Trilinear Curriculum

Amid the currents and cross-currents, with some colleges trying to hold the line against the encroachments of professional education, trying to remain "pure" even though, as mentioned, they have long since been "defiled," with other colleges having abandoned the old line of defense and seen most of their arts and sciences programs and general education overrun by careerism, a college of character offers a curriculum that explicitly provides for humane studies and skills training to start out together, without sacrificing their separate functions; remain in balance and run on parallel tracks; then later come together in advanced general education and integrative studies.

Two of three main themes featured in this curriculum are familiar: general education and vocational education or, as stated above, humane studies and skills training. The third theme, integrative education, is widely lauded but seldom achieved. Its function is not that of general education any more than it is vocational education. Its service is cross-disciplinary, involving the interconnectedness of things.

One useful way to carry out this integrative function is through seminars, classes, and independent study dealing with the moral and ethical ramifications of both general and vocational studies. More on this subject later.

Aside from developing the students' moral and ethical sensibilities through the integrative studies component of this curriculum, the purposes of the other two components are essentially those stated in good college catalogues across the nation. Henry Rosovsky, Dean of the Faculty, Harvard University, stated in 1976 several objectives for the Harvard core program that almost every American educator could endorse as appropriate for the arts and sciences:

1. An ability to "think and write clearly and effectively."
2. An "informed acquaintance with the mathematical and experimental methods of the physical and biological sciences; with

the main forms of analysis and the historical and quantitative techniques needed for investigating the workings and development of modern society; with some of the important scholarly, literary, and artistic achievements of the past, and with the major religions and philosophical conceptions of man."

3.   An awareness "of other cultures and other times."
4.   "Some understanding of, and experience in thinking about moral and ethical problems."
5.   "Good manners, and high esthetic and moral standards."
6.   "Depth in some field of knowledge" (reported in *Chronicle of Higher Education*, 1981, p. 1).

The problem arises not so much in the statement of broad objectives, whether the objectives are those listed by Rosovosky or, as an alternative, the six categories of experience presented by Boyer and Levine in *A Quest for Common Learning* (1981). The problem emerges when educators try to reach agreement on the actual organization of the curriculum, on the means by which we would achieve those ends. We are adept at putting meat on the bones when sitting at the dinner table; we are much less skilled at fleshing out a general education curriculum that serves specific goals.

Colleges and universities have, to be sure, overblown programs in general education. The surfeit happens when educators make general education a smorgasbord of trade-offs and patch-ons, until the curriculum becomes a pitiful collage without coherence. Changes in such places come by accretion, until some external influence, usually fiscal, requires us to change more dramatically, most often to cut back.

Faculty in a college of character are willing to assume the heavy and dangerous responsibility of working together to determine what is taught, rather than leaving such a decision to the individual or to chance or to external pressure groups. They are willing to determine how what is taught can be used not only to help a student learn one subject well and to prepare for a vocation but how to integrate and synthesize that knowledge in order to apply it to sociopolitical, moral, and ethical issues.

Following is an outline of a trilinear curriculum that deserves consideration by an academic community that shares the goals of a college of character. Note: *vocation* here means a calling, a summon to a mission, and is not to be confused with its familiar but distorted use in a vocational-technical sense. A college employing the trilinear curriculum will offer career education, preprofessional courses, and some professional training, but all such teaching and learning will be to foster *vocation*.

In Table 1, the units of credit assigned to the areas of concentration appear to be more rigid than is intended. They are meant to suggest a distribution but, obviously, administrators and faculty can adapt this curriculum to their institution and adjust the units of credit accordingly.

Table 1. Trilinear Curriculum (Semester Calendar)

	General Education (40 units)	Integrative Education (40 units)	Vocational Education (40 units)
Precollegiate Senior year	basic studies and education for citizenship		basic skills, reading, writing, computation, rhetoric
Collegiate First year	General Education (10–12 units)	Electives (8 units)	Vocational Education (10–12 units)
Second year	General Education (10–12 units)	Electives (8 units)	Vocational Education (10–12 units)
Third year	General Education (8–10 units)	Integrative Education 10–12 units)	Vocational Education (10–12 units)
Fourth year	General Education (8–10 units)	Integrative Education (10–12 units)	Vocational Education (10–12 units)

General Education. The basic purpose is to give the student adequate exposure to the six Carnegie "experiences":

1. Shared use of symbols.
2. Shared membership in groups and institutions.
3. Shared producing and consuming.

4.   Shared relationship with nature.
5.   Shared sense of time.
6.   Shared values and beliefs (Boyer and Levine, 1981).

Also, some general education courses should be organized around the preoccupations of youth:

1.   Self-realization or personal identity.
2.   Interpersonal relationships in their many dimensions.
3.   The claims of community, especially the institutional manifestations.

Advanced general education, that is, general education in the junior and senior years, offers an opportunity to study more complex and cross-disciplinary subjects, for example, the relationships of the humanities, science, and technology. In colleges and universities across the nation, cautious attempts are being made to link general education with modern technology. Courses in science, technology, and society are the most familiar expressions of this effort. Too often the superficiality of these courses is matched only by the student's lack of prior preparation. The trilinear crossing curriculum allows more time and improves prospects for useful learning having as its goal a technologically literate citizen capable of quantitative and analytic thinking, using applied mathematics and the computer. Elting E. Morison, professor emeritus at the Massachusetts Institute of Technology and an American historian, has made the point that, through general education, undergraduate students "should become engaged in the unfinished business of the outlying society—the problems not yet solved, the questions not yet answered" (Koerner, 1981, p. 16). Topics of importance include the new means of procreation, the exploration of outer space, the production of energy. They all originate in technology but, says Morison, "they lead out to every corner of human endeavor—economic arrangement, political structures, institutional design, communications networks, social organization, and the condition of individual lives" (Koerner, p. 16). The trilinear curriculum plan is better suited than most others to meet this need.

Integrative Education and Electives. During years one and two, electives may be taken in areas of student curiosity and exploration, with no particular obligation to relate these courses to vocational or general education. The student takes one or two such courses each semester.

Integrative education, as compared with electives, is featured in the junior and senior years and entails problem-theme-oriented courses, cross-disciplinary and, if possible, in seminar format. At this level, advanced general education and integrative studies blend together. There is an equally strong connection between advanced vocational education and integrative studies. The two tracks running parallel in the freshman and sophomore years merge to sponsor the third element in the junior and senior years.

Vocational Education. The student gets early contact with his or her presumed vocational preference, an introduction to the chosen field of study and career expectations, by taking up to two courses per semester during the freshman and sophomore years in the career sector of the curriculum.

Advanced vocational education in the junior and senior years builds on introductory courses taken earlier. It is possible, however, for a person changing professional or vocational plans during the first two years to complete a major at the upper-division level without sacrificing commitments and sequences in those other two components of this curriculum. Alternatives balance obligations.

The transfer student represents a special problem if he or she comes into the college having had educational experience inadequate for the comprehensiveness of this curriculum's challenge. However, there is some flexibility, and accommodation for many transfer students will be possible.

Any good liberal arts college fulfills, under the terms of its own form of organization, many of the obligations described herein. By the skillful use of problem/theme courses—"Darwin, Marx, Freud"—and other cross-disciplinary stratagems, the need for advanced general education and integrative education is partially met. Attention is also given, in such colleges, to the sociopolitical and moral-ethical ramifications of many fields. However, the trilinear schedule goes further and digs deeper than to other curricula.

Preprofessional education in this curriculum starts early and continues throughout the four years of study. Integrative education, with its focus on the moral and ethical dimensions, replaces most electives and becomes the centerpiece. The college provides a variety of ways to meet this requirement so that the factor of student choice or the notion of curricular tailoring is not lost, but the integrative component of the trilinear curriculum is more visible, more comprehensive, more pointed or intentional than is the case elsewhere. Finally, under the terms of this proposal, the general education program is not only turned vertical rather than horizontal, running from freshman to senior year on a track parallel to integrative studies and vocational education, but also is elevated in status to full parity with other curricular components. By design, advanced general education includes much of the subject matter that, under a more conventional schedule, is the jurisdiction of departments, where it may be limited to departmental majors working toward the B.A. General education is carried to advanced levels and taught to older students by faculty who can synthesize knowledge from their specializations with other subjects, progressing from the specific to the general. The college's goals of curricular interconnectedness and specificity are met in two ways: through courses in which students and faculty move from general subject matter to specific specializations and in which faculty and students advance from their disciplinary specialties toward inferences and general applications.

The trilinear crossing curriculum modifies the traditional idea that a proper college curriculum must be divided into three sections—general education, specialization, and electives—by reducing the emphasis on free-choice electives and by building up integrative education. Although two of the three tracks in this curriculum are familiar—general education and vocation or career education—that third rail is the live, charged element. Integrative education following on electives is a change in degree that, properly implemented, enriches and transforms the total college experience.

There are scores of individual small-scale examples of integrative teaching and learning that, without straining the resources of most colleges, could be incorporated into this third component of the curriculum. Across the nation, two or three faculty members will, now and then, as mentioned earlier, join together in cross-disciplinary teaching with a multidisciplinary approach to selected problems and themes. Love and work (Freud and Weber), individual and community (Buber), continuity and change (Marx, Einstein, Russell), home and family (Mead, Durkheim, Jung) exemplify subject-matter pairings. (Such efforts are seldom long-lived because the rewards and sanctions of departments, divisions, and institutions are seldom behind them. In the college with a trilinear crossing curriculum, by comparison, there would be no doubt about the institutional commitment, and the attendant rewards and sanctions should be strong enough to satisfy the most skeptical faculty member.)

Following are two more elaborate curricular plans, one that has been used and a second that deserves consideration. The older one integrates teaching and learning from specific historical epochs while the newer one draws on the currently fashionable institute model.

The Historical Epoch Model. An idea that originated at the University of Wisconsin in the 1920s under Alexander Meiklejohn, one that enjoyed an influence out of all proportion to its size, was, in the sixties, revived and extended by Professor Joseph Tussman at the University of California, Berkeley. He developed a program of study available to lower-division students willing to accept a prescribed curriculum that transcended the personal preferences of faculty as well as students. Everybody agreed to study the same things at the same times. The community members would move forward together. (The description given here is distilled from Tussman's account of his Berkeley experience, as reported in his book *Experiment at Berkeley,* 1969.)

The Greeks provide the exemplary episode, with attention focused in the first semester on Thucydides' account of the Peloponnesian War. Homer is in the background. Aeschylus, Sophocles, and Euripides are commentators. Plato reaps the lessons. These and other readings supplement the historical record. All are examined with the confidence that, together, they provide an introduction to ourselves, one that helps us not only to know ourselves but to transcend ourselves and our limited circumstances. Weekly seminars then may concentrate on the ways in which current problems and themes are illuminated by these historical developments, the students thus learning that their concerns are variations on enduring themes—war and peace, order and chaos, freedom and authority.

The second semester features study of selected works from seventeenth-century England. Through the King James Bible, Shakespeare, Hobbes, and Milton, a powerful cultural strand of Western civilization—the Judeo-Christian tradition—is deliberately examined. And this program of study, combined with the work of the prior semester, brings the student into confrontation with one of the crucial realities of Western life: the Hellenic-Hebraic tension in our culture.

The second year of the historical epochs integrative course of study is devoted to America—the early covenant, the Constitution, the establishment of the laws and the courts, and finally, contemporary problems.

It should be noted that the core concerns in this historically oriented program are moral rather than scientific; normative, not descriptive. Although the program is more reflective than experiential, more bookish than activist, it is always related to sociopolitical, moral, and ethical realities.

Unquestionably, the Tussman experiment challenged the adequacy of the conventional organization of knowledge and attacked the current curricular problems of American higher education root and branch. No patching and pasting here. It was not regarded as introductory to the established disciplines or to upper-level specializations; it had its own integrity. This approach to teaching and learning still shows promise and has vitality. It could be adapted into the integrative component of the college curriculum, lower division or upper division.

The Institute Model. In marked contrast to the historical epochs construct is the institute model. Based on the university research center or institute, this undergraduate plan deliberately maximizes opportunities for professionally oriented faculty to do what they want to do and for students desiring a certain course concentration to pursue what they want to study, yet within the context of the integrative program of the college.

The shared commitment of all institute participants would be to research defined as disciplined inquiry. Students would learn not only the style of intellectual endeavor in a particular field of knowledge, but also the meaning of conceptual inquiry and the way in which values infuse all scholarly efforts. The institute would aim to train students, through technical work, to be capable of critical, independent thought and yet to be aware of the philosophical and social implications of scientific work and modern technology.

Another goal would be to provide education in apprenticeships while seeking to improve apprenticeship itself. This might be achieved by allowing faculty associated with the institute, who could serve two- or three-year terms, to declare their research interests and invite a few undergraduates to participate in them. A strong student who was prepared to spend two years in the program might be given the privilege of organizing his own team around a declared research interest with an appropriate faculty person as resource person or research associate.

All research project proposals would be prepared by an "originating researcher" (faculty or student), a "research associate" (faculty or student, but the opposite of the preceding), and a "contextualist," a student or graduate student who would put the project into historical, theoretical, and social perspective.

All project proposals would be submitted for approval to the institute's "research committee," which would evaluate each proposal by three criteria: the research design, that is, purposes, methodology, theory, and expected outcomes; the project's potential for accomplishing the general education objective in the context of specialization; and the appropriateness of the proposed research for the institute's integrative program(s) of research. (As a way of assuring that institute research projects were interlocking and thus mutually supportive, and that projects were in areas of available resources and of current social significance, the policy committee would name one or more "programs of research," within which particular projects would be located.)

One theme for programmatic research might deal with problems and possibilities in transnational, technological society. Is it true, for example, that the main feature of technological society is not merely rapid change, but creative destruction? Professors Schaar and Wolin have affirmatively answered that question. They emphasize that this society's urge for immediacy is insatiable, that its nature is to destroy not only traditional patterns of behavior and old-fashioned values, but the attitudes and interests of the day before yesterday. These authors see evidence everywhere of the destructive compulsion of technological society: "Modern production has obscured the sun and the stars, and it has also made the cities unlivable. It chews up great forests and drinks whole lakes and rivers, and it consumes man's religions and traditions and makes nonsense of their notions of the aims of education. It periodically slays legions of men in war and it daily mangles the spirits of others in meaningless labor. The only aim of the civilization is to grow, and to grow it must consume. As [Jacques] Ellul has shown, the process must run until it consumes those who think they run it—until man is absorbed into technique and process" (Schaar and Wolin, 1969, pp. 5–6).

Is this a valid representation of the character and consequences of technology, or is it just another example of man's tendency to fear change and to long for earlier and simpler times, to engage in romantic regression? Does this version of science and technology allow us too easily to transfer responsibility for our condition to the behemoth who "chews up great forests and drinks whole lakes and rivers," rather than face responsibility for the future with the confidence that human beings can still control machines and shape cultures?

One of the great intellectual tasks confronting the college today is evaluating aspects of technological civilization. A program of research in an institute that both organized the undergraduate learning experience of certain students and provided research opportunities for some faculty could concentrate on the interrelated components of this massive subject. The task would be partly a critical one: to examine what technological civilization has done to our language, literature, art, politics, work, morality, and religion. It would also be retrospective: to expose historical choices that have brought us to this condition, to examine the progressive effect on science as it has come to serve the ideology of technology. Ultimately, the task should lead beyond criticism to re-creation, to putting the pieces together so as to illuminate conditions that must be understood if the consequences of our acts are to be anticipated and alternative courses of action are to be devised.

Possibilities for programmatic research themes are not, of course, limited to the technological society. The conservation of the natural environment, the creative uses of leisure, the acceptance of women at full parity are also among possible themes for research programs.

Research done by undergraduate students would usually involve secondary, not primary, sources; produce soft, not hard, data; and culminate in synoptic, not new, knowledge. But the recasting of conventional forms of knowledge, the synthesizing of heretofore isolated data, the progressive development of research interests into programmatic designs relevant to sociopolitical conditions are not only legitimate intellectual tasks, but stand among the most demanding challenges presently confronting scholarship.

Research experience might bring "old" knowledge to the undergraduate students with the weight of newness and could help them to learn that scholarship is process, involving the past and future as well as present. The plan allows faculty to communicate with students from a position of special competence and with the contagion of personal enthusiasm, yet challenges them to justify their research interests to sensitive students who want learning to be personally meaningful and socially purposeful.

The following features are common to both the historical epoch and institute models:

- Each plan tries to counter existing curricular weaknesses: subject-matter fragmentation or idea isolation; outdated and inaccurate notions of how people learn—teaching as telling, learning as rote memorization, the student as an information storage and retrieval unit; mistaken thinking about what constitutes success in learning—success by numbers or unit quantification, the highest grades to the best game players.
- Both models try to replace these weaknesses with strengths: relatively small, but not necessarily expensive, primary interest groups; students and faculty participating in shared learning experiences understood as process more than product, as dialectic rather than didactic engagement.
- The "program" in each curriculum option replaces the linear course system. Competition between classes, with attendant pull-

ing and tugging, is reduced at least in this track of the curriculum. The student devotes a significant period of time to a single ideational conception. Both plans represent some aspects of modern scholarship and the realities of human life more accurately than is possible by present departmental specializations. Each proposal is in many ways traditional and conservative; perhaps that is why they may appear innovative and radical.

Moral and Ethical Priorities

In the upper-division curriculum, when the student is completing preprofessional training and is working on advanced general education and integrative studies, it is time for another education principle of the college to become evident: the moral and ethical dimension of the student's advanced program of study.

Issues confronting the student as a person are, at their core, moral and ethical, as are many issues confronting colleges and universities. And, as the college proposes to address consciously its own moral and ethical dilemmas, so the student must prepare for the same responsibility in personal life.

Despite the presence of moral problems in every human relationship, the idea that a college should promote attention to them cuts against the grain of contemporary values. American society has rejected traditional authority in favor of the experts and celebrities of the culture of no-context interpreting the history of no-history. On the grid of 200 million, moral conflicts are resolved by the expanding coterie of control, that coalition of authorities from the multinational corporations and federal-state government. And on the grid of the individual, the solitary person thinks for himself or *thinks* he thinks for himself. At the surface and in the moment, he appears to take responsibility for his actions while actually deferring to the experts.

Such relinquishing of moral decisions, whether intentional or not, involves a bigger dilemma than most of us realize. There is a desire to substitute a new basis of authority for the old déclassé authority of the church. There is also a vague realization that the state can only govern on the basis of a generally accepted morality fed by religion or pseudo religion—for example, Communism. Religion has, historically, been the motive force and lodestar for the culture, but more recently, religion has fallen into the orbit of the culture. Americans tend to discard a discredited tradition, and yet, like astronauts circling the moon, people are still living off the capital or legacy of that which they left behind. As moderns, we cannot settle for what religious leaders once thought about morality—their principles were often wrong, resulting in slavery and the subjugation of women. Nor will it work to insist on one authority such as Jesus, Marx, objective analysis or the scientific method, existentialism or humanistic psychology (Wilson, Williams, and Sugerman, 1967, pp. 23ff.). We need ethical principles that will help us judge the claims of leaders, philosophical ideas, methodological procedures, moral codes, dogmas, attitudes, visions. But where do we get those principles? Or how do we develop our own?

Perhaps, some education leaders suggest, given the need as well as the problems, we should introduce into the college curriculum a course on ethics (of which, in fact, there are comparatively few) or delay this action until the time of the professional school program and inject a course on ethics into that curriculum (of which, in fact, there are comparatively many).

Another alternative, much in vogue during the seventies, was to feature courses or programs in "values clarification" or "stages of moral development." These approaches are much too bland to have much benefit for students and, paradoxically, too dangerous to be an appropriate institutional emphasis. Why? Because of the underlying and unexamined assumptions of such programs. William Bennett and others have exposed the liberal, individualistic, relativistic, pseudoscientific bias in most of the "values clarification" and "stages" literature (see Bennett, 1980; for another perspective, see "Applied Ethics," 1980).

Is every attempt to probe the substance of moral and ethical dilemmas doomed to failure, at least in this culture with its commitment to pluralism? It does appear, in truth, that when dealing with moral issues we tend either to dig a few deep holes in a few selected places, take our stand, and thus get positioned at that specified location, becoming fixed or sectarian; or we throw everything together, insisting that we are all alike, continuing our mistake until hell freezes over and we find ourselves skating on thin ice, circling round and round without a sense of the center or the circumference.

Nevertheless, difficulties in efforts to formulate an ethic for a college of character are no greater than the dangers of our present situation. We need not believe the skeptic's contention that nothing can be known for certain (nothing except the skeptic's premise that nothing can be known). We need not acquiesce to the transcendentalist who insists that the only help worth having comes from outside ourselves, more specifically, from somewhere up above. We need not collapse into a sauna of bile nor try to build a ladder to the sky. Help comes from beneath our feet, as Renford Bambrough has said, from this world and human experience, at least for those persons who will pick up their spade and get to work.

The quest for moral certitudes yields progress slowly, partially because it is poorly understood. It proceeds step by step, from one point of reference to another. If you ask for directions to Columbia, Missouri, we must agree on the location of another place, Kansas City or St. Louis, from which to start, so that I may guide you by use of our shared spatial knowledge to your destination. So it is in the realm of ethics. We move from the known to unknown territory, thus progressing not toward moral certainty but moral certitudes. In searching for a definition in a dictionary, you will be most effective if you have experience with words, some range in your vocabulary. You must know something about what you want to learn in order to learn more about what you want to know. As progress can be made in defining words by persistent use of a dictionary, so progress can be made in formulating standards for a college. Jesus, Archimedes, William Wilberforce, and Martin Luther King, Jr., made progress in the moral and ethical realm as much as Newton and Einstein made progress in the realm of science (Bambrough, 1969, p. 126). It can still be done.

Teaching is about how to make choices. The ethical impulse in teaching is to tell about how to go about acquiring the material and then building the edifice of a belief. As the ancients said, good teaching is a sculpting process. To that, we add, a sculpting process using the stuff of earth and man to an end that transcends the basic material yet does not forsake this world. Bartlett Giamatti, president of Yale University: "The teacher chooses. The teacher chooses how to structure choice. The teacher's power and responsibility lie in choosing where everyone will begin and how, from the beginning, the end will be shaped. The choice of that final form lies in the teacher's initial act" (Giamatti, 1980, p. 24). Giamatti does not believe that amid all this sorting and choosing a teacher should sculpt the contours of another's mind. I see no way to avoid that effect. A teacher who will not run the risk of shaping the contours of a student's mind, doing that shaping as carefully as possible, is, to change the image, as floundering but dangerous as a shark without fins. The teacher is the leader in making choices that influence the development of the student's skill in making choices—and probably affects the choices the student makes.

At the heart of integrative education in a college of character is a concern for moral challenges and responses. Stated even more uncompromisingly: Integrative education capable of meeting contemporary needs is moral education. It is education for character.

Advanced general education has an objective to work through a study of practices—historical, social, whatever—in order to get at motivations and purposes; wherein facts are important but no more so than the meanings attached to the facts, wherein the question of "how" is always followed by "why" and "so what"; wherein the particular is important insofar as it illuminates the ideal; wherein intentions no less than behavior are a focal point of concern.

Max Weber's famous book *The Protestant Ethic and the Spirit of Capitalism* (1904/1977) has remained the crowning glory of the historical and philosophical school of German sociology. This book is about the *ethic* of a religious movement and the *spirit* of an economic system. Weber was never interested merely in the facts of history, nor even in the forms of social and economic systems, but rather in the detection of the ultimate impulses behind the attitude and behavior of human beings.

Weber's discourse points to what advanced general education should be about, that is, detecting the ultimate motivations. Nothing could be more important now.

But how do we uncover and deal with the ultimate impulses behind attitudes and behavior, especially from the launching pad of the subject-matter specializations and within the abilities and orientation of faculty? An answer follows, suggested by the content of three provocative books. One of the books is in the social and behavioral sciences, the second in the natural sciences, and the third in the humanities. However, a teacher could employ classical as well as contemporary approaches.

I refer first to William Wilson's book *The Declining Significance of Race* (1978). Wilson argues that educated blacks are experiencing unprecedented economic mobility while the black lower class remains in desperate condition. Thus, Wilson (a black sociologist at the University of Chicago) joins Franklin Frazier, Daniel Patrick Moynihan, James Boggs, and others in warning that two black communities have developed in America, one affluent and perhaps even privileged, one poor and getting poorer.

Economic status is more important than race in determining access to power and privilege. Whites prefer to associate with middle-class blacks than with poor whites. And middle-class blacks prefer to associate with class-equal whites than with poor, underclass blacks.

Americans have entered a new stage of race relations, Wilson insists, with changing patterns of discrimination, and with evidence of growing class-based arrangements that assure underclass subordination.

A competent teacher can employ this thesis to launch discussions with students about the basic motivations behind human behavior.

Edward Wilson's book *On Human Nature* (1978; also, review by Richard Currier, 1978) illustrates a perspective on morality from the vantage point of natural science.

Wilson is a materialist who can imagine no inherent purpose for human life beyond the essential activities of survival and reproduction. Morality and ethics, he insists, are simply neurophysiological response systems that evolved to promote the survival of the human groups in a harsh, uncertain world. How, he asks, are we to fashion moral guidelines in a future world where human survival and reproduction will already be assured by the scientific and technological establishment?

Wilson's answer is that the charting of human destiny must no longer be entrusted to the ruminations of philosophers, the inspirations of spiritual leaders, or even the deliberations of legislators. The helm, he says, should be taken instead by an impending confederation of biological and social scientists. Only then, he claims, will the people be able to shift from the blind gropings of emotion and intuition to "precise steering based on biological knowledge."

You may wonder whether Wilson belongs with the steerers or in steerage in light of his views on human nature. Wilson (pp. 121ff., 169ff.) says:

- Human beings are innately aggressive.
- Men and women are genetically programmed to behave quite differently from each other.
- Human altruism is based almost entirely on calculating self-interest.
- Religion is here to stay for the simple reason that human beings have an irresistible need to be indoctrinated and subordinated by systems of unquestioning belief.
- And finally, we should renew our sagging faith in the Promethean ideal and seek our liberation through the expansion of knowledge and power.

Here, in sociobiology, we find a controversial way to unite the natural and social sciences in the search for the ultimate impulses behind attitudes and behavior.

A short comment about a third book, in the humanities. Like the others, it approaches moral issues through an established field of study. John Murray Cuddihy, in *No Offense: Civil Religion and Protestant Taste* (1978), examines the general religion of America, the "civil religion." He shows the effects of that religion now, asserting that American civil religion has become fundamentally a religion of civility—founded on the rock of cultural pluralism and conspicuously supporting religious toleration. Diversity of belief and practice should be accepted not as a necessary evil but as correct and desirable. The style of this national religion is inoffensiveness. Sectarian divisiveness, according to the canon of the civil religion, is heresy. Despite its style, the new orthodoxy can become offensive when confronted by that old heresy, as evidenced by the

New York Times editorial reaction to the Moral Majority in the election of 1980 ("Private Religion, Public Morality," 1980).

The American religion of civility serves another function: it legitimizes the cultural drift toward role differentiation, specialization, and professionalism for individuals as well as the popular emphasis on the distinction between public behavior and private experience.

Are we content to live by the tenets of a religion based more on survival than on significance? To do so eliminates the prospect for significance without actually assuring survival.

An assertion about the humanities generally, as compared with religion specifically: Except for the purposes of research and in the training of specialists, functions that can be carried out by selected universities, the humanities should not be studied in isolation, not as ends unto themselves. Literature, art, history should be studied in relation to human life. In a liberal arts college, the emphasis should never be on textual analysis or isolated theory without analysis of its connections and meaning. The humanities illuminate life, extend human understanding, provide illustration and precedent, and guide the formation of good judgment.

The National Endowment for the Humanities should put the emphasis not on subsidizing scholars—the proper responsibility of universities—but on bringing the humanities to students and to the people. Too much of the time, NEH has misplaced its emphasis. Thus it has contributed to charges against itself, especially to those stating that it is a symbol of elitism and a service to those who need it least. The Endowment is, at its best, an instrumentality by which the riches of the humanities are given to the citizenry in order for the people to make better sense of their own lives by learning about the lives of other people, to transcend what has gone before by knowing more about the deficiencies of that past, to better use their own resources and those of the humanities. The humanities and arts are understood to be tools as much as treasures, to be studied relationally, especially regarding their moral and ethical significance.

The previous discussion offers ways to get the tumblers on the vault door to fall into place so that entry can be gained to that domain where the moral and ethical issues and the ultimate impulses for human actions are to be found. The point behind these illustrations is that there are manifold ways of enriching teaching and learning with the moral implications of almost all subject matter in the curriculum of a college of character. Such a college offers the best prospects for a crucial specialization—understanding the interconnectedness of ideas and events, thinking and talking together across the disciplinary lines in more synoptic policy formulation.

One change in emphasis that would benefit the college: a moral emphasis throughout the curriculum, but especially in the upper-division years and in the integrative studies component, coming after the student has had exposure to subject-matter specialization and vocational training as well as to general education, when the student is prepared to deal with the moral dilemmas of "love and work" (Freud).

Another beneficial reform: a trilinear curriculum—general education, vocational education, integrative education—with these emphases starting early in the student's course of study and continuing throughout, in order that the endemic anxiety of students and parents about career preparation and the relevance of the college program of study can be relieved by experience, even as general education's importance is made evident through its direct connection with both vocational training and integrative studies. (For a variation on the themes of the trilinear curriculum, applied to a university, see Hill, 1982.)

A professional development program for faculty members and administrators that emphasizes the personal or spiritual enrichment of college leaders and the necessity for teaching to be understood as a vocation and not as a job can bring meaning and delight back into the profession of teaching as well as strengthen the college for its leadership role in society.

Leverage for Change

Has the conventional, guild-oriented socialization of faculty become so persuasive that nothing can be done to change it? Is the virus that must be eradicated from the academic body politic so resistant to treatment, so virulent, that it will not only survive all attacks but also destroy its attackers?

Some observers of colleges throw up their hands in despair at any attempt to change faculty and administrators. Faculty commitments to subject-matter specializations and departmental loyalties are, critics say, too deeply embedded—these commitments provide whatever security and mobility are left to faculty in a time of retrenchment. Administrators are mainly managers and, as such, prefer orderly and predictable arrangements. This is why some administrators are content to work in the context of collective bargaining and union contracts: it makes life more manageable. Most administrators and many faculty are so conditioned by the adversarial posturing associated with professional roles that it is, according to observers, futile to promote *communitas,* good will, and mutual trust. Administrators have, as stated, programmed themselves for institutional management, and, consequently, it is absurd to expect them to retrain voluntarily for education leadership. Administrators who attempt such a change would encounter an identity crisis because the effort would involve repudiation of the style as well as substance of a professional life with which they have been identified and satisfied. They could not swallow the criticism implicit in such a transformation, nor could they find the courage to regroup around new rewards and functions.

If colleges were still wheeling and dealing in the bull market of the sixties, with faculty polishing their credentials while administrators stored bags of money and issued dazzling growth statements, if conditions had not changed so drastically, it might be necessary to accept the critics' assertions that leverage is lacking to generate major reforms in education leadership. But the bears, not the bulls, dominate today's market—most signals flash "sell." Like the automotive industry, the education business is hardly in a position to merchandise its wares with old, unbending sales plans. External influences are effecting internal changes. The question for all colleges except those with the highest endowments is not Can faculty be made to change? or Will administrators change? but Will changes now occurring destroy the essential functions of faculty and corrupt both faculty and administrators to the extent that they allow their colleges to become shopping malls selling tawdry goods?

Faculty in most colleges can be forced to accept changes. Administrators are easily seduced. Yet no sensible leader wants to intimidate faculty or manipulate administrators. What does it profit a man to prove that educators are no more courageous than politicians or that they are as vulnerable to influence as people in business? Strong-arm tactics and arm twisting turn a community upside down, making it as ineffectual as a turtle on its back.

There are other and better ways to effect changes and to enlist the resources of professional educators without destroying their spirit. Faculty may have been thinking small and acting defensively because those responses were appropriate for the challenges put before them. Recall the responsibilities delegated to faculty by trustees and presidents of many colleges: "Manage the curriculum," "Oversee educational programs"—"and do it within the terms of retrenchment." No wonder faculty guard their turf so ferociously. They have so little of it. No wonder agendas for faculty meetings are filled with trivial items. Having no part in the formulation of policies that they are expected to carry out, faculty labor over details they can control.

An observer looking at higher education in America, more pointedly at liberal arts colleges, would get the impression that things are winding down. Maybe Zeno's Paradox has come true— educators are tired travelers who have discovered that they can at best cover no more than half the distance to their destination each day and that, consequently, they will never arrive. They are condemned to take smaller and smaller steps into eternity, always short of their goal.

Administrators and faculty members who care about liberal arts colleges or about humane teaching and learning in undergraduate education must be encouraged to think more comprehensively, more courageously, more persistently about the college as a whole, about a better future (not just more of the same), about what should be done in order for the college to become what we want it to be: a college of character.

Time-servers look only from the past to the present, calling educators to plan for the future by moving cautiously and proceeding incrementally, but we need ideas that go beyond immediately available options and familiar strategies and tactics. An example of the scale and daring required for this era, albeit an example on a plane and with a magnitude dwarfing available options in education, was given by Jonathan Schell in a three-part essay on the nuclear revolution and its threat of human extinction. Schell's essay spelled out not only the chilling terms of nuclear war but an audacious challenge to transform world politics and world goals. Nuclear disarmament and conventional arms disarmament, not control, were called for, and then, as though that weren't enough, Schell added: "If we accept both nuclear and conventional disarmament, then we are speaking of revolutionizing the politics of the earth. . . . we must lay down our arms, relinquish sovereignty, and found a political system for the peaceful settlement of international disputes. . . . In sum, the task is nothing less than to reinvent politics: to reinvent the world" (1982, pp. 102–103).

Was Schell hooted down? By some, yes. By others, no. His essay energized town meetings in New England, expressed a concern shared by students and faculty across the nation, and boosted the morale of Americans and Europeans who were members of various movements to save human life on this planet. By telling the story of bombs that can destroy everything, by refusing to settle for conventional thinking, by daring to spell out the extent of the changes required to transform government in order to save the world, Schell contributed to the debate in Congress and to the education of the people.

This example should not be exploited or turned into a caricature: The threat to American colleges is not the same as the nuclear threat to mankind. This essay is not, and cannot become, Schell's essay. Yet there are questions confronting leaders in higher education that are life and death issues. The survival of some colleges is in question. Moreover, the contributions of colleges to the education of citizens and leaders who must make the most awesome decisions, about nuclear war among other things, are also in question. Dare we think narrowly? Dare we not think daringly? Faculty and administrators should be encouraged to extend the range of their vision, deepen the critical examination of their traditions, and pick up the pace in their movement toward significance. Where much is expected, much will be given.

Rather than submitting to changes imposed willy-nilly from the outside, and rather than fighting a rearguard action inside to defend tight faculty and administrative specializations that encourage role separation to the point of isolation, faculty and administrators should accept the reforms of a college of character and put their minds and hearts to the task of making that community a corrective force in a society of increasing authoritarianism and the threat of despotic government.

What is at stake, finally, is not control of faculty salaries and job descriptions or recognition for emerging administrative professions, but the willingness of faculty and administrators to work through and across their specializations, to work with students and campus personnel, with trustees and alumni, with leaders from churches and synagogues and other institutions in the larger community, to effect changes that will prepare the college community to deal with social and moral issues of incalculable importance to all mankind.

8

Building Alliances Among Constituencies

If a college is to have character and to stand as a countervailing force to the emerging national culture of control, its leaders must strive to establish an alliance that rallies the resources of that college and others. It will be hard enough for the college community to put its own house in order or to go it alone in academe or society. With all the help the college can get, it will still be David against Goliath.

The alliance must involve other independent colleges and colleges within universities—private, public; church-related, secular. Character for a college is not defined in any one way, despite the occasional appearance of such a claim in this book, but wherever character has been achieved, it will be evident. Those institutions that have a noticeable distinctiveness are candidates for this alliance. There will, of course, be limits to tolerance. An airplane's piston engine is not mounted on the same wing with a jet engine, even as two jet engines on the same wing are not expected simultaneously to generate forward thrust and reverse thrust.

The Range of the Connections

The alliance should also include institutions and agencies other than those committed to formal education. Resources beyond

155

the campus are essential to the achievement of common goals. Following are some suggestions concerning linkages, beginning with more familiar and accessible ones—those with the so-called precollegiate sector as well as those with the postcollegiate—and then proceeding to those in the community at large. This is simply a sketch of possibilities offered in the spirit of the statement by T. S. Eliot: "These are only hints and guesses, hints followed by guesses."

School-College Connection. What a contribution could be made, to cite one point of contact, if college leaders and school leaders would work together to outline a sequence of study for the 50 percent of high school graduates who move on from school to college. At present, there is little collaboration, more conflict than cooperation. Higher education's educational requirements are stated and the precollegiate sector is expected to adapt. There is work to be done here, and liberal arts college leaders should specialize in developing this connection. The notion of articulation is not new, but the idea of leadership for its achievement coming from the liberal arts colleges, rather than the associations or universities, is fresh and noteworthy.

College–Graduate School Relationships. This is another area that needs reexamination and reform.

Although graduate school enrollments are declining, graduate school pretensions persist. With fewer and weaker students, graduate faculty still maintain the charade of offering a research-oriented, scholarly degree. Actually, most graduates of these narrow programs, with their generally trivial research assignments, never advance into scholarly careers featuring research. Most graduate programs should have an orientation balancing research and teaching. Most graduate programs should be more interdisciplinary—in Michael Beloff's phrase, cross-pollinated and fully fecundated!

If the undergraduate college attends to the interconnectedness of things, and graduates of this type of college continue to go to graduate school, then the connection between undergraduate and graduate programs of study deserves special attention and should be improved. The graduate school as well as the college has plenty to gain from a healthy relationship. And the college could take the lead, make the contacts in its geographical area, and live by the adage "To persist is to prevail."

But what torque does a college of the arts and sciences have with a graduate school in a major university? Plenty. Undergraduate programs in those universities subsidize graduate-level teaching and research. In addition, liberal arts colleges outside the university are sources of students. Indeed, they are staging areas for securing recruits and giving them basic training before sending these students off to, shall we say, officers' training school. The graduate school faculty must have sufficient numbers of recruits lined up or, alas, these distinguished scholars and researchers accustomed to working exclusively within their specializations and almost exclusively with selected advanced trainees will have to offer more than an occasional course for undergraduates and may have to teach nonmajors. When Moses came down from the mountain, the disobedience and lack of respect by the people so enraged him that he smashed the stone tablets. That epochal incident has been repeated countless times when the university's senior faculty leave the heights of their labs and seminars and come down to the masses in the classroom. Consequently, university faculty leaders might be available for negotiations with representatives of those colleges that provide much on which the university heavily depends.

What changes would faculty leaders from a college of character seek to encourage in graduate schools? Among the changes sought is one that would make graduate work, and the Ph.D., a truly philosophical program of study. Most teaching majors, graduate students, and Ph.D. candidates do not proceed into research careers, nor do they have the luxury after they become teachers working with a few graduate students in a narrow specialization. They teach more than they research. And they often teach introductory courses for nonmajors as well as majors. These faculty members would be happier and more useful to the colleges if their graduate-level study had been more contextual, cross-disciplinary, applied, philosophical. Encouragement in this direction would be a service to the universities who provide the teachers as well as to the colleges at which those teachers usually work.

Another area of shared concern, shared because the effects are as significant for the college as for the graduate school, involves the socialization of students in the undergraduate disciplines as well as the graduate specializations. The typical situation is untenable because it is morally indefensible. The student selects a discipline or, sometimes, is lured into one. (Will a nonassigned student opt for a major in philosphy if we entitle our introductory course "The Philosophy of Love"?) The faculty members of the department into which that student comes, affected by expectations of the disciplinary guild and their own graduate school experiences, introduce the student to a professional socialization, complete with initiation rites and baptism by immersion in work if not by fire, which may be consistent with what the student will encounter in graduate school but which is not consistent with the ideals of the college nor with the best interests of the student as a person. It is the beginning of a process of assimilation that threatens identity and integrity. The university in general, and the graduate school in particular, is organized for the convenience and advantage of senior faculty. The extent to which the undergraduate student is conditioned to be a student assistant exploited in teaching assignments, to do the non-productive scud work on research projects, and to feed the ego of various mentors, is the extent to which professional traditions and procedural arrangements have become moral dilemmas that need to be discussed by the parties involved. We will have plenty on our plates if we will sit at table together.

College–Professional School Linkage. The connection between the college of liberal arts and professional schools other than the graduate school is another area requiring analysis and change. During most of this century, the growth of professional schools and professionalism has profoundly affected the undergraduate curriculum. Programs for majors have become dominated by national professional organizations and made into entryways for professional schools. The survival of the arts and humanities is threatened by the dominance of preprofessional and professional values.

One consequence of the weakening of arts and sciences education and the strengthening of professional training has been the loss by students of the skills of contextual thinking as well as the loss of moral sensibilities. Partially to compensate, professional schools add a token course in ethics or provide a reading list of appropriate books.

Nobody is satisfied. And the question that persists is, Could the orientation and themes, the concerns and subject matter of the arts and sciences, be pushed up into professional education even as professionalism has been pushed down into undergraduate education? A revised and improved linkage must be forged, offering a special opportunity to the type of college that has made the relationship of ideas and deeds its specialty.

As there is no longer any reason for leaders in liberal arts colleges to be intimidated by university graduate schools, so, now, leaders in the colleges should consider joining together to negotiate improvements in the relationships of the college with certain national professional associations.

Many problems arise for a liberal arts college committed to general education as much as to subject-matter specialization or, even more, for a college committed to something like the trilinear-crossing curriculum with emphasis on integrative and general education as well as vocational specialization, when national professional associations set undergraduate curriculum requirements that seem to be numerically excessive and qualitatively suspect. For example, programs in accounting may require sixty hours of courses for the major. Forestry, agriculture, and nursing are programs that make heavy demands on the time of the undergraduate. Why should a national association promoting, say, business administration be able, within its membership, to set undergraduate requirements that impinge heavily and inequitably on students and faculty in the college? Are sixty units really necessary? Are there other appropriate ways of meeting the concerns of leaders in the various professions, concerns presently met by stipulating such a high number of hours in the specialization that students have almost no time for electives?

Colleges of character, working together informally or through available regional and national organizations, such as a state association of independent colleges, should arrange meetings with representatives of professional associations to collaborate in designing undergraduate courses of study that foster general and humane learning as well as career or professional education.

College leaders need not fear the doomsday predictions of faculty or administrators that failing to play ball with the professional associations will compel students to bypass the liberal arts college and go to a university where larger blocks of time for specializations are readily granted. Many students and parents, and leaders in enlightened professional associations, favor an undergraduate education in the liberal arts. They can be expected to support efforts to achieve better balance in programs of study for students.

The College and Colleges of Arts and Sciences in Universities. The undergraduate college in the complex university, that is, the college of arts and sciences, stands among the resources available to the freestanding liberal arts college striving to become a college of character. There are opportunities for connections between these institutions.

A college of arts and sciences in a large university subsidizes graduate-level programs and provides students for graduate specializations in much the same way the liberal arts college serves as a feeder institution for the research-oriented university. The prospect of reforming graduate education in America would increase if these two types of undergraduate colleges joined forces to influence the specialistic pattern of graduate schools and to make the connectedness of fields of study the chief characteristic of graduate education.

Faculty in the university's college of arts and sciences are more likely to be under the influence of the intoxicating elixirs of research and scholarship, narrowly defined, than are faculty in a liberal arts college. However, graduate enrollments are down, external funding reduced, and the spotlight is on other actors. Consequently, university faculty who were in the past trying to eliminate or sharply limit their services in the college of arts and sciences are now more receptive to that association—in order to keep the feeder lines open and thereby generate graduate-level FTE, as well as to secure teaching assignments in undergraduate departments that will substitute for the research, laboratory, and graduate seminar assignments preferred by these faculty members.

Most university administrators are eager to facilitate even an expedient connection between the college of arts and sciences and the graduate school because it is the best way to make use of faculty whose courses would otherwise be undersubscribed.

Not all faculty members in the undergraduate college of the typical university are content to breathe the so-called value-free atmosphere of a research university which, seen from a distance, with any detachment, is as polluted by the fallout from corruptions of science and technology as the air over Los Angeles is polluted by smog. These faculty still care about teaching and learning and about the whole person in a fragmented culture. They are kindred spirits despite their location. Some of them are leaders in their universities, strong swimmers against a heavy tide. Persons who have combined research and scholarship with their commitment to teaching and service will be leaders in the alliance that is needed to contend with dysfunctional forces in society and to prepare colleges for a new culture.

Now is the time for leaders in liberal arts colleges, working with like-minded faculty in university colleges of arts and sciences, to press the case for the reform of graduate and professional education. They can ride the tide "that, taken at the crest, leads on to glory."

One modest reform that faculty and administrators in these differing yet reconcilable institutions would promote would be an expansion in the use of an existing but little-used degree program— the Master's in Liberal Arts. Available in perhaps forty universities, it is a cross-disciplinary program of study, usually attractive to adults who are less concerned about job skills and more interested in the meaning of their personal experiences and public responsibilities.

A rise in the utilization of the MLA degree would have advantages not only for an adult clientele returning to the university in larger numbers but also for the reform of connections among disciplines in the institution. It would be a start. Progress could also be made if the university installed a parallel degree program: Bachelor of Liberal Arts.

There is at least a modicum of truth in the assertion that the liberal arts are wasted on the young. Adults most likely to be candidates for the MLA or the BLA will probably be receptive to the idea of liberal education. These persons grew up at a time of greater support from parents and teachers for the arts and sciences: the tradition of the liberal arts is their tradition. Having established themselves professionally, as members of the middle class, they want teaching and learning configurations that deal with personal development and civic responsibility.

The College and the Learning Society. The connection between the college and the learning society is another possibility for
collaboration awaiting development. There is an educational system,
one that combines technical training with education in the humanities and social sciences, developing rapidly in business and industry.
The first objective in this system of education is the expansion of
technical training, the growth of programs for professional development of middle-level executives, the establishment of corporate or
nonuniversity universities. What is less well known is the second
side of this new system—where elements of general and liberal education are becoming integral to educational programs in business
and industry.

The issue, finally, is not whether Americans will get something akin to general and liberal education during the next two
decades. They are going to get it—from the media, through neighborhood activities, under the egis of business and industry, churches
and synagogues, libraries, museums, and social agencies. The issue
for educators is the extent to which they and their institutions will
actively contribute to the general and humane education of Americans and the extent to which they will contribute to its substance
and quality by taking the lead in establishing proper linkages between their colleges and nontraditional institutions in this learning
society.

For an example of connections—the connection with the
learning society in particular—consider Guilford College, near
Greensboro, North Carolina. An old-line liberal arts college
(founded 1837), the third-oldest coeducational college in the nation,
Guilford has drawn on its Quaker heritage to achieve a degree of
interrelatedness that provides a contemporary model for colleges
that propose to live "in connection" with resources surrounding the
campus.

Hearing that the Greensboro YMCA was planning to build a
branch facility on the Guilford side of the city, college officials
worked out an agreement with YMCA officials to raise $3 million
for a college physical education center that would be shared with the
YMCA. Benefits of this connection? Instead of two appeals for corporate and individual support for two facilities that would inevita-
bly provide certain overlapping services, local corporations and

benefactors could be asked to make one donation for a facility capable of meeting the needs of both groups and drawing college and community closer together. Now, with this facility in use, Guilford students meet business leaders and senior citizens—on the courts, in the pool. Schoolchildren from the community move across the campus to the "Y." There is maximum interaction and very little friction. An outdoor basketball court, lighted, is a gathering place for youth from the town as well as the college.

Guilford College offers an educational program called "A Month of Sundays" involving an invitation to parents, extended through local schools, to bring daughters and sons to academic courses taught by Guilford faculty, 2:00–4:00 P.M. on Sundays. The cost is nominal, the learning benefits for precocious children and youth are considerable, the modest financial supplement for faculty is appreciated, and the benefits for Guilford College in terms of its connection with schools and parents in the larger community are invaluable.

Adjacent to the campus of Guilford College is a retirement community. Senior citizens attend campus events—films, lectures, various cultural activities—and some students from the college provide educational services at the retirement community. This connection is another manifestation of Guilford's determination to be an intergenerational community.

Here, then, are three examples of one college's efforts to bring people and institutions together. There are, of course, other ways Guilford College works at being an extended community, even as other colleges show their commitment to this objective in a variety of ways. (Franklin and Marshall offers noon seminars for in-town professionals.) And wherever such contacts are made, the objective of alliances that will strengthen both college and society is served. Strengthening and extending such alliances is part of the business of a college of character.

There is yet another connection. For the purposes of this essay, it may be the most important one.

The Church-Related College

Prospects for the development of institutional character are best in the private, church-related college. Evidence of character, as defined here, is less likely to be found in research-oriented, complex universities. They have another tradition, another set of objectives, another agenda. Nor are the so-called comprehensive universities likely to take the lead. They are consumer-minded, emphasizing high-demand programs and salable arrangements, not education philosophy and unitary institutional purposes.

The prospects for a college of conviction, it must be added, are not bright for public institutions. These schools are products of the culture of pluralism and a tradition of accommodation. The very word *character* bespeaks judgment and choice, ideational discrimination, creeds and norms—themes with which public institutions feel uneasy and prefer not to be identified.

Chances for distinctiveness are best among church-related colleges still called liberal arts colleges. As stated in an earlier chapter, they are small enough to be responsive to efforts to effect change. They are vulnerable now and likely to be attentive to a plan for institutional distinctiveness. They have sufficient resources— human and financial—to implement ideas.

Persons skeptical about the ability of church-related colleges, or colleges in the so-called independent sector, to respond creatively to the challenges that face higher education generally as well as other social institutions, should review the positive, not just the negative, aspects of this education tradition.

It was from the private sector that the initiatives for higher education came in this country. Francis Wayland, in 1835, then president of Brown University, made this point and also defended the initiative of religious leaders in the administration of the college:

> Our country in all its older settlements, is well supplied with colleges and universities, of course, when compared with those in older countries, in an incipient state. But, I ask, by whom were these institutions founded, and endowed, by legislative or by individual benevolence? The answer is, almost universally, by individual benevolence. And whence came that individual benevolence? The answer is equally obvious: It came from the religious. The legislatures of this country have never done for even professional education one tithe of what has been done by the various denominations of Christians

among us. In many cases, the State has done nothing; at best it has generally done but little, and I fear it is too true that even that little has been done badly. The colleges in this country are, in truth, almost strictly the property of the religious sects. You may judge, then, how decent as well as how modest is the intimation, not always too courteously given, that religious men ought not to busy themselves quite so much in the management of institutions of learning [Wayland; 1835/1961, pp. 242–243].

In America, churches and colleges grew up together, nurturing one another. The earliest and the best of the colleges were, with few exceptions, established by the churches. And it was from the college that the churches got their leadership. The churches planted colleges throughout the Midwest and South as though they were corn and cotton. The states were slow and timid by comparison, at least until after the Civil War and the launching of the land-grant universities.

We should remember that the colleges in the private sector, most often those with a Christian tradition, contributed significantly to the culture from which they have derived so much. Most of the enduring reforms and innovations in the development of higher education were products of institutions under private auspices. Between 1876 and 1910, Johns Hopkins University and Clark University led the way in the transformation of the American university. It was Harvard University, under Eliot, that gave national visibility to the free elective curriculum. Columbia, Harvard, Chicago, and Brown were, at various times during the twentieth century, leaders in general and liberal education, even as Princeton had been late in the prior century. It is a safe generalization that colleges and universities in the private sector have been able to do in three years, whether the task was building new campuses or changing curricula, what the public institutions required five years to achieve.

If one looks for examples of high quality in teaching and learning, research and scholarship, governance and student services, fund raising and alumni activities, most often the illustrations will be from private colleges and universities.

When criticism of the political status quo and the creation of social alternatives are the focal points of concern, the contrast between private and public institutions is less evident. City College of New York in the thirties was an institutional leader, as was the University of California, Berkeley, in the sixties. The University of Wisconsin has a tradition of sociopolitical involvement. Nevertheless, some of the most courageous criticism of the McCarthy era, the Southeast Asian War, and racial segregation came from people in private colleges and universities.

Despite the various contributions of colleges and universities, particularly those in the private sector, there is no escaping the acknowledgment that the general movement of both private and public educational institutions in the twentieth century has been toward diversity in structures and functions but conformity in purposes and assumptions. Today, with some exceptions, church-related colleges and universities are not significantly different from public and secular educational institutions. The possibilities are there, but the performance fails to meet the challenge.

Church-related colleges may be less bureaucratic—as a consequence of small size and unusual leadership, not church affiliation. These colleges may be places that are first-name friendly, downright nice environments resulting from a tradition of cordiality or respect for persons, but not from church connection. This same warmth and friendliness has been a feature of the University of California, Davis. These and other virtues are found in nonchurch environments and are often absent in church-related institutions.

Church-related colleges as a category of educational institutions are not, by definition alone, different and better. These colleges are not uniformly noted for clarity of purpose, institutional integrity, value-oriented education, innovation and experimentation, or a sense of community.

Liberal arts colleges generally, and church-related institutions specifically, are not ready to take positions of leadership in dealing with the ethical crisis on campus. Nor are these schools ready to stand up to external pressure any more than are public institutions.

American University, a Methodist-related institution in Washington, D.C., had an endowment of $10 million in 1980, while 97 percent of its operating budget came from student tuition and fees. This is an extreme case, but it is common for colleges and universities in the private sector to be 75 to 85 percent dependent on student tuition and fees for operating budgets. And then, 30 to 50 percent of tuition income to the institution may be from state tuition equalization programs and targeted federal support for students. Harold Howe has indicated how important that subsidy can be: "While student aid from state and federal governments is of considerable assistance to public colleges, it has become the life blood of much private undergraduate education. Without it, hundreds of private institutions would close" (1979, p. 29). It turns out that the colleges are about as independent as a baby in a pram being pushed across a busy street.

If administrators at state universities must be responsive to politically sensitive issues and to thin-skinned politicians, the administrators of private universities must be responsive to business and professional interests represented on their boards as well as to wealthy benefactors.

The faculty member in the private institution received his advanced education, in all probability, at the same universities as his public counterpart, receiving not only the same technical and methodological training but also the same guild socialization. The administrator attended the same management seminars. Nor is there any reason to ascribe moral superiority to representatives of the private sector. With only a few exceptions, these leaders have not made better use of academic freedom or institutional independence (Martin, 1969).

Nevertheless, among the options available, the best prospects for the emergence of character are in the private, church-related liberal arts colleges, especially if they use the resources of churches and synagogues. Alert people in the religious communities are not afraid to join with the college community in the search for answers to America's moral dilemmas. Leaders in churches and synagogues are usually well educated, respect higher education, and recognize the need for alliances in overcoming the perils confronting religion as well as education. One down-to-earth advantage is that church-related colleges have formal connections with constituencies and communities. Such affiliations have been viewed as burdensome by many of the colleges, as something to be terminated or at least "secularized." Now, however, colleges that have had only a nominal church connection are trying actively to revive and improve that relationship. Necessity has generated this inventiveness. The presence of a church constituency is an asset for student recruitment and a source of benefaction and conference allocations. Far from being a drain on the college, this connection is seen as an important form of support.

Presidents hear from the experts that up to 25 percent of the liberal arts colleges will be forced to merge or close because of declining financial support from government, a smaller pool of student applicants, and widespread uninterest in the liberal arts. Predictions of this sort put the fear of God in presidents and motivate them to return to that sanctuary where people of God if not the Holy Spirit are found, and where the sons and daughters and dollars of God's people may again be directed to support that institution again called the church-related college.

There is more than a pragmatic reason for this connection; in fact, it may well be that the best reason for such a connection is ideological or even spiritual. Churches and synagogues, as well as the college of character, exceed business and industry in seeing human beings as more than units of measure or markets even as they transcend those empirical sciences that see *human nature* as a lyrical term for the effects of external causal laws. These religious and educational organizations are bonded together by a commitment of basic importance, as expressed by Roger Hausheer (1979, p. xvii): "Men are defined precisely by their possession of an inner life, of purposes and ideals, and of a vision or conception, however hazy or implicit, of who they are, where they have come from, and what they are at. And indeed, it is just their possession of an inner life in this sense that distinguishes them from animals and natural objects."

Leaders in churches and synagogues need the intellectual resources in colleges and universities if the people are to deal with infinitely complicated social, political, and military issues—for example, the threat of nuclear war, the necessity for nuclear disarmament, the warding off of extinction for human life at least in the Northern Hemisphere. And leaders in the colleges, given their tendency toward theoretical orientation and idealism unencumbered by attachment to reality, need the people with farms and businesses and payrolls who are often practitioners of the churches. It will take the best efforts of poets and artists, philosophers and historians, scientists and politicians, technicians and theologians, priests and rabbis, parents and shopkeepers and common-sense folk to dismantle that doomsday machine. This is not a partisan political issue. It is an issue of survival for us all. It is not an issue for campus radicals that will alienate church members with a conservative bias. In fact, the surge of antinuclear war protests in 1981 and 1982 was generated mainly by leaders in religious orders and denominations, not in colleges and universities. It is an issue to which sane people can relate, and because it is a moral imperative, the best place to make that connection and get it moving is among the people of the churches and the colleges—working together.

If the nuclear threat does not seem sufficiently threatening to justify a coalition, then consider recombinant DNA, prospects for behavior control, fetal research, and psychosurgery. Should there be any limits to the scientific search for a comprehensive understanding of human nature? Here, again, we have issues of the utmost importance about which persons of ability and sensitivity differ. The challenge is to bring the best resources of the college and university, the church and synagogue together in order to assure an omnibus approach to problems of monumental social and moral importance. Nowhere is there a better opportunity for substantial connections than in the church-related college.

Connections such as these will be crucial to success for those persons who hope to form, during the eighties and nineties, centers for creative responses to the moral crisis on campus and in American society. Although connections with individuals who are like-minded can be made everywhere, with persons of many orientations and affiliations, the best opportunity for structural or institutional linkages is here, with churches and synagogues. It is better than any connection these colleges can arrange with labor or management, with professional organizations such as law and medicine, with volunteer groups, and with the media or the arts.

Can constituency leaders and campus leaders work together? On a level about alumni giving or the annual fund campaign? On matters more important than the recruitment of athletes or reducing the consumption of beer in the dormitories? The possibility is real.

Following are several suggestions for the church-related college community that is ready to begin cultivating character.

Activities—Small and Large

Colloquia. As a way of moving beyond intentions to action, leaders in graduate and professional education and in the college of arts and sciences could be united in a colloquium on "ethical dilemma in the contemporary university." One presentation would deal with selected dilemmas: case studies of issues confronting faculty, students, and administrators. Another presentation could show historic as well as contemporary connections—religious, political, social—within which the moral guidelines of the institutions have been drawn. And yet a third presentation would present policies and procedures for dealing with these dilemmas. The benefits of such a colloquium would be several, not least the visibility and evidence that the college, as sponsor, has this concern and is doing something about it.

Assuming a measure of success, college leaders could proceed with a second colloquium, including among the participants several church and synagogue leaders and representatives from community organizations. The same general theme of moral dilemmas could be used, but in this instance, attention would focus on issues in the community and on the ways these dilemmas reach from community to campus and back again. This colloquium could be one of a series, with varying membership and topics, as a way of forging linkages and building alliances.

Following is an idea of sufficient scope or magnitude to engage most of the resources on campus and in the larger community for a long period of time.

Education in Public Policy for Adults. The older adult, meaning that person beyond the traditional 18–22-year age college student, has in recent years been courted actively by most colleges and universities. Programs have been offered for the person who wants to advance technical skills, to qualify through education for salary increments, or to develop a new competency or leisure time activities and hobbies.

There is, however, another area where much work remains to be done, for the benefit of the person as well as the good of society. I refer to the civic education of adults or, as mentioned here, education in public policy for adults.

Democracy depends for its success on participation of informed citizens. In this nation, given customarily low levels of involvement in political campaigns and elections, given the widespread marginal literacy of citizens regarding social and political life in America, and given the ever greater complexity of international affairs, it is mandatory that the education of citizens continue in a disciplined way beyond the years of formal schooling. If high school civics classes were effective, which they are not, and if college courses in state and federal government or in U.S. history were effective, which they are not, it would still be important to involve adults in continuing policy-oriented studies of local and state issues as well as national and international issues.

Colleges of character are best suited for this responsibility. Their faculty members are more likely to be effective teachers than are the research-oriented professionals in universities. The college is committed to cross-disciplinary, integrative study, and, therefore, the motivation and the skills necessary for issue-oriented work with adults are available at this institution. This type of college also has the resolve to forge connections with other institutions and agencies in society—museums and libraries, health clinics, and social centers, churches and synagogues, businesses and industries. Finally, the scale of the college is usually small enough to allow for that community to formulate policy and to move it through governance procedures to implementation, without so much time elapsing that the impetus is lost or so many program compromises being made that the outcome bears no recognizable connection with the original intention.

What could actually be done? Scattered efforts around the nation, mounted usually by organizations other than academic institutions, suggest a program in this area and ways of getting started. Several foundations have seminars and workshops for state legislators, federal judges, school board members in which the educational ramifications of public-policy decisions are discussed. Although these efforts, and other foundation activities focused on corporate executives, show ways of working with leaders in major professions, it is important to look also into the work done by several foundations with local community leaders. Citizenship education for adults, or education in public policy directed to adults, is a challenge whose time has come and for which a response can be made.

College leaders could negotiate with local corporations for release time of middle-level and junior-level executives to take courses offered, at company expense, during the lunch hour at the plant or work site, or afternoons, in the last hour of the workday, with half of that hour donated by management and half drawn from the private time of the employee. Major corporations are now granting sabbaticals to selected executives for participation in community projects. Sensing that education in social and political issues, or in the moral and ethical dimensions of public policy, relates to the vitality of the work ethic and to general productivity, corporate leaders should be easily persuaded that it is in their best interest to cooperate with the college in courses that educate workers for responsible citizenship. (No educator will miss the implications of such activity for social indoctrination or for institutional independence for the college in the context of sociopolitical interdependence.)

Several national unions have contracts with employers that include education provisions: money set aside for the education of employees in job skills and in subject matter that nearly qualifies for the liberal arts. In these and other existing arrangements are opportunities for the introduction of citizenship education for adults.

It would also be possible for college faculty to hold problem- or theme-oriented classes in churches and synagogues, community centers, public libraries and museums. Television and radio, videotapes and videodiscs provide a technology of dazzling potential for projects of this type.

The Carnegie Foundation for the Advancement of Teaching, in the Seventy-Fifth Anniversary Essay, presented by Ernest Boyer and Fred Hechinger, emphasized the importance of citizenship education of adults (Boyer and Hechinger, 1981). Their challenge is drawing a response. The college of character should not miss this opportunity to join the movement and lead in bringing quality and substance to the endeavor.

Within the College. Among specific activities worthy of attention by members of the campus community are: First, concerning institutional accreditation, the self-study of the college could be directed to ways to change an outmoded liberal arts college into a comprehensive college and a college of distinction. Second, the trilinear and crossing curriculum could be fleshed out and adapted to the special purposes of the college. The integrative collegiate seminars could be designed, as well as cross-disciplinary courses that feature social, political, and moral connections.

Faculty members who serve on accreditation institutional self-study teams or as site visitors to other colleges should receive credit in their professional files just as they would for professional services such as consulting or publishing.

Criteria for professional advancement in the college, especially at the level of the faculty, should serve institutional objectives more than individual preferences or the norms of professional guilds. Leaves of absence and faculty sabbaticals should be more purposeful, that is, more related to the values and objectives of the college. Sabbaticals and paid leaves of absence have proven to be so expensive and, often, only marginally valuable for the college; perhaps time formerly spent in the professional soft-shoe shuffle that characterized too many sabbaticals and the money spent by the college in so many counterproductive ways can be channeled into activities that benefit the community. It is, once again, a matter of priorities.

Other tasks, even details, that take on an importance out of proportion to their inherent size include:

- The catalogue of the college should be rewritten to stress provisions for the achievement of the old and new purposes.
- Brochures and general publicity used by the admissions office and the development office should be designed and written to state the themes of importance.
- The faculty handbook and the handbook for nonacademic personnel must be rewritten.
- Key personnel—admission staff members, leaders in the development office, student personnel staff, alumni officers—should be involved in the sequence of activities as full participants.

• High school principals and counselors should be briefed on the direction of the college and on the school-college connection.

In planning for substantive change in the college, it is as important to enlist leaders and groups outside the institution as it is to work with faculty, students, and administrators. Regardless of theme—curriculum innovation, governance change, student life, institutional mission—there will be elements of the theme and elements of the task that can best be advanced through involvement of business experts, parents, alumni, trustees, church and community leaders.

There is, to be sure, a legitimate division of responsibility; for example, trustees delegate to the faculty, through the president, responsibility for the instructional program of the college. There should be respect for professional expertise, for example, the investment policies governing the endowment of the college should not be decided by a voice vote at the annual alumni picnic.

Too much has been said, however, about the sanctity of delegation and the authority of expertise. Some aspects of the instructional program of the college are proper agenda items for all elements in the college community. The investment policies of the institution should be reviewed by representatives from that community, other than the investment committee of the trustees. Professional specialization must not be allowed to become the nemesis of community unity.

When educators plan change in some aspect of the life of the college, they almost always concentrate attention on people within the college. They set up faculty workshops, arrange for colloquia, and run the items past trustees. The emphasis is internal, not external. Perhaps that approach should be reversed. Changes of consequence in higher education have usually come about in response to external pressure.

If the goal is to turn a liberal arts college into a comprehensive college, transform the course of study by use of the trilinear curriculum, greatly improve the professional development program, and activate various institutional connections, especially those with churches and synagogues; if the aim of the innovations is to move a college along the road toward achieving character, it is at least as important to work with leaders off campus as with those on campus. This is the way to effect change and to prove that the community is not a precious enclave but a powerful assembly.

Will college personnel cooperate, especially in endeavors that send people off campus and are time consuming? Faculty members have been willing to go off campus to professional meetings of colleagues in their field—in part because they thought rewards and sanctions resulted from such participation. Now, at a time when institutional loyalty takes precedence over guild loyalty, and when rewards and sanctions can be made to reflect this shift of emphasis, perhaps faculty will be able to find the time for these other valid forms of professional activity.

Furthermore, given the reality of declining financial support from federal and state sources, and the subsequent need for increased funding from business and industry, many colleges and universities are encouraging faculty leaders to make themselves available to corporate executives for the purpose of "selling" research and other services. Academic researchers who only a decade ago were unwilling to be tainted by association with big business are now actively soliciting contracts and facilities. It should be no harder to get faculty members to relate to church and synagogue leaders, particularly when faculty are reminded that these community groups are important sources of students as well as finances for the colleges. If university researchers can do the impossible, relate to and strike contracts with business representatives, college teachers can do the improbable, relate to and work out connections with church and community representatives.

These have been suggestions, large and small, about ways to develop character in a college. Many other activities relate to this task, and their definition and implementation are left to the reader's wit and ingenuity. Not that useful ideas and effective utilization come easily. We should remember that when T. S. Eliot spoke of "hints and guesses, hints followed by guesses," to that he added

"and the rest is prayer, observance, discipline, thought and action"
(1970 p. 199).

> *If you want an institution to move faster in the
> direction in which it is going, dangle the carrot
> out in front and wave the stick behind.*
> *If you want the institution to change direction,
> even reverse itself, wave the stick out front and
> point in the new direction with the carrot.*

9

Potential of the College of Character

This long essay began with four statements: A college president expressed the management mentality, a no-nonsense market approach to institutional survival at the risk of institutional character; a faculty member reminded us that demographic prognostications are often wrong and at this time, despite dire predictions, the established ways of organizing the college curriculum as well as the familiar ways of teaching and learning are holding up quite well; an education reporter, skeptical if not cynical, presented evidence that gangrene has set in at liberal arts colleges where leaders kept telling each other that the canonical body of opinion is still healthy; finally, a student who has learned to manipulate the system and intimidate faculty revealed a recondite way to acquire requisite credentials.

The problems presented by those statements are part of a moral crisis in American college and university life of such magnitude that every other problem pales by comparison. What is at stake is nothing less than the integrity of educational institutions and their programs, degrees, and authority in society. Also endangered is the integrity of those persons—faculty members, administrators, students, trustees, service personnel—responsible for the day-to-day work of this enterprise. Institutional and personal integrity are higher education's most precious possessions. That they are threatened now justifies the stark assertion that colleges and universities are experiencing a moral crisis.

The notion of crisis here, there, everywhere, is burdensome. Many people recoil at hearing yet again that education in America is in crisis. Cry wolf too often and you cry alone. But how can we deny the realities of our situation? Education as we have known it in this country is threatened by financial as well as ideational strains even as civilization as we have known it as threatened by the mounting prospects of nuclear war. However burdensome to contemplate, a crisis, another crisis, is upon us, some of it emanating from the educational institution outward beyond the campus, but most of it entering academe from the outside (Schlesinger, 1982). It would be more accurate, in fact, to say that a moral crisis in society is contaminating educational institutions. For example, such problems as program contradictions at the level of government, the erosion of neighborhood standards, the ineptitude of home and church, and chicanery in business not only fuel a moral crisis in society but also shape conditions on campus that engender discontent. Educators tout the contributions of scholars and basic research to society. They are reluctant to acknowledge, however, that society is often active while the college is reactive; society contributes or corrupts while the college receives and reacts. Crisis breeds crisis.

The situation, in society and in education, can be neither ignored nor explained away. The moral crisis in America must be contained, relieved, reduced in scope and penetration. This challenge is now drawing a response. Indeed, several proposals are evident. What remains to be done is to choose among them, or be chosen, and thereby be saved or damned. In this essay, one comprehensive response has been described, a macro plan countered by a second and more modestly scaled response calling for manageable beginnings toward education reforms in undergraduate colleges, reforms that also show potential for the transformation of society.

Here is a restatement of both alternatives, that is, the massive final solution and the focused incremental probe.

The Divided Society Reunited

One word that describes our nation is the word *immense*. Not that America is all that big, at least from the perspective of satellite pictures of the earth: it is big, but not immense. Rather, it is the *concept* of American life that has become huge to the point of being immeasurable. We live on the grid of 200 million, as George W. S. Trow said. And when we try to think about the size of the grid, and life on it, we are impressed by an immensity of scale—a megatonic scale, a billionic scale.

A second word to describe our world is the word *intimate*. The universe for many Americans has become their inner world, the world of the self and selves within the self. This is the grid of the unit of one, the place of the solitary individual who, finding the external world incomprehensible because of its scale and complexity, turns inward only to discover new immensities. When standing among the masses, this person is a "dependent variable," defined by experts and their surveys, a cipher or unit of measure, a set of characteristics. Hence he admires the celebrity who is able to rise up from the grid of 200 million, at least for a moment, and send back a reassuring smile that helps the lonely person cope with isolation, at least for the moment. But this individual also discovers, or is told by his examiners, that he is a spore—capable of developing into a new individual unlike the parent. Exploring the layers of the self, as long as there are discoveries, seems even better than watching celebrities. More accurately, certain of those therapists, analysts, pastors, and counselors help the individual watch, examine, report on himself. Hence, intimacy characterizes this inner world.

To the extent that government is government by experts and celebrities, it bridges the two grids of contemporary life. The president speaks on television as a remote "talking head." Yet the disembodied head speaks to the people, to each person, in terms of immensity and intimacy. He spans the gap. But the straddle is fatiguing, even for the president and the government. The strain shows in the government's inability in working with Congress, not on television, to get consensus for a program of national reform that will meet the needs and interests of the masses and their institutions as well as the solitary individual and interest groups. Democracy is threatened.

Inflation and recession race back and forth across the two grids, energized by the spirit of acquisitiveness and the insatiable materialism that characterize capitalism. This flashy coming and going covers a multitude of sins, and yet enough gets through to

embarrass the government, which hears voices of conscience de-
nounce disparities between the wealthy and the poor. Capitalism is
threatened.

Two major institutions that traditionally have mediated between the claims of the one and the many, between the person and
the state, between the two grids, are the church and the school.
Indeed, they not only adjudicated differences between the separate
elements but also had a magnetism that pulled the claimants together. They were once a force encouraging unity and coherence.
Not today. Religion no longer draws the person and the state toward
itself and each other. Education no longer bridges the gap or recon-
ciles the differences. Religion follows the culture and does not lead
it. Education still serves, as education must always serve. But it does
not span the elements in the culture. It connects awkwardly via
rocky detours down through the canyon and riverbed that separate
the grids.

Disappointments on the mass scale, particularly the inability
of most people to experience success on that plane, are conspicuous
and tragic. Citizens turn away from government. Twenty-seven percent of the potential voters can elect a president. People look elsewhere for meaning and satisfaction. Retreat into your inner recesses,
some say, if you cannot prosper in the public world. The advice of
these therapists and psyche handlers, however, leads to endless
mucking around in the bogs of the human heart, at best resulting in
attention to dreams from a now-discredited past or misty visions of a
more creditable future.

The deep history of a discredited past has no appeal, to be
sure, for some people. Despite the problems that attend the present
culture—the impersonality of public life and that feeling of over-
whelming immensity, the internalization of the individual with its
insistence on instant intimacy—a lot of people are now better off
than they were in the past. The civilization of no-culture and history
of no-history are preferable to a culture and a history of slavery and
genocide.

In Great Britain today there is a sadness among many subjects, a palpable grieving for a beloved but fading culture. They are
dismayed by multiplying troubles: a staggering rate of unemploy-
ment, race riots in London, Liverpool, and elsewhere, civil war

marching on Ulster, rising crime rates, political parties in disarray. But there is another evidence of decline that is the hardest of all to accept. The British are grieving mainly, as Jane Kramer has written from London, "for the decency they have always held, as an article of faith, to be a particularly *English* quality, for the civility, the fairness of mind and spirit, that they believe is finally what sets them apart from millions of swarming and disreputable Europeans just waiting across the channel to corrupt them. They seem to be suffering from a loss of faith in the British character" (1981, p. 91). However, what the British call character is seen by many people, particularly the poor and the racial minorities, as blatant class consciousness. England is the most class-oriented society in Europe. Now change is coming, and a whole new class of men and women is demanding a share of power, demanding a turn to run the country. Character in Britain, these newcomers have concluded, has more to do with class pretense than with moral convictions even as civility is thought to have more to do with the control of mind and spirit than with fairness and decency. Persons of this persuasion, British or American, remembering so much in the past that was a source of abuse to them or their forebears, would rather risk an uncertain future for the sake of a few small gains in the present.

Other people believe that the present situation is not so different from the past. Perhaps one third of the population of major American cities is consigned to a permanent underclass. For every O. J. Simpson who makes it big in intercollegiate and professional athletics, moving from player with talent to celebrity with big bucks, there are thirty or more black athletes who end up back home in the pool hall, on the streets, with neither money nor education. We still have a separate and unequal society—racially, socially, economically, educationally. We have a class-conscious, gender-conscious culture. Given the extent of these divisions, and their persistence, this nation embraced the best option in sight: the culture of pluralism. And we have pushed pluralism to the point of contradiction, unintentionally reviving that social doctrine expressed in the catch phrase "separate but equal."

Esteemed education statesmen, Alan Lord Bullock and others, believe that a divided society is the setting within which education must originate and work. That is, to be sure, where educators must start. But is it where we must end? A new breed of leaders say no: education, government, and the economy need not be stopped by our divisions and related problems. We are divided but we can become united. There are prospects for a more creditable tomorrow. There are not only dreams of the past but visions for the future.

One source of confident leadership with a plan for the future in this time of crisis are the kinds of organizations that are becoming dominant planning center of our epoch—the multinational corporations. Their international headquarters are often called campuses; their training programs for the development of leadership constitute the growing edge of higher education in America. These corporations are not only money-making institutions but also research, teaching, and service institutions. They have an ideology as well as resources, contacts as well as power. They work together. The Trilateral Commission and the Roundtable group are examples. Executives of the multinational corporations are not paralyzed by complexity nor overcome by modesty. Government may be in ideational conflict and seem unable to reach a political consensus equal to the challenge of major reforms, but these leaders are prepared to redefine social roles and recast political relationships until America gains a revitalized government. Following is a review of the way they think and possible effects in the future.

Discipline Democracy. This country is always changing. Now national attitude is shifting from the notion of progress toward the idea of consolidation. For the next several years Americans will undergo a period of exceptional adjustment, rediscovering values that have been embedded in our tradition but, after a period in which they were subsumed, are emerging in force and moving toward a position of renewed dominance.

In the seventies, single-issue political coalitions threatened the two-party system in the United States. In the eighties that two-party system further attenuates as factionalism intensifies. These developments must not be allowed, the new leaders believe, to destroy social order. They see the black and white middle class, led by the so-called meritocratic elite, using the resources of the government and, even more, those of multinational corporations, uniting behind issues of shared concern to effect the consolidation and sanctioning of a new civil politics that parallels the more familiar civil religion in America. There will be two political parties, but behind the separate and seemingly sectarian rhetoric, there will also be a shared commitment to social diversity and to the retention of, for as long as possible and to the degree possible, the appearance if not the substance of the American way of life.

There will be toleration for single-issue coalitions as long as they operate within the limits of tightened state policy. Special interest groups such as antiabortionists, "Feed the hungry" advocates, civil rights supporters, "Save the redwoods" crusaders, as well as coalitions of people concerned about energy and environmental protection or the status of women or racial and ethnic minorities, will continue to exist and will demonstrate that American public life is still pluralistic. But the fundamental societal needs—energy, food, fossil fuels, work, markets, technological development, education, class status, health services—constitute the boundary markers that are likely to be used by the new coalition of control to define the limits to pluralism. Those who threaten access to these resources, try to explain away these needs, or deprecate these satisfactions exceed the limits of diversity and try to negotiate with the nonnegotiables of America's social philosophy, that is, disciplined democracy.

The guardians of the civil politics of the future will not be the Democrats and Republicans but, rather, the multinational corporations working with state and federal government. And the people will acquiesce. When the standard of living is reduced, when personal safety and jobs are not assured, when the individual's importance and identity are jeopardized, then, for all these reasons and for others as old as Plato's time and never better stated, man will look for a savior—perhaps in the form of an autocrat, or even a tyrant, as Plato warned, or perhaps in the form of the state coupled with transnational businesses, as seems more likely now given the size of our problems and paucity of individual leaders.

Ray Allen Billington, historian and senior research associate, Huntington Library, San Mateo, California, has written: "American society as it has been known may be in the late afternoon of its life . . . and one of the major political consequences of this may be increasing governmental control over everyday life as scarce resources steadily dwindle. It may be a very long twilight. . . . There's going to have to be a permanent readjustment in mentality, and I'm afraid it's going to take years or decades or even a century of agony before we adjust to it" (1979, p. 24).

Because our values as a community are in conflict, because that which is acceptable to some citizens under the extended rubric of diversity is unacceptable to others in this diverse society, we are not likely in the near future to find a national leader who can both conform to the ideals of participatory democracy and bridge the differences among contending interest groups. More likely will be the emergence of cadres of control, chiefly anonymous leaders from business and industry with management and systems skills but also with a global perspective; oligarchical leaders with a passion to save democracy in a more disciplined form, to assure the continued growth of corporate capitalism, and to protect the American way of life, albeit again in a revised form; eclectic leaders emerging from corporations based in those nations that can be called the "seven sophisticates": the United States, the United Kingdom, France, West Germany, Italy, Canada, and Japan.

From near chaos in the eighties to control under corporate managers working with government bureaucrats in the nineties, to the eventual emergence of demogogic leadership in a small oligarchy of control in the early twenty-first century. . . . Is this not the likely and alarming sequence of events?

Regarding government, then, the key word of the emerging response will be *control*. America's experience with disintegrating authority, along with the fragmentation of our political consensus, compounded by the social divisiveness that frustrates initiative and saps energy—all have frightened the citizenry sufficiently to cause them to accept more centralization, despite nostalgia for decentralization; more control, after an affair with liberty; so-called disciplined democracy. Control is a necessity for a complex society. In Manhattan, it is not necessary to control the importation and sale of pencils: supply and demand suffices. But it is necessary to control Con Edison and the real estate developments, to control energy and land use.

We the people are now refining the social philosophy of controlled entitlement, a philosophy of slightly reduced expectations for ourselves and considerably reduced expectations for other people; a political philosophy preferring discipline and order to liberty and opportunity; a moral philosophy favoring probity over permissiveness, and consolidation or qualitative refinement after a period of expansiveness and quantitative wantonness. Such philosophy is for a nation adopting a defensive, protective posture, a nation hunkering down.

Planned Capitalism. If disciplined democracy is one reformulation expected in the next twenty years, one of several that will influence higher education, here is another: A changed political philosophy for America will join a changed national economy. And as the changed public philosophy will be characterized by what can be called "disciplined democracy," so the main characteristic of the changed economy will be "planned capitalism." The historic movement of the national economy from competitive capitalism to corporate or monopolistic capitalism will, in the 1980s and 1990s, culminate in comprehensive, systematic planning. The purpose of this tightening of corporate capitalism will not be to remedy the various moral failures that have attended capitalist growth, although capitalism embraces certain reforms. The effort, at base, will be to protect and promote additional growth—in the People's Republic of China, or wherever—as long as possible. The growth will be restrained, but growth nevertheless (Heilbroner, 1961, p. 71; also see Barnet, 1978).

Planned capitalism will be designed by the same coalition of forces that will restore discipline to democracy and revive the civil religion—the multinational corporations working with government and supported by the media and arts, the military, most churches and synagogues, most colleges and universities. (For more on the ways an epoch reveals itself through its art, and how art can be made to serve the culture, see Hughes, 1980.) This planning by the coterie of control will look from one angle like socialism and from another like fascism. It will in fact have elements of both—some benevolence, more authoritarianism; some sharing, more tightfistedness. And it is the price most Americans are willing to pay to assure another twenty years of growth.

Enlivened Pantheism. Because America is so divisive in its racial and ethnic mix, in social characteristics, in the educational attainment of the people, and because levels of human motivation, ability, and skill vary so greatly, there will be no return during the next two decades to religious sectarianism as the national religion, despite the efforts of the "electric church" and evangelical Christianity. Furthermore, the variety of religious experience has helped entrench the culture of pluralism. Nor is the old civil religion, with its simplicities, likely to be revived. Too many people do not believe in the sovereignty of God, although they may still secretly yearn for new evidence of America's manifest destiny. As for the religion of civility—that faith in no-faith, except fairness—it simply will not do in this unfair world.

There will be a compromise on the issue of whether religion should continue to serve culture or whether culture should again express religion. And this compromise will provide a national religion—the current variation of Franklin's "Publick Religion"— that can be called an enlivened pantheism.

Old forms of pantheism were bland, with no hooks or handles. Their advocates were content to assert that the universe, taken as a whole, is God and that there is no God other than the combined forces and laws manifested in the universe. Enlivened pantheism will be not only the latest expression of a theology of pluralism but also its most substantial expression—a pluralism sensitive to transcendence as well as tradition, and to the need for a religion that is personal or relevant to the individual even while expressing the collective faith of the nation-state (Bellah, 1978, p. 367).

Religion and education have always been expected to serve the state, and to the extent that they do so, the state, as it has in the past, will support them. Universities are good places for research and training—in the service of national policy. Colleges are good for citizenship education and socialization of youth—with the values and weights for both set by the state. Churches and synagogues are effective in guiding an individual through the holy moments of life: birth, confirmation, marriage, family, death. These religious institutions also bless the political and economic institutions of the nation-state, sanctifying their endeavors. Such are the functions of religion and education—or so say the new leaders.

Some of us believe that this sequence of events in government, the economy, religion, and education will set the course for authoritarianism in this country and may go beyond to prepare the land for totalitarianism. Cultural pluralism and a theology of pluralism represent, despite America's best efforts, a peace of exhaustion. Cultural pluralism is the best we can do with what we know about who we are. It is more of an expedient than a principle. Like law or the regulations of government, it is what happens when the fabric of a society has been rent asunder. Laws and "regs" are not the natural, healthy, invariable culmination of a complex social organization. Rather, laws and "regs" are necessary but regrettable coping mechanisms. They help us control negative human tendencies and protect against social breakdown.

So, too, with modern religion, this theology of pluralism and its enlivened pantheism—controlling man while giving him the appearance of control; playing down man because he is such a small part of the universe, yet dignifying him because he is first among living organisms; protecting the natural world so that it can be exploited more systematically; acting as conscience to the controlling state while serving as part of that mechanism of control.

Educators with humane convictions, no more than the dominant network of control, can accept a divided society in which cultural pluralism is allowed to broaden mindlessly until it encompasses cultural contradictions and moral absurdities, extremes that destroy any possibility for a focused definition of mankind or a coherent program for achieving a humane culture. But we, unlike this secular leadership, believe that democracy and capitalism will be served best when religion and education have freedom; when Judaism and Christianity and higher education can bring criticism and creative alternatives to the ideologies and programs of the state; when colleges and universities in particular are centers of independent thinking and models of intentional communities. This emphasis is old and honorable. The need for it, however, is new and urgent. We believe that the best hope in America for the creation of a countervailing force is in religion and education, in colleges and universities working together with churches and synagogues. But what can we do, those of us who believe that education and religion should provide an alternative force to the culture of control? Where can we start, those of us who favor a focused, incremental approach to institutional reforms that may point the way to social transformation?

A Countervailing Force

One point at which to begin responding to that emerging authoritarian society is development of what has here been called a

college of character. Start with the college. Proceed later with the
university. Both are needed, as are churches and synagogues, but the
college is the most available instrumentality while the university is
less accessible and quite inflexible. The college, particularly the
church-related college, provides a fertile setting for what is most
needed now—the planting of a metaphysics for higher education
that will enable the institution to respond to the ethical crisis on
campus and in society.

In the mid-sixties, Philip Phenix, Distinguished Professor of
Philosophy and Education at Teachers College, Columbia University, wrote an article entitled "The Moral Imperative in Contemporary American Education." Professor Phenix asserted that the central
issues of that time were neither technical nor political but moral
concerns—questions of conscience. Vietnam was the immediate
issue, but it symbolized a wide range of social and personal problems having to do with race, poverty, drugs, sex—anxieties that
could not be relieved in conventional ways. Phenix said: "Americans
are becoming increasingly aware that material and technical approaches to these issues do not suffice, that without a moral basis
and the morale that flows from it, typical American practicalism
and activism prove impractical and stultifying" (1966, p. 6).

And so the search for remedies was intensified. At the very
time metaphysics was widely scorned, it was needed, and Americans
groped for ethical norms and standards of value with which to han-
dle those persistent problems. Only a few people resorted to the
authority of nihilism, denying that there are any uniform standards
of right and wrong, asserting that the human endeavor lacks shared
purposes. Many more people accepted in the seventies the authority
of the individual, a viewpoint or orientation expressed by existentialism, and leading to the conclusion that human beings are infinitely varied, with values nothing more or less than artifacts having
no significance beyond that assigned to them by disparate individuals. A third point of view, receiving new attention in the early eighties, asserts that there are objective standards or values that are
known, that can be taught, that provide clear and unambiguous
norms of judgment for human conduct. Finally, there is a modifica-
tion of that more absolutist position, one useful to us now, a moral
theory that, in my judgment, should be the foundation of the force

countervailing the doctrines of authoritarian control. Here is Phenix's description of it: "The theory that the moral demand is grounded in a comprehensive program or 'telos' that is objective and normative, but that forever transcends concrete institutional embodiment or ideological formulation" (p. 10). What is required, then, for members of the needed countervailing force is commitment to this quest, to the progressive discovery of what they ought to know and do; commitment to the pursuit of truth "through the partial and imperfect embodiments of it in the concrete historical institutions of society" (Phenix, p. 11).

The college is one of those institutions and is now an undervalued resource in the search for a theology of education and a metaphysics for education and society. Furthermore, a college of character can demonstrate to other colleges the values of a community that makes no claim to absolute certainty but tries to live by provisional certitudes.

What else can a college do that would contribute to making it a force for reform not only of higher education but eventually of society at large? The college of character, I have argued, provides a deep history in this time of no-history. It also challenges members of the education community to venture out to the edge of the known context to stimulate criticism and creativity. This community changes at the growing edge of knowledge but maintains a vital center or healthy core of basic convictions from which every activity in the college derives energy and direction.

How do we go about changing a college among colleges into a college of character? First, we must change the public image of this institution from liberal arts college to comprehensive college, so that it escapes the preciousness of that old label while gaining recognition for the full range of its services and its true concerns. Assumptions and purposes must be examined, then clarified and presented in the institutional mission statement as well as made the basis for the school's professional development program.

Second, we must change the curriculum of the college to allow general education and vocational education to progress together, and then to blend so that the college's commitment to integrative education and to the examination of the moral dimensions of all subject matter can be carried out at the upper levels of a student's program of study. Finally, the college of character will feature, not conceal, its connections with churches and synagogues, business and industry, precollegiate and postcollegiate institutions of learning, constituencies and local community.

A college that wants to change will shake off its burdensome inferiority complex. Its suffering self-image is exemplified by faculty members who yearn to leave the college and "advance" to a research university, mistakenly assuming that the university's threadbare status symbols and its old pecking order are still relevant to their professional success; or by those faculty who would leave this college and "condescend" to go to a community college, assuming that better salaries will compensate for the community college's poorer working conditions. The faculty of a college of character now share the opportunity to build a potent community that will be more intellectually invigorating than the isolating environment of the university and a more unified community than is possible amid the anything-goes orientation of the community college. Also, at a time when changes in undergraduate education are needed, faculty members and administrators of a college of character can make changes within enduring institutional commitments in half the time required to effect lesser changes among its institutional competitors.

With such changes a liberal arts college can outgrow its sagging posture of apology. No longer is it necessary for the college to imitate the model of the research university, where the ever-tightening specializations are surpassed only by the pretensions of the professional guilds. Nor is it necessary for the college to imitate the model of the community college, where the range of community services increases as the commitment to standards of higher education decreases. The college of character stands between, in contact with both extremes, because it provides the crucial synoptic function in education: Integrating the disciplines to form a comprehensive response to problems requires synthesizing skills every bit as important as the analyzing skills featured in the university, even as a commitment to the search for purpose and meaning in human life is every bit as useful as the community services of the community college.

In the *Chronicle of Higher Education,* at the annual meetings of national associations, leaders in higher education admonish their colleagues to relate scholarly endeavors to other areas of cultural and intellectual life, to make their disciplines less isolated and more intelligible (for one example, see "A Disconcerting Philosopher . . . ," 1981). Where are the academic professionals who can most effectively respond to these admonitions? In the liberal arts college, particularly the college of character, where the curriculum is organized and the professional rewards and sanctions are weighted to achieve these goals. Other worthy emphases and objectives are to be found in the college—achievement of a coherent institutional mission, clarity concerning the meaning of the baccalaureate degree, and vitality in the educational community. The college provides the best environment in which to effect these gains.

While no college or university is independent, the liberal arts college is in the best position to achieve the sort of balanced interdependency with its sponsors and constituencies that results in its achieving a good measure of independence.

The university, remember, is dependent on government research contracts, on state and federal grants and loans, and, increasingly, on commissions from business and industry, particularly multinational corporations. The community college is dependent on local and state funding, on state and federal grants and loans, and, increasingly, on its ability to train the support personnel, the second or third-level functionaries for local business and service organizations. The liberal arts college is not dependent on government research contracts, although the college is, like the university and community college, too dependent on state and federal grants and loans. The college is not dependent on ties that bind the college to business and industry or multinational corporations. Nor does it try to offer—if it is truly a college—any and all services requested by interest groups in the local community.

As a generalization, the prospects for a good measure of independence are better for a liberal arts college working with its particular sponsor(s) and its limited constituency than for a university or a community college working with its larger, diffuse, more pluralistic, often public sponsors and constituencies. Universities have been mobilized, nationalized, coopted by state and federal influences. Community colleges have never claimed independence and have always been a "dependent variable." Liberal arts colleges were, for the most part, at one time, arms of the churches. Many of them later became semi-independent and essentially secular. Today, they are returning to their sources to reestablish an old relationship, but with new dimensions, elements, and responsibilities. These colleges have a chance, now, to persuade sponsors and constituencies to give them more freedom and independence than universities or community colleges have, in order for the liberal arts college to do what the others cannot do—prepare leadership that will have a humane orientation as well as specific skills, leadership that will express the values of a college of character in order to meet the needs of a society in great peril.

> *The light dove, cleaving the air in her free flight,*
> *and feeling its resistance, might imagine that its*
> *flight would be still easier in empty space.*
>
> Immanuel Kant

Begin Again

Certain colleges and universities will in the eighties go on as before regardless of changes now shaping a new culture. These traditionally oriented institutions still have enough support, self-confidence, and momentum to proceed through a floodtide of change as a well-sealed car navigates flooded streets.

Other colleges and universities have shown in recent years their addiction to and dependence on change. They are often non-traditional institutions, and in the future as in the past, they can be expected to embrace proposed changes in higher education as quickly and mindlessly as the traditional institutions will reject them.

There are perhaps 700 colleges and universities, nearly one fourth of the total, where faculty, administrative, and constituency leadership recognizes that the characteristics of the nation's culture in the next ten to twenty years will affect the character and activities of institutions of higher education. They will see that changes in society necessitate changes on campus, that colleges for a new culture cannot be stagnant.

Leaders in this third category of colleges will examine social or external changes from the standpoint of their college's perception of its place in American society. They will then weigh the significance of those external changes against appropriate internal changes for the college. Reforms within the institution of higher education generally result from changes outside it. But the way life outside is perceived and applied inside, to governance, curriculum, student life, and faculty development, is among the responsibilities and benchmarks of leadership for a college of character.

A new social philosophy is developing in America, authorizing more control, herein referred to as *disciplined democracy*. The national economy is changing, legitimizing both expansion and restraint, herein called *planned capitalism*. The civil religion in America is again evolving, still promoting cultural pluralism but constraining it, too, herein called *enlivened pantheism*.

These developments have effects for colleges—for general education, that part of the educational experience shared by all students; for specialization and professional studies; for the purposes of all institutions of learning; for faculty development programs; for all connections, including relationships with other institutions of society such as the church and synagogue.

The reverse is also true. What happens in the college influences society. A clear, relevant statement of institutional purposes, a definite philosophy of education, will help students, parents, and the constituency read and critique the social philosophy spreading across political life in America. The investment policies of the college, the relationships between trustees of the college and interested corporations, the treatment on campus of support personnel—in brief, the economic policies of the educational institution—will encourage the campus community and its large connections to develop an appropriate response to the economy of control favored by leaders from multinational corporations. The social and ethical standards at the college, as well as the general ethos of the place, will affect the way that graduates and friends as well as students and faculty evaluate the civil religion in America.

If hundreds of colleges become colleges of character, they will influence community colleges and universities. No less affected will be other institutions—churches and synagogues, formal and informal community groups—that have so much in common with the college. Beyond all that, and equally important, the political state and the business corporations will take notice and react. The dangers for the college in daring to differ must not be minimized. But the dangers of fully submitting to the agents of control, that is, capitulating to an authoritarian state, are greater and must be emphasized. Also, there is the possibility that a new constellation of influences can be created by this movement initiated in the colleges, a set of influences that will prove by their positive effects that these colleges for a new culture are able to affect that culture even as it affects the colleges.

Much of the content of this essay may, of course, be irritating to the reader. It goes against the grain of so many familiar elements of American life—by calling for restraint rather than free expression, for community rather than solitude. The effects of several proposals herein can be viewed as limiting, confining, restrictive. There is, however, another way of assessing these proposals. The outcomes can be viewed more positively than negatively. Consider the beneficial effects of a community of conviction and, to heighten the impact, apply those effects to our own lives:

- We will escape the disabling influences of America's recent past: the "paralysis of analysis," the mood of existential despair; the emphasis on the problematic, the paradoxical, and the contradictory in human experience.
- We will be freed from narcissism, worship of our own navels, rampant individualism, and radical subjectivism.
- We will escape untenable commitments—to unrestrained materialism, planned obsolescence, raw competition; to momentary or fleeting allegiances, faddism, and the trendiness of passing superficialities; to certain forms of *hubris,* such as America's "manifest destiny," "watchman for the world," and other nationalistic extravagances.
- We will renew our connection with solid, enduring, freshly im-

portant commitments—to marriage, home, kin; to other contrac-
tual relationships that prosper not on legal details but on loyalty,
trust, and good will; to communitarianism and neighborhood,
the social order, and other restraints that liberate; to tradition and
continuity—the beauty of that which endures and provides
stability.

- We will revive and refurbish some struggling but honorable
  coalitions involving college and church, faith and learning. We
  will regain respect for the four cardinal virtues even as we guard
  against the seven deadly sins. No longer will we constantly emphasize the perils that attend traditional ways of thinking and
  acting because, instead, we find that in vast areas of life the old
  ways are the best. To be sure, there have been abuses and excesses
  and mistakes. But we have come to the conclusion that risks
  generated by most new cultures are greater than the risks in some
  of the old traditions. To find value in renewing our connection
  with the past does not mean that we must forsake the best developments of the present. There have been gains as well as losses of
  late, and it is a positive sign that we can distinguish between
  them.

- We will be released, as members of centered communities, at this
  time of an emerging culture of control, from the tightening grip
  of fatalism—to nuclear destruction, to the irreversible pollution
  of the environment, to the death of this planet. The revival of the
  notion of restraint and limitation extends to include control of
  the destructive forces of man as well as the destructive forces of
  nature.

The emphasis on a measured or paced response is not a negative but a positive development. It encourages discipline and makes
enduring relationships possible. Although it can stifle creativity, it
can also give a person the stability necessary for creativity. Personal
freedom can be exhausting and, worse, tyrannical—intimidating,
draining, paralyzing in its effects. More crimes have been committed
in the name of freedom than of any other ideology.

The revival of the notion of social responsibility, interdependence, sharing, personal restraint in the interest of social
growth, is a positive development. As we do not begin our lives

alone and do not want to die alone, so we should not live our lives alone. We are meant to live in relation to other like-minded persons. Community is a constraint that frees (Goodwin, 1974).

More specifically, that is, with application to higher education, it is fortunate that attention to core curricula and general education has reawakened. We take heart in that attention is, more and more, concentrating on the deeper elements of professional development as well as on the basic assumptions of educational programs; on the relationships between disciplines and their application to social urgencies; on the concept of the teaching profession as a vocation of service rather than a mere occupation.

The likelihood that business and industry, colleges and universities, social and religious and political organizations will interact more frequently with one another is also an encouraging development. We are, after all, in the soup together. Together we can get out, not by climbing over one another but by helping one another.

It is right to emphasize not our separateness and competitiveness as educators—that inclination to make our mark by criticism and to establish our skill in adversarial disputation—but, rather, to emphasize our commonalities and our potentiality for harmony and the benefits derived from cooperation.

Finally, despite the emphasis in this essay on shared experiences and collective judgments, change begins with individuals who examine their own lives, their immediate environment, and the collective opinions of people they trust, and then, from what they can learn of the larger world and its wisdom, and incorporating into the equation any dream or vision that seems relevant, begin to act.

It is time for us, individually and collectively, drawing on the traditional wisdom of mankind and on nontraditional insights of contemporary leaders, to begin the task of shaping colleges worthy of being called colleges of character. And, at least for the time being, we must find our satisfactions in the striving. In the last paragraph of his last published lecture, *Create Dangerously*, Albert Camus summed up this way of winning:

> One may long, as I do, for a gentler flame, a respite, a pause for musing. But perhaps there is no other

peace for the artist than what he finds in the heat of combat. "Every wall is a door," Emerson correctly said. Let us not look for the door, and the way out, anywhere but in the wall against which we are living. Instead, let us seek respite where it is—in the very thick of the battle. For in my opinion, and this is where I shall close, it *is* there. Great ideas, it has been said, come into the world as gently as doves. Perhaps then, if we listen attentively, we shall hear, amid the uproar of empires and nations, a faint flutter of wings, the gentle stirring of life and hope. Some will say that this hope lies in a nation; others, in a man. I believe rather that it is awakened, revived, nourished by millions of solitary individuals whose deeds and works every day negate frontiers and the crudest implications of history. As a result, there shines forth fleetingly the ever threatened truth that each and every man, on the foundation of his own sufferings and joys, builds for all [1961, p. 272].

> *Not fare well*
> *But fare forward, voyagers.*
>
> T. S. Eliot

References

"And Man Created the Chip." *Newsweek,* 30 June 1980, pp. 50–56.

"Applied Ethics: A Strategy for Fostering Professional Responsibility." *Carnegie Quarterly,* Spring/Summer 1980, *28* (2,3), 1–7.

Arendt, H. "The Crisis in Education." In *Between Past and Future.* New York: Viking Press, 1961, pp. 173–196.

Arendt, H. "Home to Roost." *New York Review of Books,* 26 June 1975, pp. 3–6.

Arrowsmith, W. "Thoughts on American Culture—and Civilization." In D. N. Bigelow (Ed.), *Schoolworlds '76—New Directions for Educational Policy.* Berkeley: McCutchan, 1976, 151–176.

Bambrough, R. *Reason, Truth and God.* London: Methuen, 1969.

Bambrough, R. *Conflict and the Scope of Reason.* Hull, England: University of Hull, 1974.

Barnet, R. *The Giants.* New York: Simon & Schuster, 1978.

Barth, J. *The Floating Opera.* New York: Doubleday, 1956.

Bellah, R. "Civil Religion in America." In *Beyond Belief.* New York: Harper & Row, 1970, pp. 168–189.

Bellah, R. "Commentary and Proposed Agenda: The Normative Framework for Pluralism in America." In "Dilemmas of Pluralism: The Case of Religion in Modernity." *Soundings*, Fall 1978, *61* (3), 355-371.

Bellah, R. "Cultural Vision and the Human Future." In "Knowledge, Education and Human Values: Toward the Recovery of Wholeness." *Teachers College Record*, Spring 1981, *82* (3), 497-506.

Bennett, W. J. "Getting Ethics." *Commentary*, December 1980, pp. 62-65.

Berlin, I. *Concepts and Categories.* New York: Penguin Books, 1981.

Bettelheim, B. "Reflections: The Uses of Enchantment." *New Yorker*, 8 December 1975, pp. 50-114.

Bettelheim, B. "The Ultimate Limit." In *Surviving and Other Essays.* New York: Knopf, 1979, pp. 3-18.

Billington, R. A. *New York Times*, 1 July 1979, Sect. 1, pp. 1, 24.

Bok, D. *Beyond the Ivory Tower.* Cambridge, Mass.: Harvard University Press, 1982.

Boorstin, D. *The Fertile Verge: Creativity in the United States.* Washington, D.C.: Library of Congress, 1981.

Booth, W. *Critical Understanding: The Powers and Limits of Pluralism.* Chicago: University of Chicago Press, 1979.

Bouwsma, W. J. "Models of the Educated Man." *American Scholar*, Spring 1976, *44* (2), 195-212.

Boyer, E., and Hechinger, F. *Higher Education in the Nation's Service.* Washington, D.C.: Carnegie Foundation for the Advancement of Teaching, 1981.

Boyer, E., and Levine, A. *A Quest for Common Learning.* Washington, D.C.: Carnegie Foundation for the Advancement of Teaching, 1981.

Buber, M. *Between Man and Man.* Boston: Beacon Press, 1955.

Camus, A. "Create Dangerously." In *Resistance, Rebellion and Death.* (J. O'Brien, Trans.) New York: Knopf, 1961, pp. 249-272.

Carnegie Council on Policy Studies in Higher Education. *Three Thousand Futures: The Next Twenty Years for Higher Education.* San Francisco: Jossey-Bass, 1980.

Chronicle of Higher Education, 20 April 1981, pp. 1, 13.

Cleveland, H. *Humangrowth: An Essay on Growth, Values and the Quality of Life.* New York: Aspen Institute of Humanistic Studies, 1978.

Committee on the Objectives of a General Education in a Free Society. *General Education in a Free Society: Report of the Harvard Committee.* Cambridge, Mass.: Harvard University Press, 1945.

Conroy, F. "Oscar Peterson." *Esquire,* September 1981, pp. 68–70.

Cuddihy, J. M. *No Offense: Civil Religion and Protestant Taste.* New York: Seabury Press, 1978.

Currier, R. "Another Step for Mankind." *Chronicle of Higher Education,* 16 October 1978, pp. 8–9.

"A Disconcerting Philosopher Challenges the Pretentions of His Discipline." *Chronicle of Higher Education,* 9 December 1981, pp. 25–26.

Durant, W., and Durant, A. *Dual Autobiography.* New York: Simon & Schuster, 1977.

Einstein, A. *The World as I See It.* (A. Harris, Trans.) New York: Philosophical Library, 1949.

Eliot, T. S. "The Dry Salvages." In *Four Quartets* in *Collected Poems.* New York: Harcourt Brace Jovanovich, 1970, pp. 191–199.

Eliot, T. S. "Choruses from 'The Rock.'" In *Collected Poems.* New York: Harcourt Brace Jovanovich, 1973, pp. 147–171.

Ferrater, M. J. *Unamuno: A Philosophy of Tragedy.* (P. Silver, Trans.) Berkeley: University of California Press, 1962.

Fiske, E. "Winds of Change on Morningside Heights." *New York Times,* 28 September 1980, pp. 38–48, 84–86.

FitzGerald, F. *America Revised.* Boston: Little, Brown, 1979.

Geilker, C. D. "You'll Never Know It's a Computer." *Archive* (William Jewell College), May 1979, 7 (3), 24.

Gellner, E. *Legitimation of Belief.* Cambridge: Cambridge University Press, 1974.

Giamatti, B. "The American Teacher: A Gift of Giving." *Harper's,* July 1980, pp. 24–25, 28–29.

Gunn, G. "Elevating Good Manners to a 'Civil Religion.'" *Chronicle Review,* 2 October 1978, p. 12.

Goodwin, R. C. *The American Condition.* Garden City, N.Y.: Doubleday, 1974.

Gouldner, A. W. *The Future of Intellectuals and the Rise of the New Class.* New York: Continuum/Seabury, 1979.

Hausheer, R. In I. Berlin (Ed.), *Against the Current.* New York: Viking Press, 1979, pp. xiii–liii.

Heilbroner, R. *The Future as History.* New York: Grove Press, 1961.

Hersey, J. "The Triumph of Numbers." *Atlantic Monthly,* October 1980, pp. 78–84.

Hill, P. "Communities of Learners." In J. Hall and B. Kevles, *In Opposition to Core Curriculum.* Westport, Conn.: Greenwood Press, 1982, pp. 107–133.

Howe, H. "What Future for the Private College?" *Change,* May/June 1979, pp. 28–31.

Hughes, R. *The Shock of the New.* New York: Knopf, 1980.

Hutchins, R. M. *The Idea of the University.* Chicago: University of Chicago Press, 1944.

Hutchins, R. M. *The University of Utopia.* Chicago: University of Chicago Press, 1953.

James, W. *Pragmatism.* New York: Longmann, Green, 1928.

Jencks, C., and Riesman, D. *The Academic Revolution.* Garden City, N.Y.: Doubleday, 1966.

Kirkwood, R., and Uchitelle, S. *The Danforth and Kent Fellowships: A Quinquennial Review.* Mimeographed. St. Louis, 1976.

Koch, A. *Philosophy for a Time of Crisis.* New York: Dutton, 1960.

Koerner, J. D. (Ed.). *The New Liberal Arts.* New York: Sloan Foundation, 1981.

Kramer, J. "A Reporter in Europe—London." *New Yorker,* 11 May 1981, pp. 91–124.

Langer, S. *Philosophical Sketches.* New York: Mentor Books, 1964.

Lapham, L. "Has Humanism Been Emptied of Its Meaning?" *Wall Street Journal,* 19 March 1982, p. 27.

Lippmann, W. "The University." *New Republic,* 28 May 1966, pp. 17–20.

Martin, W. B. *Conformity: Standards and Change in Higher Education.* San Francisco: Jossey-Bass, 1969.

Martin, W. B. "The Ethical Crisis in Education." *Change,* January 1974, pp. 28–33.

Martin, W. B. "The Limits to Diversity." *Change,* December-January 1978/1979, pp. 41–45.

Martin, W. B. *Common Ground.* St. Louis: Danforth Foundation, 1979.

Martin, W. B. "The-Narrow End of the Cornucopia: Lessons on Equity from the Danforth Fellowship Program." *Change,* January-February 1981a, pp. 35-37.

Martin, W. B. "Why Won't Accreditors Investigate the Abuses in College Athletics?" *Chronicle of Higher Education,* 26 January 1981b, p. 64.

Marty, M. "The American Tradition and the American Tomorrow." In S. Sardmel (Ed.), *Tomorrow's American.* New York: Oxford University Press, 1977, pp. 134-155.

Mead, S. *The Lively Experiment.* New York: Harper & Row, 1963.

Moberly, W. *The Crisis in the University.* London: SCM Press, 1949.

Moynihan, D. P. "State vs. Academe." *Harper's,* December 1980, pp. 31-40.

Nock, A. J. *Theory of Education in the United States.* New York: Arno Press, 1969. (Reprint of 1932 edition.)

"Notes and Comments." *New Yorker,* 26 September 1977, pp. 27-28.

Papert, S. "New Cultures from New Technologies." *BYTE,* September 1980, 5 (9), 230-240.

Phenix, P. H. "The Moral Imperative in Contemporary American Education." In *Perspectives on Education.* New York: Teachers College, Columbia University, 1966, pp. 6-13.

Pole, J. R. *The Pursuit of Equality in American History.* Berkeley: University of California Press, 1978.

"Private Religion, Public Morality." *New York Times* (editorial), 5 October 1980, p. E18.

Reston, J. "Washington." *New York Times,* 9 September 1981, p. A31.

Rice, R. E. "Dreams and Actualities: Danforth Fellows in Mid-Career." *AAHE Bulletin,* April 1980, pp. 3-5.

Rieff, P. *Fellow Teachers.* New York: Harper & Row, 1972.

Riesman, D. *Constraint and Variety in American Education.* Garden City, N.Y.: Doubleday Anchor, 1959.

Rosovsky, H. *Chronicle of Higher Education.* 20 April 1981, pp. 1, 13.

Roszak, T. *Where the Wasteland Ends.* Garden City, N.Y.: Doubleday, 1972.

Sapir, E. "Culture, Genuine and Spurious." *Culture, Language, and Personality: Selected Essays.* Berkeley: University of California Press, 1970. (Quoted in Arrowsmith, 1976, p. 156.)

Sargeant, W. "Profiles: 'Presence'" *New Yorker,* 26 January 1981, pp. 40–60.

Schaar, J., and Wolin, S. "Education and the Technological Society." *New York Review of Books,* 9 October 1969, pp. 3–6.

Schell, J. "Nuclear Arms." *New Yorker,* 15 February 1982, pp. 45–107. (Part III of a three-part essay, later published as *The Fate of the Earth.* New York: Knopf, 1982.

Schlesinger, A., Jr. "American Politics on a Darkling Plain." *Wall Street Journal,* 16 March 1982, p. 28.

Schorske, C. E. "Community Experience and Cultural Creativity: Basel and Vienna." Unpublished manuscript, November 1980, pp. 1–33.

Schorske, C. E. *Fin-de-Siecle Vienna: Politics and Culture.* New York: Vintage Books, 1981.

Schumacher, E. F. *Small Is Beautiful.* New York: Harper & Row, 1973.

Sheed, W. "A Thought a Day Isn't Enough," *New York Times,* 29 June 1982, p. E19.

Sontag, S. "Civilization as Tragic." *New York Times,* 8 February 1976, p. 36.

Steiner, G. "De Profundis." *New Yorker,* 4 September 1978, pp. 97–99.

Thomas, L. *The Medusa and the Snail.* New York: Viking Press, 1974.

Thomas, L. "On the Uncertainty of Science." *Harvard Magazine,* September-October 1980, pp. 19–22.

Tillich, P. *The Protestant Era.* Chicago: Phoenix Books, University of Chicago Press, 1957.

Trow, G. W. S., Jr. "The Decline of Adulthood." *New Yorker,* 17 November 1980, pp. 63–171.

Trow, G. W. S., Jr. *Within the Context of No-Context.* Boston: Little, Brown, 1981.

Tussman, J. *Experiment at Berkeley.* New York: Oxford University Press, 1969.

Unamuno, M. *The Tragic Sense of Life.* (C. Flitch, Trans.) New York: Dover, 1954.

"Wanted: A History that Pulls Things Together." *Chronicle of Higher Education*, 7 July 1980, p. 3.

Wayland, F. "A Discourse Delivered at the Dedication of Manning Hall, the Chapel and Library of Brown University." 4 February 1835, Providence, R. I." In R. Hofstadter and W. Smith, *American Higher Education Documentary History* (Vol. 1). Chicago: University of Chicago Press, 1961, pp. 242–243.

Weber, M. *The Protestant Ethic and the Spirit of Capitalism.* New York: Scribner's, 1977. (Originally published 1904.)

Wilson, E. O. *On Human Nature.* Cambridge, Mass.: Harvard University Press, 1978.

Wilson, J., Williams, N., and Sugerman, B. *Introduction to Moral Education.* Baltimore: Penguin Books, 1967.

Wilson, W. J. *The Declining Significance of Race.* Chicago: University of Chicago Press, 1978.

Whitehead, A. N. *The Aims of Education.* New York: Macmillan, 1959.

Yeats, W. B. "The Second Coming." In *The Collected Poems of W. B. Yeats.* New York: Macmillan, 1959, pp. 184–185.

Index

A

Administrators: change by, 150–154; delight and meaning for, 105–106; leadership by, 94–98. *See also* Presidents
Agreement: importance of, 7; and pluralism, 14; societal, disintegration of, 15–16
American University, financial situation of, 166
Anarchy, academic, crisis of, 29
Apprenticeship, in institute curriculum model, 140
Arendt, H., 5, 23, 199
Aristotle, 46
Armstrong, J., xxiv
Arrowsmith, W., 10, 199
Augustine, 104

Authoritarianism: authority distinct from, 121–122; expanding, and leadership, 102
Authority: authoritarianism distinct from, 121–122; basis for, 14, 67; character related to, 20; emancipation from, 99–100, 101; of individual, 9; of teaching, 120–122

B

Bailey, R., xxiv
Bailey, S., xxiv
Bambrough, R., 53, 75, 145, 199
Barnet, R., 185, 199
Barth, J., 11, 76, 199
Basel, creativity in, 58–59

Oklahoma, University of, and athlete's transcript, 25
O'Neill, K., xxiv
Oregon, University of, scandal at, 123
Ought, concern for, 116

P

Pantheism, enlivened, 185–187, 193
Papert, S., 53–54, 203
Parnell, D., xxiv
Pascal, B., 76
Passion, role of, 77
People's Republic of China, 114, 185
Perlman, I., 51
Peterson, O., 19, 62
Phenix, P. H., 188, 189, 203
Plato, 183
Pluralism: and agreement, 14; cultural, assumed mandate for, 68–71; culture of, 9–10, 23; and enlivened pantheism, 186; freedom related to, 122–123; and tolerance, 34
Pole, J. R., 76, 203
Powell Hall (St. Louis), as symbol of capitalism, 32–33
Presidents: flexibility of, 93–94; leadership by, 91–94; synoptic function of, 92–93. *See also* Administrators
Princeton University, leadership by, 165
Probity, imposed, crisis of, 29–30
Process, commitment to, 13
Professional associations, and curriculum requirements, 159–160
Professionalism: and fragmentation, xviii; and leadership, 87; limitations of, 90–91; triumph of, xvii–xviii; true, and teaching, 114, 125
Pruitt-Igoe (St. Louis), as symbol of capitalism, 32–33

Q

Quality, standards related to, 123–124
Quehl, G., xxiv
Querencia, concept of, 57–58

R

Reason: faith related to, 53–55; scope of, in college of character, 74–76
Reed College, and character, 73
Religion: civil, 33–35; of civility, 35–36, 148–149; concept of, 74; and enlivened pantheism, 185–187; for faculty, 116–119; national, crisis in, 33–37, 180
Reston, J., 30–31, 203
Rice, R. E., 96, 203
Rieff, P., 122, 203
Riesman, D., xvii, xxiv, 41, 202, 203
Roosevelt, F. D., 20–21
Rosovsky, H., 132–133, 203
Roszak, T., 118, 119, 203
Roundtable group, 182
Royal Palace, Amsterdam, 42

S

St. John's College, and character, 73
St. Lawrence University, mission statement of, 79–80
St. Louis, Missouri, and economic crisis, 32–33
St. Mary's College of California, and character, 73
St. Olaf College, and character, 73
Sapir, E., 10, 203–204
Sargeant, W., 20, 204
Schaar, J., 140–141, 204
Schell, J., 153, 204
Schlesinger, A., Jr., 178, 204
Schorske, C. E., 58–59, 204